How to Analyse Texts

How to A...
language ...
language-...
– spoken, ...
which can ...
ent levels.

This textbo...

- three ...
  use, ar ...
- a wide ...
  China ...
  digital ...
- objecti...
  sugges...
  studen...
- a comb...
  section ...
- a comp...
  links ar ...

Written by t...
Texts is key ...

Ronald Ca...
English at th...
Routledge ...
Linguistics ...

Angela Go...
Education ...
Language A level at a national examination board. She has taught English across different sectors of education and at universities both in the UK and abroad. Her research interests include language and creativity, and the language of new technologies. She has written and edited many books and articles on English language, including the Routledge Intertext series.

'Without a doubt the most practical and innovative textbook on text analysis on the market. Not only do Carter and Goddard provide clear explanations of theoretical concepts, but they also provide concrete advice about how to go about the practical work of collecting and analysing a range of different texts. A superb introduction to text analysis for beginning students and a useful resource book for more advanced students and researchers.'
Rodney H. Jones, *City University of Hong Kong*

'This user-friendly book covers a wide range of carefully chosen text types and genres, and takes a modern approach to text analysis. *How to Analyse Texts* is a fantastic resource for students on undergraduate English Language courses.'
Mario Saraceni, *University of Portsmouth, UK*

'A delightful coursebook marrying the study of a range of modern, multi-modal, electronic, creative and ludic texts with the core tools of descriptive linguistics. This highly useful yet accessible introduction will serve the next generation of students of media and modern English language very well.'
Rajend Mesthrie, *University of Cape Town, South Africa*

'This impressive introductory textbook guides students step by step through the intricate processes of understanding and interpreting texts.'
Carmen Rosa Caldas-Coulthard, *Federal University of Santa Catarina, Brazil, and University of Birmingham, UK*

How to Analyse Texts

A toolkit for students of English

Ronald Carter and Angela Goddard

LONDON AND NEW YORK

First published 2016
by Routledge
2 Park Square, Milton Park, Abingdon, Oxon OX14 4RN

and by Routledge
711 Third Avenue, New York, NY 10017

Routledge is an imprint of the Taylor & Francis Group, an informa business

© 2016 Ronald Carter and Angela Goddard

The rights of Ronald Carter and Angela Goddard to be identified as authors of this work have been asserted by them in accordance with sections 77 and 78 of the Copyright, Designs and Patents Act 1988.

All rights reserved. No part of this book may be reprinted or reproduced or utilised in any form or by any electronic, mechanical, or other means, now known or hereafter invented, including photocopying and recording, or in any information storage or retrieval system, without permission in writing from the publishers.

Trademark notice: Product or corporate names may be trademarks or registered trademarks, and are used only for identification and explanation without intent to infringe.

British Library Cataloguing in Publication Data
A catalogue record for this book is available from the British Library

Library of Congress Cataloging-in-Publication Data
Carter, Ronald, 1947- author.
How to analyse texts : a toolkit for students of English / Ronald Carter and Angela Goddard.
  pages cm
Includes bibliographical references and index.
1. Linguistic analysis (Linguistics) 2. English language--Textbooks for foreign speakers. I. Goddard, Angela, 1954- author. II. Title.
P126.C375 2015
410--dc23
2015005536

ISBN: 978-0-415-83679-1 (hbk)
ISBN: 978-0-415-83680-7 (pbk)
ISBN: 978-1-315-68322-5 (ebk)

Typeset in Akzidenz Grotesk and Eurostile
by Saxon Graphics Ltd, Derby

To Jane and Adrian

Contents

Acknowledgements x
Texts xii
Introduction 1

PART I
Foundations: researching texts 5

1 Your materials 7
2 Gathering more materials 10
3 Sizing up the job: questions, scope and focus 15
4 The right tools for the job: research methods 20
5 Preparing the ground: reading and note-making skills 32
6 Analysing 35
7 Reporting: writing about texts 36
   Review your skills 37
   Commentaries for Part I 38

PART II
Drilling down: how texts are structured 41

Section A: Graphological and phonological levels

8 Definitions 44
9 Language as a semiotic system 45
10 What are the rules? 47
11 Signs and symbols 49
12 Sounds and symbols 57

13	Speech, writing and multimodality	71
	Review your skills	76
	Ideas for assignments	76

Section B: Lexical and semantic level

14	Introduction	81
15	Frequent words	82
16	Words and morphemes	87
17	Forming words	89
18	Words and semantic fields	95
19	Words and word families	99
20	Words and multiple meanings	101
21	Connotation and collocation	104
22	Words and metaphors	111
23	Lexical cohesion	114
	Review your skills	118
	Ideas for assignments	118

Section C: Grammatical level

24	Introduction	123
25	Grammar and cohesion	125
26	Grammar and representation	128
27	Grammar, speech and language change	139
28	Grammar and politics	146
29	Conversational grammar	151
30	Texting grammar	153
31	Creative grammar	155
	Review your skills	159
	Ideas for assignments	160
	Commentaries for Part II	162

PART III
Building Up: texts and contexts   **187**

32	The dimensions of texts: place and time	189
33	Textual perspectives and point of view	201
34	Texts as discourses: culture and gender	205
35	Dialogues: genre and intertextuality	211
	Review your skills	214
	Ideas for assignments	215
	Commentaries for Part III	216

A checklist for text analysis	219
Corpus resources and projects	222
References	230
Links to online references	232
Further reading	235
Glossary/Index	238
List of texts	247

Acknowledgements

The author and publishers would like to thank the following copyright holders for permission to reproduce the following material:

Extract from "Lonely Planet Georgia, Armenia & Azerbaijan" (2012) reproduced with kind permission of Lonely Planet.
"Dove of Hate" reproduced with kind permission of Brainbox Candy Ltd and Andy McKay.
Street sign reproduced with kind permission of the National Capital Commission, Canada.
From The Independent, 11/05/2013, "More than words", Rhodri Marsden. Reproduced with kind permission.
Extract from Ladder of Years by Anne Tyler (Vintage/Random House, 1996), reprinted with the permission of HSG Agency as agents for the author, and the Random House Group. Copyright © 1996 by Anne Tyler Modaressi.
Excerpts from Carter, R. et al. (2007), *Working with Texts*, Abingdon: Routledge. Reproduced with kind permission of Taylor and Francis.
Texts from art'otel Berlin reproduced with kind permission.
Excerpt from Thurlow et al. (2004), *Computer Mediated Communication* reproduced with kind permission of Sage Publications.
"Conchas Barrachas" from *Ceviche: Peruvian Kitchen: Authentic Recipes for Lomo Saltado, Anticuchos, Tiraditos, Alfajores, and Pisco Cocktails* by Martin Morales, text © 2013 by Martin Morales. Used by permission of Ten Speed Press, an imprint of the Crown Publishing Group, a division of Random House LLC, and by permission of Orion Publishing Group. All rights reserved.
Volvo advertisement reproduced with kind permission of Volvo Car UK.
"Just out of bed…" napkin reproduced with kind permission of Rodney's Oyster House Corp.
Photographs of Pokhara and Lisbon reproduced with kind permission of Martin Phillips Educational Consultancy.
Simple promise warranty card reproduced with kind permission of simplehuman.
"Like" card reproduced with kind permission of Fourth Wall Brands.

Extract from The Guardian 13/12/2012, "TV review: Escape from Colditz", Sam Wollaston. Reproduced with kind permission of Guardian News and Media Ltd.

Niedecker, L. *Popcorn-can cover* in "Lorine Niedecker, Collected Works" (2004), Oakland: University of California Press.

Cover of South China Post Magazine 24/07/2014, reproduced with kind permission of South China Morning Post Publishers Ltd.

Extracts from "Orange the world in sixteen days" and "UN Women ad series reveals widespread sexism" reproduced with kind permission of United Nations Publications.

Extract from "Goodness Sakes" booklet reproduced with kind permission from Pret a Manger.

Extract from Boyd, W. (2007), *Ordinary Thunderstorms* reproduced with kind permission of Bloomsbury Publishers Plc and Harper Collins US.

Extract from Child, L. (2010), *61 Hours* reproduced with kind permission of the Random House Group and Darley Anderson.

Text from Marriott Hotels reproduced with kind permission of Marriott Hotels International, Ltd.

Cover of Times Higher Education issue 2029, 15/12/11, reproduced with kind permission of TES Global.

Advert from Clas Ohlson, reproduced with kind permission of Metro and Clas Ohlson.

Corpus examples have drawn on the Cambridge English Corpus, (Cambridge University Press) the British National Corpus and Cobuild English Corpus (Collins Publishers) and are reproduced here by kind permission. All examples are (c) the publisher.

Every effort has been made to contact copyright-holders. Please advise the publisher of any errors or omissions, and these will be corrected in subsequent editions.

ADVISORY BOARD

Manon van der Laaken, University of Amsterdam, The Netherlands
Alastair Henry, University West, Sweden
Philip Chan, Hong Kong University
Sibusiso Clifford Ndlangamandla, UNISA, South Africa
Nomsa Zindela, UNISA, South Africa
Sonia Zyngier, Federal University of Rio de Janiero, Brazil

Texts

The texts for analysis and exploration in this book are taken from a wide range of sources and from different parts of the world. These include, for example, advertisements; travel writing; poetry; novels; newspaper reviews and articles; instructions; menus and recipes; everyday signs, symbols, and notices; informal conversations; new – and older – forms of digital communication; political speeches; letters; computer generated corpus concordances and frequency lists; and many more. A full list of texts is given at the back of the book, with page numbers for ease of reference.

Introduction

MAKING THIS BOOK WORK FOR YOU

This book aims to be, as its title suggests, a toolkit for active enquiry into language use in the many texts that surround us. It will provide a range of starting points for you to think about language patterns, both in terms of how texts work internally and also how they construct and reveal the wider culture that produces them.

Because there is much more to say about texts in different parts of the world than a single book can ever describe, the working method for this book is to provide you with useful frameworks and approaches and give you plenty of texts to practice on. You can then go further by replacing the texts and using the toolkit for the analysis of texts from different **World Englishes** and from contexts where you live, study and work.

Applying the ideas in this book will mean being active in collecting texts for yourself and analysing them. A toolkit is something to be used, not just described. The belief running through this book is that while learners need to be given tools and shown how to use them, real skills are only developed in practical applications and activities.

Being active about learning is easy to say – it's something we would all want to be – but this idea needs breaking down further. **Part I** of this book will take you through a series of careful steps in order to help you set up some good learning routines. It will help you to have some resources to hand and some confidence when you are asked to branch out on your own and do some independent work.

Parts II and III are more about explicit frameworks for analysis, and ideas for how to put the material you will be constantly collecting to good use. **Part II** has a more text-internal perspective, with explanations of some of the structural aspects of language that frequently need to be understood in order to describe how a text works. **Part III** is more text-external, focusing on some of the more contextual aspects of interpretation. Both of these perspectives are essential to a good analysis. Each Part and Section has a set of aims at the start and a learning review at the end. As well as frequent activities, there are many ideas for assignments, where suggestions are made for longer term and more sustained investigations.

The book offers models for how to write about the language perspectives covered, both in the main part of the text and in the form of commentaries at the end. When key terms are first used in the book, they are emboldened and defined in the glossary at the end. At the end you will also find a summary checklist, which will act as a set of prompts for analysis, helping you to recall the different aspects you have worked on during the course of the book.

New methodological approaches to text analysis are being developed all the time by academic researchers. A relatively recent phenomenon is the development of language **corpora** (singular – **corpus**), which are digital, searchable collections of millions of words. There are explanations of these new resources as the book progresses. There is also a special section at the back of the book where different corpora are listed and a range of projects and activities are suggested.

How you use this book is obviously up to you. The book is divided into its three different parts specifically because we are aware that language courses vary tremendously from place to place in their emphasis, even within one community, and also that your own starting points are likely to be different from those of a fellow student. But however you use the book, we believe that as a whole it offers something distinctively different from many other textbooks. Acting as a flexible support to active enquiry, and approaching language as a creative resource for human communication, this book views texts of all kinds – from Shakespearean sonnets to public bathroom notices – as complex pieces of communication and therefore worth analysing.

TEXTS AND DISCOURSES: DEFINITIONS AND APPROACHES

The terms 'text' and '**discourse**' are increasingly used interchangeably, but there are subtle differences between them and they have very different origins and histories. 'Text' has been used more in arts and humanities subjects, while 'discourse', and its plural 'discourses', have their origins in the social sciences.

The terms have had a different scale of reference, reflecting the preoccupations of their different subject bases. While a 'text' has been seen more as a single artefact, 'discourse' has tended to refer to more extensive communication – a cluster of repeated representations, or interactions of some length and substance. The term 'discourses' as used in social science refers to whole patterns of thinking, knowing and behaving that are built up within a society from repeated occurrences of viewpoints expressed in particular ways.

The different orientations suggested by the terms can be exemplified with reference to SMS usage. We talk about 'text messages' (or 'txt messages', where people are at pains to distinguish SMS from other kinds of text), referring to the digital artefacts we compose on phone keyboards. But we can also talk about 'the discourse of SMS', in which case our focus moves away from individual compositions towards a larger-scale view of the nature of this form of communication. Such a shift moves us beyond the finer details of the language features towards a greater understanding of who might use the communication, and where, when and why they might do so, as well as the longer-term social implications of its use. It is the aim of this book to bridge these different areas of focus, emphasising not just how texts work internally but how they are connected with the wider world that produced them. In other words, our theoretical approach is discourse-analytic: we will be taking a discourse perspective on the texts that we analyse.

'Text' has also traditionally referred primarily to written communication, whereas 'discourse' has focused more on spoken language. Older textbooks on 'discourse analysis', at least within language studies, are likely to be looking primarily at conversations, speeches and other types of talk. However, in more recent times the two terms have moved closer together, with both 'text' and 'discourse' encompassing more than simply written or spoken communication. New forms of digital communication have aided this broadening of focus, encouraging ideas about the inter-connectedness of speech and writing rather than seeing them as different, discrete systems. For example, Twitter users produce 'tweets', communication symbolised as birdsong (endorsed by Twitter's bird logo) – but tweets are messages that, like SMS, are keyboard products. The increasingly **multimodal** nature of our modern communication systems takes us beyond any easy or narrow conceptualisations of speech (or sound) and writing (or symbol).

In keeping with this broader view of communication as multimodal, this book will cover aspects of spoken and written language, but will not divide its coverage into sections on that basis. Of particular interest throughout the book is the intertwined nature of speech and writing, so that aspects that have historically been associated with particular types of communication are brought into view more generally. For example, the dimensions of space and time, which form the focus for some of the work in Part III, are seen as significant for texts of all kinds, and links are made not only between spoken and written texts but also between literary texts and many other kinds of communication.

While we certainly do not ignore important visual elements, such as images, that form an integral part of many messages, the central concern of this book is with language in the verbal sense. Part II explores aspects of language patterning that recur across many different texts, helping to form the basis for an analytical toolkit. Part III situates language in broader dimensions of context, enabling the different tools in the kit to be selected for particular purposes.

Although the different parts of the book do prioritise different aspects of analysis, the approach of the whole book is to see texts not as isolated artefacts, but as part of the social texture of any community. There are many texts for you to work on, and equally many suggestions for activities that will enable you to look around your own community and understand more about its textual output. This will help you to take a broad, discourse-oriented view of the texts that are part of your daily life and that both reflect and construct its realities.

Part I

Foundations

Researching texts

Aim: Part I will help you develop the research skills that are fundamental to the academic work of text analysis.

CONTENTS: PART I

1. Your materials
2. Gathering more materials
3. Sizing up the job: questions, scope and focus
4. The right tools for the job: research methods
5. Preparing the ground: reading and note-making skills
6. Analysing
7. Reporting: writing about texts

   Review your skills

   Commentaries for Part I

CHAPTER 1

Your materials

Developing a spirit of enquiry starts in your own location. Research is not necessarily about leaving familiar territory – some of the best work is done on home soil. At the core of all good research is the ability to stand back from what is known and see it afresh. This can be done in any context, familiar or not.

However, standing back from language is never easy, because it seems so natural to us. The activities that follow are designed to get you looking at yourself anew – as the source of some good language materials.

> **A LANGUAGE INVENTORY**
>
> Answer the questions below, making an inventory as you go. At the end of this process, you will have a profile of yourself as a resource for ongoing text analysis.

Activity 1.1

1.1 YOUR OWN LANGUAGE DEVELOPMENT

Make a list of any material you have, or have access to, that relates to your younger self. For example:

Early reading books	Teachers' reports	Diaries
Old comics and magazines	School exercise books	Games
Greetings cards	Collections, eg football cards, cards about toys	
Recordings of yourself	Letters, eg to a penpal	

Examples of your digital communication, eg emails, SMSs, social media posts.

1.2 YOUR FAMILY AND FRIENDS

Make a list of any people in your immediate social circle who are interesting or intriguing from a language point of view. For example:

- Do you have younger relatives or friends who are themselves using or producing any of the material above?
- Do you have any relatives or friends in occupations that use a specific type of language?
- Do you have any older relatives or friends who have kept material from years ago – for example, sports articles, greetings cards etc.?
- Do you have friends from different communities who use language in distinctive ways?

1.3 YOU NOW...

- Do you belong to any groups or take part in any activities that have their own forms of language?
- Do you do any work that involves you in using language in a certain way?
- Do you collect, read and/or write particular sorts of material?
- Individuals are said to have their own 'idiolect', or set of linguistic fingerprints that are uniquely their own. Give some examples of language habits or expressions that characterise your idiolect.

1.4 ...AND YOUR ATTITUDES

Everyone has an attitude to some aspect of language or another. What are some of your pet loves and hates about language? What are some of the things that make you laugh, think, feel confused, cry? Read the list below, and add any further items that you feel strongly about:

- The way people speak on mobile phones
- Shop names
- Gravestone inscriptions
- Family conversations
- Sign language
- Advertising language
- Language and stereotyping
- Political speeches
- Occupational language – e.g. legal language, scientific language
- Children's expressions
- SMS
- The way people communicate online – e.g. in blogs, on Twitter, on social media

- Language and 'political correctness'
- Terms of address – e.g. words used to women
- Swearing
- Song lyrics
- Personal ads – e.g. the language of internet dating sites
- The language of some rituals – e.g. weddings, funerals
- Language use in some specific contexts – e.g. at the hairdresser's, at the dentist's
- Communication with animals – e.g. the way people speak to their dogs
- Graffiti
- Conversations between strangers at bus stops or on trains
- Greetings
- The language of junk mail
- Bias in newspapers
- The language of some magazines
- Certain types of literature
- Road signs
- Greetings cards
- The language of birth announcements or obituaries
- Some new words and expressions
- Particular **accents**, dialects or languages

When you feel you have exhausted all the topics here, write a summary for yourself of all the different language resources you could tap into, and all the different language areas that provoke a reaction in you.

Your summary is, in effect, a description of you as a language resource. It shows some possible sources of texts, and it also shows some areas where doing research could be rewarding for you. Research questions that arise from something you find personally affecting – whether that's pleasurable, or annoying – can be powerful because you care.

This completes the first layer of your toolkit.

CHAPTER 2

Gathering more materials

Simply sticking with your existing resources will not give you a way to develop further. You need to plan for how you will go about collecting new sources of language use.

Here are some ways you can add to your raw materials:

2.1 RECORDING

Keep a note of interesting examples of language use that you see and/or hear as you go about your everyday life. There are times when we all wish we had had a way to record a conversation that unfolds near us, perhaps on a bus or in the street. However, even if the conversation itself proves elusive, it is still possible to record some elements of it in a notebook or notemaking tool on a phone or other device. Try to make a note of what it was that you found so interesting.

Of course, recording sound and/or video has become far easier with mobile digital technologies, and there are many examples of undercover recordings that are made by investigative journalists attempting to expose what they see as corruption or bad behaviour of some kind. However, academic research ethics also warn us against doing anything which causes harm to individuals during the process of research, particularly if those individuals are vulnerable – for example, if they are very young, elderly and infirm, mentally ill, or powerless in some way. Ideally, if you want to record people in conversation, you should ask the permission of the speakers. However, researchers recognise that the very act of doing this can alter what would otherwise occur naturally, for example by people saying what they think you want to hear, or by being on their best behaviour. This idea of the researcher affecting the results of their own research is called the **observer's paradox**. Sometimes, a compromise position is reached where recording is covert (if it really has to be) and then permission is asked afterwards – and may be refused. In any case, whatever is transcribed for public view must not reveal any details about the participants' lives, such as their names, where they live, where they work, and so on.

While recording or photographing individuals always requires some thinking about ethical behaviour, capturing images of inanimate objects is more straightforward. It may get you some puzzled looks, but there's nothing to stop you photographing signs, notices and objects that are on public display. However, items in galleries, museums and private collections have their own rules and you need to abide by whatever terms are in operation.

SWEDISH TRAIN SEAT

An example of a picture taken spontaneously. These Swedish train seats are covered with faux graffiti – the fabric has the handwritten names of the Swedish royal family (for example, Kristina, Viktoria, Sofia). Would it be ok to sit on the names of your country's rulers?

Text 2.1

NOBODY WAS HERE

Here is another example of something seen in passing, this time a piece of real graffiti photographed in a public square in Paris. The writer seems to be playing with the traditional tag of 'X was here'. They claim to be nobody, and in so doing they are creating a paradox because somebody must have written the language.

Text 2.2

WATERSTONES

Text 2.3

Here is an example of a text that has been professionally produced. This poster, from a UK bookshop, is interesting from a language perspective because it assumes that readers know a particular type of saying ('You can take the X out of the Y, but you can't take the Y out of the X'). This expression means that you can physically remove someone, but the context you've removed them from stays in their hearts and minds. An example could be 'You can take a girl out of school but you can't take school out of the girl', to mean that you can make a girl leave school but she will always be interested in learning.

Encouraging readers to interact with a text is a well known strategy used by advertisers to draw attention to a message. However, this text uses the routine pattern in a clever way, by suggesting that not only is the saying so well known that it doesn't need repeating, but so is the idea that books represent a lifelong enrichment for children.

GONE TANNING

Text 2.4

Here are two further texts from different parts of the world that use references to other texts (termed **intertextuality**) as a starting point for their own creative language use. The first text, right, is from a shop selling beachwear in Lisbon, Portugal. The sign announces that the shop is closed by referring intertextually to the phrase 'Gone fishing', implying that the writer is enjoying himself elsewhere. In using the phrase 'Gone tanning', the suggestion is that the author is on a beach somewhere.

CI GUSTA

The second text, right, is from a food outlet specialising in ice cream and light lunches in Chennai, India. The shop is called 'ci gusta', part of a **global** company whose headquarters are in Italy. The carrier bag uses an intertextual reference to the phrase 'Have a good day' – originally American English but now used in many other countries too. 'Have a food day' is ci gusta's international slogan, used on their website as well as on their packaging.

Text 2.5

2.2 ARCHIVING

Having established the idea that you need to look around constantly for interesting texts, the next issue is how to store them. You may well end up with a variety of text types – paper notebooks, cuttings from newspapers and magazines, junk mail, digital notes on a phone, tablet or computer, sound files, video clips, photographs, screen grabs, saved internet chats and web links, to name but a few. How you organise your collection is up to you, but you will need a system that is searchable and logical. For example, you could store particular text types all together, so you have all your photographs in one digital file, speech transcripts in another; and scanned paper cuttings in a third. Or you could file your texts by theme and put texts of different types under particular headings. As an example of the latter, see below, taken from a real researcher's archive. This collection could be entitled 'interesting shop names: men's clothes', with details of the names, sources, dates, and places, as well as the questions raised by each example.

14 GATHERING MORE MATERIALS

Text 2.6

RESEARCHER'S ARCHIVE

Interesting shop names: men's clothes

The Throttleman: Pamplona, Spain, 1998.
'The word 'throttle' sounds quite frightening as it's an old word for strangling someone. I wonder how Spanish people understand it? It also refers to an accelerator on a motorbike so maybe it suggests speed – perhaps it's only older native speakers of English who would know the other meaning?
www.throttleman.es

Pull and Bear: Galicia, Spain, 2000.
This seems like an odd combination of words. Does 'pull' mean 'pullover'? Does 'bear' refer to an animal, or are both words verbs (i.e. pull something, bear a weight)?
www.pullandbear.com

Paul and Shark: Amsterdam, 2009.
An Italian clothes shop with an odd pairing of a man's name and a frightening predator. Bears, sharks – is there a theme here?! Would you have a store called 'Tom and Squirrel', or 'John and Hedgehog'??
www.paulandshark.it

The links provided for each of the shops raise a further question about how digital texts are best stored. Obviously, if there is a possibility that a website may change, then creating a screen grab and storing it is the safest solution. Although news and magazine sites often have their own searchable archives that you can return to (sometimes for a fee), and Google and YouTube can help you to recover a multitude of lost links, saving and assembling a collection of links under specific headings can become a valuable resource for later use. There are many different kinds of free digital storage spaces available where links can be collected, tagged and organised to suit different needs: current examples include Zotero, Delicious, Evernote and Pocket.

Speech data recorded as sound files make their own specific demands on researchers, first to store, and then to transcribe. Transcription conventions vary in their level of detail, depending on what the research question is. Links to some information about transcription are given on the Links page at the end of the book (p232). Internet chat transcriptions can be simply saved as Word files before closing the chat window.

CHAPTER 3

Sizing up the job

Questions, scope and focus

3.1 QUESTIONS

Parts II and III of this book include many activities where research questions have already been set up for you. However, there will be occasions where you want to set your own agenda, and there are some generic questions that frequently come into play regardless of the precise focus of the research.

WH-question words can seem very minor, but can address important questions in text analysis:

- WHAT?

What happens in a text is always going to be of interest, regardless of the research question. Pointing to a text's features is part of the way that you structure an analysis, as they form evidence for your interpretation.

As you move away from the 'what?' question towards the other 'wh' questions, you are moving from describing what is in a text to considering some of the reasons for the language choices that are in evidence.

- WHO?

If you are looking at speech (or any other real-time interaction, such as an online chat) then the question of who the participants were, and how they related to each other, will be a significant factor in the language choices that they made. For example, two people who know each other well are likely to be less formal than two strangers.

Written texts may not appear to have participants in quite the same way as speech, but they do have implied communicators. Writers, consciously or subconsciously, create a **narrative** voice to address their audience, and this voice can make many assumptions about who you are as a reader. In this way, a written text can in fact have many 'WHOs' – a real writer, an imaginary **narrator**, a real reader, and an implied reader, as well as the characters who might populate the text itself. There is more extensive coverage of this question in Part III of this book.

- WHERE?

The physical setting for a conversation or text is also an important determinant of language choices and meanings. People who know each

16 SIZING UP THE JOB

other well enough to use very informal language might not use that language if the setting is very formal — for example, a courtroom or lecture theatre. Context can be powerful in other ways too.

TSUNAMI

Many public notices only make sense because they occur in a particular place: for example, warning signs such as the one here are placed only at strategic points where readers might need to take action (in this case, the Californian coastline).

A further aspect of location is the key question of the **point of view** or perspective that any text sets up. For students of language, this refers to how a topic is presented — for example, which details are left in the background and which are **foregrounded**. The idea of perspective, like the word perspective itself (from Latin perspicere, to look intensively), traces its origin to the visual arts — art, photography and other types of visual communication. Every verbal text sets up a position from which ideas are viewed as surely as an image does.

LISBON

This is a mosaic in the centre of Lisbon, photographed from the top of an adjacent building, showing Portuguese voyages of discovery. Compare this point of view with the perspectives that were available to the people standing on the map.

More exploration of the importance of placement is provided in Part III of this book.

- **WHEN?**

The time of a text occurrence is also an important factor. Language changes constantly, as do our attitudes towards different expressions. Older texts can reveal a lot about the values of a previous era, and the language of that era might not be acceptable today. On the other hand, it's important not to assume that the modern era is somehow superior or has all the best tricks. It might surprise you to learn that Richard II, who was king of England from 1377–1399, was rather fond of something called a 'tostee', a toasted sandwich. This link is to a cookbook called 'The Forme of Cury', written in 1390 by some of the chefs at his court. (The word 'cury' was the medieval English term for cookery.) This archive is explored again in Part II, Section B: Lexical and Semantic Level.

http://www.bl.uk/learning/langlit/booksforcooks/med/tosteehome/curytostee.html

Time is also a factor in terms of the status of particular language varieties, with some 'World Englishes' such as Sri Lankan English or Afro-Caribbean English gaining recognition as distinctive varieties of English only relatively recently.

There is further exploration of the concept of time as it relates to texts in Part III of this book.

- **HOW?**

This question is all about how the language choices in a text work – how they connect with each other and build into a pattern that can be read or understood in particular ways. Answering the 'how' question involves interpretation: there is no single right answer to a question about how a text works. This is because different readers will see different things in a text, depending on what an individual brings to the text from his or her own cultural background and personal experience.

- **WHY?**

Why is the language as it is? This is a question that can take us beyond the text and into many different sociocultural aspects, reflecting the discourses that are current in any culture at a specific time, including ideas about what is appropriate for different audiences and purposes. Answering this question demands extra tentativeness, as there can be many complex reasons for the nature of any particular text. Complexity should not be off-putting: recognising and showing complexity, where it exists, is a hallmark of high quality research.

A practical exercise can help to get you thinking about the usefulness of applying the 'wh' questions to a text.

18 SIZING UP THE JOB

Activity 3.1

USING 'WH' QUESTIONS

Choose a text to focus on. This could be something you have collected yourself, or something that has been included in this book up to this point. Go through the 'wh' questions in turn, answering each one by thinking about its relevance to the text you have selected. At the end of the process, you should have produced a wealth of ideas about the nature of your text, as well as learning that some questions may be more useful than others, depending on the text involved.

Here is an example, to help you get started. The notes below were written by a student of English language. You can still focus on the 'ci gusta' text yourself, as you may not agree with what is written here, plus there is more to say about this text.

> The 'ci gusta' carrier bag.
> This text is interesting because of its use of English in an international context, so my focus to start with was on the 'where' question. But this is linked to the 'when' question, too, because English seems to be used a lot more now than it was years ago, as a form of international communication. But I also think the 'who' question is important, because the carrier bag has been produced by the company as their form of advertising. Whoever was given this became a walking ad for 'ci gusta'. But I've noticed that the bag has the company's website on it, so the bag is not the only form of advertising that they do.

3.2 FOCUS AND SCOPE

Deciding that some questions should take priority is the same thing as determining a focus. The term focus is no different in text analysis from how it functions in photography, where it means adjusting your sights to get as sharp a picture as possible of a specific area. Focus is, in turn, closely connected with scope, which is about how much of the rest of the picture to include. Scope is often determined by focus: if the focus of the enquiry is clear, then the scope of the study shouldn't be too difficult to work out.

TELESCOPE

Think about the visual analogy below — if you get the focus right on a telescopic image, then its surroundings become clear. However, you should remember that there is still a world outside of the image you have trained your sights on.

Text 3.3

There is no fixed pathway for a language exploration, and you can see from the student's notes on the 'ci gusta' text earlier that one idea can lead to another. This particular student starts with the idea of international English, but then moves on to focus on the nature of advertising. So a suggested focus for him/her would be to look at the use of English in the advertising material of international companies. The scope of a study is partly determined by how big a part an independent study plays on any particular course. Nevertheless, whatever the level of study, students are rewarded for the detail of their analysis, and it is better to limit the amount of material chosen. In this case, limiting the scope to one company, perhaps comparing its paper-based advertising with its online version, could yield some interesting results. The student's own commentary shows that this variation is something that interests him/her.

The suggestions made here are just that — suggestions. There is no right or wrong approach, but clear and realistic aims and plans are important.

CHAPTER 4

The right tools for the job
Research methods

4.1 WHAT IS A RESEARCH METHOD?

A research method is simply how you go about finding out answers to the questions you have posed. Since language is all around us, you need to decide how to capture some language and fix it for study. In doing that, you are automatically using a method. As well as referring to how you collect material, the term 'method' also refers to how you do your analysis.

This book as a whole supports a research method called text analysis or discourse analysis, and although there are many sub-fields within that method, there are certain ideas that are shared.

A commonly-held view is that text analysis relies on interpretation – that is, a reading or story by the researcher about what is going on in a text. Different schools of text or discourse analysis place different degrees of emphasis on how much a researcher's own perspective can be relied on, and argue about what it means to carry out an 'objective' text analysis. However, no text or discourse analysis is a hands-free activity: it involves human beings observing the behaviour of other human beings (or their own behaviour).

The approach of this book is to equip you with as much expertise as possible in identifying and describing aspects of language, so that you can point to them as evidence for the reading you give of any text. Some aspects of language are well known to play a part in constructing certain meanings and impressions, and these will be outlined in detail. On the other hand, meanings are not fixed, so there are times when the same language feature can produce a very different effect. As well as your developing ability to recognise language features, therefore, you need an understanding of how aspects of context can help to shape meanings and understandings. The two-part nature of the method being proposed here is reflected in the division of the rest of the book into Parts II and III.

Text or discourse analysis is sometimes referred to as a **qualitative research method**, and this is contrasted with **quantitative** approaches. Qualitative research aims to give an account of the nature of things – what things are like in a certain domain of human activity. It can be very small scale, even to the point of focusing on a single individual as a case study. Quantitative research is much more concerned with large-scale patterns, and is often used in scientific research studies involving whole populations of individuals – for example, to test new medical treatments. While the finer details are missing in quantitative research, information gathered from so many people can produce a level of reliability, at least about general trends.

The two approaches described above are not mutually exclusive. Although text analysis is qualitative in nature, that doesn't stop an analyst from counting occurrences of features. There are also many useful tools, such as dictionaries and language corpora, that themselves are based on quantitative methods to some extent. These types of resource are a supportive addition to the text analyst's toolkit, because they are able to draw on many examples in order to suggest how words and expressions are habitually used. A language corpus is a large body of items ('corpus' is Latin for 'body') which have been collected together from a variety of sources and stored electronically. Because corpora are computer-based, they can be searched, so it is possible to select a particular word and search for it, producing a range of examples of how it has been used in different texts. It is possible to call up a few words either side of the item being searched, providing a little bit of the context for a particular word. A list of such lines is termed a **concordance.**

Corpora will not do your analysis for you. There are also issues about what corpora contain; for example, if the collection is mainly sourced from newspapers and formal spoken language, then casual expressions are unlikely to be represented. However, what you can begin to see when you use a corpus is that sometimes words occur in predictable patterns, having regular 'friends'. This idea of frequent co-occurrence is called a **collocation**. Collocations can infuse a word or phrase with a certain set of **associations**, or **connotations**, and can help to explain why a writer might prefer one term to another for a particular text.

Getting access to some corpora can be expensive, but some allow free searches which will offer you a range of examples which should be enough for a regular text analysis. References to the nature of corpora will occur throughout the book, and more substantial information about different corpora is given at the back (see *Corpus resources and projects*, p218).

USING A CORPUS

This activity will give you a flavour of how corpus searches can help you. Imagine that you are analysing a text where a writer has chosen to use the word 'chat' rather than a synonym such as 'discussion'. You are aware that chat seems less formal than discussion, but you would like to know more about how the two terms are used more generally.

Activity 4.1

COBUILD 'CHAT' AND 'DISCUSSION'

Below are two searches from an original database called Collins Cobuild (Collins Birmingham University International Language Database). The searches were based on the terms 'chat' and 'discussion'.

What patterns of usage do you notice for the two terms?

Look at the words surrounding the searched items – do they tend to be different? If so, how?

For example, is there any evidence that 'discussion' might occur in more formal contexts than 'chat'?

```
           of re wine and joins in the sex-chat [p] Todd and I would like to
     far away from him to have much of a chat. [p] It wasn't until the 14th that
     proper space for these youngsters to chat about their problems. [p] As you can
        all in The Lover, is jetting in to chat about her new potboiler, The Colour
      least 10 minutes, where we laugh and chat and generally put the world to
          at Camp David for a 90-minute chat and a photo opportunity, an offer
         overturn recent preference for anti-chat, for clever interviewers outwitting
          over, contact [c] telephone [/c] [h] CHAT FROM THE CHAIR [/h] [p] At long
                  and now we share a drink and chat. He reached out [p] Auberon Waugh,
  office writer came to pay a visit and chat. He had been to a great Heathen
     not appropriate. Once your child can chat more easily to familiar friends, you
       shaking. Did you just want to have a chat, or what?" In one burst I said, `I
        perhaps when you've got more time to chat. Our new Caller Display service
              him to her private suite for a chat over a drink. It was a perfect
      course meal interrupted by `rest and chat periods with more bevvy [p] Mary
            gay men. For more information or a chat ring 071-837 3337 (men & women, 7.30-
              tuning in to a late-night cultural chat show on Italian television, every
         terrible, called in by mischievous chat-show producers to deflate the great
       DJ Nicky Campbell his own late night chat show [p] In November, for example,
        up artist from a popular television chat show who the president if the
              Oprah Winfrey;People Today [/h] [p] CHAT show host Oprah Winfrey claims she
     daughter about your sex life, advises chat show host Joan Rivers. `Or lack of
           Faithfull stormed off a Canadian TV chat show this week after she took a
              of famous men including Sixties chat show host Simon Dee. [p] Lainie's
               Potter plays, gay seasons, nude chat shows, the infamous After Dark
         loving are high priorities. Fancy a chat? Telephone Mailbox No 77980. [p]
         11 learn much more from a leisurely chat than a quick one. Two: I want you to
           show, where you'll have a chance to chat to some of the dancers. Please send
              You could stand beside the car, chat to whomever you wanted. It was cold
       boy, who only went into the garage to chat to the cashier, was gunned down by
          American visiting England started to chat up a pretty young thing in a bar. `
              Leaning across the gangway to chat up a young mother with her baby as
         special [p] But the fast-faltering chat-up technique still didn't get him
              and it was great to be able to chat with one's fellow translators and
         to 29th place. Clarke didn't stop to chat with the group he'd just caught,
         the bathroom with BONO, and sneaks a chat with THE EDGE and mad, bad and sad-
      anything of any value coming from a chat with Lady Godetia: her name's coming
         and telephones so that you can have a chat with a NatWest [p] insurance
          the buildings is unduly grand. [p] A chat with the court physician preceded
             life too seriously. [p] [h] Back Chat;Woman Today;Letter [/h] [p] I ADMIRE
```

practical experiment, reading and discussion. [p] [p] Theatre-going is an
of humour is a pointless topic of discussion. [p] To a large extent,
   soon as possible their unhelpful discussion [p] [h] British dons to judge
Contact Theatre); Queer Culture, a discussion about lesbian and gay arts (26
   this could lead to a more general discussion about Leo. Finding out about him
one factor which can influence the discussion about that in Poland: Catholic
He is here just to cash in on the discussion and the debates around
      that all options remain under discussion and that a shorter phase-in
   issue which transcends all other discussion. But Ayatollah Sadeq Khalkali,
         leader said he welcomes such discussion, but said it would be more
led Barak off for a more detailed discussion. Cheney repeated the familiar
   on Sunday.) Lesbian social and discussion group plus coffee bar. Meets 1st
year. It did not seem the level of discussion had been high. [p] [f] Shut up,
   MOW is stimulating thought and discussion in all these areas. It produces
   did not appear ready for serious discussion. Instead Polish sources are
Hartman has transformed the entire discussion into a debate about language. `De
   When you are orchestrating a discussion like the one between Jacqueline
   significantly at the start of a discussion of all these categories, the
   Again he begins his essay with a discussion of Chih-i's doctrine of the Three
   Gallery vote and then possibly no discussion of it would arise in parliament,"
   c 1600-1800" into a challenging discussion of the origins of nationalism
      organized a commission for the discussion of problems arising out of the
         the therapist would begin a discussion of the infant's developmental
      first became aware of it. His discussion of the irrationality of the end (
An excellent, thorough, up-to-date discussion of all the research on memory in
         the man was laudatory in his discussion of Nixon's command of
   there—there's the beginning of discussion of—of his side of this too. And
         [p] Spotlight — pre-show discussion on Loot and Entertaining Mr
   on the `passions", notably his discussion on whether `union is the effect
      researchers demanded more open discussion on euthanasia. [p] The current

---

There is a commentary on this activity at the end of Part I.

24   THE RIGHT TOOLS FOR THE JOB

Activity 4.2

TRY IT FOR YOURSELF

Cobuild research started in the 1980s, before the use of the internet became widespread. Since that time, many terms have expanded their meanings to encompass new communication technologies. For example, in the Collins Corpus from 1990–1999, uses of the word 'cloud' referred 100% of the time to meteorology, or clouds of dust or smoke. From 2005–2009, more than 60% of the recorded uses referred to computing, with the phrase 'in the cloud' referring to communication rather than atmospheric particles.

Do you think 'chat' is likely to have undergone a similar development?

Try a search for yourself: go to the BNC at the link below (the British National Corpus, comprising one hundred million words) and do some free searches on both 'chat' and 'discussion'. Do you get similar results to those you saw from Cobuild? Are there any uses of either term in new communication contexts?

http://www.natcorp.ox.ac.uk

There is no commentary on this activity because each free search will offer fifty random lines of text.

4.2 METHODS OF DATA COLLECTION

Many suggestions have already been offered about collecting and archiving different written materials. In the case of written texts, decisions are not so much about how to collect them but how much to collect. Obviously, this will depend on what the enquiry is. As the book proceeds, you will be given some guidance on how to limit the scope of your research for any particular activity.

However, there are some specific issues about capturing and presenting examples of spoken language and other types of data that operate in real time.

4.2.1 Recording and transcribing speech

Different research methods require particular methods of data collection. For example, if you want to know something about how spontaneous speech works, then you need to record some real speech. That might sound obvious, but sometimes people think they can learn about real speech by looking at fictionalised speech – for example, in novels, plays or TV ads. Looking at the dialogue in novels or plays or advertising can tell you a lot about the way the novelist or playwright or advertising copywriter has gone about their work, but you won't know about the raw materials they use until you record some of the real thing.

Speech comes in many shapes and sizes, from the very public and rehearsed, such as political speeches, to the very private and spontaneous, such as two friends chatting over a coffee at home. Speech is tricky to record clearly and transcribing is hard work, so you need to think carefully beforehand about what kind of speech you really want to capture, and why. However, just by recording and transcribing a small amount you will quickly learn that speech works very differently from writing, so it is well worth the effort. Knowing a little about how speech works will help you to write more effectively about the way some writers try to sound speech-like when you come to analyse written texts.

> **THINKING ABOUT TRANSCRIPTION**
>
> Read the transcription of the voicemail message below.
> You will notice some things about the way transcriptions are written.
> First, the transcript is not written as **sentences**, with full stops and capital letters. This is because the idea of the 'sentence' comes from writing, where we demarcate visually, using punctuation. In speech we demarcate orally, using gaps in sound. So the gaps in the stream of sound are marked using brackets, with (.) representing a normal pause for breath, and numbers representing longer pauses.
> What features do you see that are typical of some kinds of spoken language?
>
> There is a commentary on this activity at the end of Part I.

Activity 4.3

VOICEMAIL MESSAGE

hi it's Helen (.) I'm just ringing up to say a happy Christmas (.) and all that kind of thing (.) and see how you are (.) and um (1.0) I'm off I'm off to Ireland this week (.) but when I get back let's get together (.) and eat and drink and things like that (1.0) and walk maybe and do stuff (.) and all that kind of thing (1.0) so hope you're ok sweetie (.) and have a lovely time (1.0) speak to you soon (.) bye

Text 4.2

The text above is a single speaker, so there are no examples of the way that spoken dialogue involves overlaps and interruptions. Nor does it show many other aspects of sound – for example, the speaker's accent, voice quality, pitch, volume, intonation, or any other emphasis – but these would all have been there, even though the speaker knew they were speaking into a machine and not to another human being.

You should be aware that transcripts are likely to vary considerably. This is often for good reason – researchers choose their transcription markings according to what they are researching. The voicemail data was collected in order to research the way speakers organised the information that they wanted to leave; and to look at how voicemails might vary according to how familiar the caller was with the recipient. If they had been collected in order to study accent, they would have looked very different.

There are also things called 'transcripts' that are available online, as records of what people said, for example, in conference speeches or interviews. These are often 'cleaned up', in the sense of not always representing faithfully all the pauses and hesitations and normal errors that speakers make, and that we expect them to make as part of being spontaneous and genuine. Everyone knows that speeches are scripted, but we expect them to be delivered from the heart, so speakers often try to make them sound as spontaneous as possible and not rehearsed or word-perfect.

Activity 4.4

TRANSCRIPTION PRACTICE

Go to the NPR link: http://www.npr.org/2012/09/04/160578836/transcript-michelle-obamas-convention-speech, which is hosted by America's National Public Radio. You will see something called a transcript of Michelle Obama's 2012 Democratic Convention speech. The transcript is described as the text that was 'prepared for delivery', so actually it's more of a script. In any case, the written text differs a little from what was actually spoken.

Listen to the beginning of the recording and read the transcript from 'Thank you' as far as 'earth' (eight paragraphs). Now, write out the transcript putting in some markings to reflect Michelle Obama's actual speech. Here are some basic features you could note:

- repetitions and hesitations
- brackets both for normal pauses and for longer ones, e.g. (.) or (2.0)
- bold type or underlining for those words or parts of words that are emphasised more than others
- brackets for a description of any non-verbal or paralinguistic aspects

You can choose how detailed you want your observations to be, but don't annotate just for the sake of it. An approach which focuses on a lot of technical detail is called Conversation Analysis, and the transcriber Gail Jefferson developed a form of notation that many use in that particular field. If you want to use some features from that system, you can find examples on academic sites such as this one at the University of Loughborough:

http://homepages.lboro.ac.uk/~ssca1/notation.htm

> **TRANSCRIPTION PRACTICE** *(continued)*
>
> as well as on individual academic's pages, such as this site run by Sean Rintel:
>
> http://seanrintel.com/key1/
>
> When you have finished annotating, compare your version with the one written on the website. If you able to, try out the different written versions on someone who has not heard the speech. Which of the versions gives a better sense of the spoken performance? Are there aspects of the spoken performance that no amount of written markings can capture?
>
> There is a commentary on this activity at the end of Part I.

4.2.2 Other real-time discourse

Speech might not be the only real-time communication that you want to capture and analyse. Real time writing of various kinds – chat tools on social media sites, text boxes in virtual learning environments, chat windows in online games – demand the keyboard skills of typing, but also, crucially, involve turntaking and some of the other aspects associated with spoken dialogue.

It is possible to save most online chats, normally as a regular Word file. Then it may appear that the job of producing a transcript is done. Actually, however, that is not the case. Although the resulting text will be a faithful reproduction of what the participants wrote in the actual conversation, unless there are timings attached to each posting, it is very difficult to estimate how much of a pause there was between each turn. Nowadays, many chat tools include indicators that another person is writing, which can help to control the pace of turns. However, if there are no cues of this kind, those who write the fastest can sometimes end up with the most turns. This can cause the kind of confusion we rarely experience in speech. An additional issue is that in multimedia contexts, some participants may have more communication tools than others, because technical set-ups vary.

28 THE RIGHT TOOLS FOR THE JOB

Activity 4.5

TRANSCRIPTIONS OF INTERACTIVE WRITING

As a practical illustration of these issues, read the MSN chat data, below.

Alice, aged nine, is in conversation with her great aunt Angela. Alice has a webcam but Angela doesn't. This means that Angela can see Alice but Alice can't see Angela.

How do you explain this line, and what does it indicate about the way real-time writing works?

Angela: coo lovely! we are having a chicken…oh!

There is a commentary on this activity at the end of Part I.

Text 4.3

PERSONAL 'CHAT' DATA

Angela: 'elo
Angela: hey I can see you!
Alice: be back in half an hour got to hav t
Angela: what are you having for t?
[Alice is waving]
Angela: waving at you too!
Angela: what is your badge?
Angela: is it for swimming?
Alice: roast and we are having lamb and roasted beetroot mmm delicious
Alice: its a pirates in the carribean one
Angela: coo lovely! we are having a chicken…oh!
Alice: ok have a good dinner – see you later!

Just because we call real-time writing 'chat', that doesn't necessarily mean that we always write in an informal style, or even in the same style. Of course the environment will have an effect, but so too will the function of the interaction and who the participants are. As an illustration of this variety, here is a different kind of chat. This is between a customer (the same adult as in the chat above) and a provider of webspace (anonymised in the data below). The provider offers an online chat tool, and the customer is using this tool to clarify an issue with the online adviser, Graham.

How would you describe the differences between the chat below and the previous example, including Angela's language use?

BUSINESS 'CHAT' DATA

Text 4.4

Angela (13:29): I have asked to close my account. I have been sent a message about this but I can't log in and read it because you have suspended my account!

Graham (13:30): Good afternoon, I'm Graham from [name of provider] support. This means that your account is closed as you requested.

Angela (13:30): So I don't need to read the message that you have sent me and that you asked me to read?

Graham (13:33): Most likely the message was a confirmation that your account was closed.

Angela (13:34): ok, but can I get that confirmation from you, then please? Otherwise I have no evidence that it has been closed and that you have removed my credit card details.

Graham (13:36): Yes, I can confirm that your account is closed.

Angela (13:37): ok, thanks, can you send me a copy of this chat log then please?

There is no commentary on this activity.

4.2.3 Work on public views and attitudes

If you are exploring a particular discourse or issue – for example, the way literary texts or advertisements represent different cultural groups – you might decide that you want to ask others about their views and attitudes. There are different ways of doing this, including showing groups of people some material face to face and asking them how they respond to it, or setting up a questionnaire online or on paper, or blogging about the issue on your own or others' sites.

Interviewing others effectively and writing clear survey questions are skills in their own right. To develop your skills, you need to practice them. Doing a pilot study before any wider enquiry is always a learning experience. It is a common experience to find that the questions you assumed were clear are anything but, and to realise that you have in fact not covered the very issue you wanted to explore.

Activity 4.6

ASKING OTHERS

As a practice run, read through the material below, which is from a Lonely Planet *Guide to Georgia, Armenia, and Azerbaijan*. This passage is introducing Georgia to readers, and is followed by many further details later in the guidebook. The passage acts as a kind of headline and summary of what is to come. When you have read through the passage, imagine that you want to find out how different readers respond to this text.

First, decide what *you* think of the text. Is it persuasive? Is it informative? Are there terms that are unexplained or difficult to understand? What image does it give you of Georgia? Can you imagine going there and finding it interesting and enjoyable? What would be your hopes and fears about such a journey?

Once you have gathered your own impressions, identify some of the key words and phrases that you think helped you to come to certain conclusions, regardless of whether they were positive or negative.

Now, either write yourself some interview questions which you will ask another person after they have read the passage, or write some survey questions which aim to get some information from other readers about their responses.

Try out your pilot study and draw some conclusions about how well your questions worked, and about the skills needed to conduct interviews and run questionnaires.

Write up your conclusions as a set of guidelines that you can refer back to in future research tasks, and that you can share with others. If you are able to share, add any further tips to your guidelines that you learn from others.

There is no commentary on this activity.

GEORGIA

With sublimely perched old churches, watchtowers and castles dotting its fantastic mountain scenery, Georgia has to be one of the most beautiful countries on earth. This is a place where (except in the drabber, Soviet-built sectors of some towns) the human hand has much enhanced that of nature. Finally putting post-Soviet internal strife and economic stagnation behind it, Georgia is now developing its tourism potential and making the full range of its attractions safely and readily accessible to travellers. Appealing accommodation for all budgets is becoming available across the country and opportunities for exploring by foot, horse or vehicle are expanding fast.

From the snow-capped Caucasus mountains to its semitropical Black Sea coastline, Georgia abounds in natural variety. Tbilisi, the capital and by far the biggest city, has the atmosphere of an age-old Eurasian crossroads, yet it's also a 21st-century city with European-style nightclubs and eye-catching new architecture. Georgia's deeply complicated history has given it a fascinating cocktail of influences from Turkey, Russia, Persia, Central Asia and beyond, with a wonderful heritage of architecture and art. But today Georgia looks to Europe for its future and is the most Western in atmosphere of the three Caucasus countries.

Perhaps its greatest treasure is the Georgians themselves: warm, proud, high-spirited, cultured, obsessively hospitable and expert at enjoying life. This is a country where guests are considered a blessing. The abundant local wine flows freely, tables are laden with fine food and you'll never cease to be delighted by the warmth of your welcome.

CHAPTER 5

Preparing the ground

Reading and note-making skills

Reading and note-making are different but related activities. Reading helps you to acquire ideas and information, while note-making helps you to retain and revisit those ideas. Reading is always good as an activity in its own right, but if your note-making is poor, then you may well forget a lot of the ideas you come across.

There are different types of reading that you will need to do in order to produce successful text analyses. Obviously, there are close reading skills that relate to the texts themselves. Although in real life we don't regularly pore over the many texts that surround us, for purposes of text analysis you will need to be prepared to read texts several times, thinking about them from different angles and asking yourself whether there are different ways of understanding them.

You are also likely to be reading the results of searches in archives of various kinds – for example, dictionaries, thesauruses and language corpora – as well as textbooks, journal articles and other articles found online, for example on Google Scholar or on individual academics' own pages.

The reading you do will be for different reasons. For example, you may want to consult a thesaurus in order to explore the language choices in a text, because you want to know what synonyms there are for some of the terms – in other words, to explore the language choices that were *not* made. That kind of reading is different from reading an article or part of a textbook, where you will be looking for ideas about how to approach an analysis of particular types of text. For example, if you are going to analyse some comics, you will want to see what people have said about how comics work. The Further Reading section at the end of this book is designed to help you to explore in this way.

Whatever reading you do, you need to keep a record of the resources you have consulted, including the title and author of the book or article, as well as its publication details (place and date of publication for a book; date, volume, and part for a journal article; web reference and date of access for an online publication). Page numbers are important where you cite an author's actual words. There are many different guides to referencing, and different referencing conventions, but a frequently used method in arts and humanities subjects is the Harvard system. As with transcription symbols, there are examples on university websites, often as part of library pages. If you do not have a guide from your own university or college, or you are not formally part of an educational organisation, you can go online and find useful resources. For example, here is a link to a library resource called *Cite It Right* at the University of Otago, New Zealand:

http://www.otago.ac.nz/library/pdf/harvard_citeitright.pdf

If your notes are going to be useful, they need to be in a form that you can understand. That might sound obvious, but sometimes people create abbreviations and then forget what they stand for – it's the same as creating passwords then forgetting them. So if you devise a system of abbreviation, keep a note somewhere of what the system is.

While being concise, your notes also need to give you enough detail about what you've read for you to be able to express the ideas in your own words later. Summarising – sometimes called précis – is a skill that can be used in many different contexts, not just in text analysis work. So it's worth spending some time practising.

> **NOTE-MAKING**
>
> Make notes on the following, using your own words and writing no more than 50 words for each task:
>
> - Using the material in Texts and discourses: definitions and approaches (p2), write notes for yourself on how these terms can be defined.
> - Give **5** aspects of recording (p10) and archiving (p13) that are important to remember.
> - Write notes on the 'wh' question words (p15) in a way that jogs your memory about what they stand for.

Activity 5.1

Activity 5.2

USING QUOTATION

This activity is different because this time you are going to pick out some useful pieces of text to use as quotations. Quoting authors' words can be useful if you are presenting an argument or explaining an approach, but it is important to limit the number of words you take from them, otherwise it can seem as if you are not doing your own work.

Choose some useful quotations for the following, from what you have read in this textbook so far. Set out the quotations formally, giving all the details you would need to include if you were writing a formal essay:

- Explaining what a research method is
- Suggesting that recording and transcribing speech involves some special considerations
- Pointing out some issues in analysing real-time writing
- The characteristics of good notes

There is no commentary on these activities.

If you are undertaking a formal piece of research you might be required to write something called a 'literature review', and this again involves a particular set of skills. Even if you are not required to do this, you still need to show that you have read about your subject and that you know how to incorporate ideas from your reading into your analysis.

A literature review is not a list of all the things you've read, and neither is it – like a music or film review – a story of each entire text. Each person whose work you read will be offering an approach, or an argument, or a view of the subject they are writing about. Summarising their views should be an important function of your note-making. If your notes work, then you should be able to bring the writing of person x or y into your analysis at a relevant point. Relevance is the key, though. It's not a question of simply showing how much you have read, but that you have read something that's relevant to what you are doing. The Further Reading section of this book will refer you to articles and books that are relevant, as starting points.

CHAPTER 6

Analysing

In Parts II and III there is a pattern to the way that you will be introduced to the analytical areas that are covered. Explanations of concepts or areas will normally be followed up with an exercise to offer an illustration and to give you some experience of what it means in practice. Analytical activities will be supported by questions and sometimes by bulleted sub-headings, in order to give you some guidance and a pathway through the text. You will then normally be referred to a commentary at the end of a particular part, where you will find some feedback on what was considered important or salient about the feature of a text. At convenient junction points there may be a further text with a more open-ended task. At the end of each section there will be *Ideas for Assignments*, consisting of a list of ideas for more extended research activities where you will be able to put your learning to good use in a more independent way. All these aspects of the book are teaching you about how to do an analysis – how to write an analysis, as well as how to guide your thinking along more research-oriented pathways.

CHAPTER 7

Reporting

Writing about texts

Students are often unsure what style of writing to adopt when they do an analysis. There is also sometimes a mistaken assumption that there are two 'extremes' of writing, one being a very scientific style where it sounds as though no human being ever came near the activity being described, and the other being a very personal style, using 'I think' and 'in my opinion'. The former style can seem very artificial, while the latter can seem a bit pointless – after all, it's your writing and your analysis, so it's obvious that you are the one doing the thinking and speculating.

The best styles of writing for text analysis aim for clarity, using neither of these extremes but what might be described as a 'statement style', where features are described and ideas proposed, but where individuals are neither artificially excluded nor given centre stage. That doesn't mean that you can't use a passive structure (such as 'this was seen' rather than 'I saw this') when you want to; nor does it mean that you can never use 'I'. However, try to sound clear and natural rather than trying to script yourself in a forced way.

Think of a text analysis as a piece of report writing, similar to serious journalism.

> Activity 7.1
>
> **WORKING ON STYLE**
>
> It is worth looking at some examples of 'statement style' that have already been used in this book. The extracts below acted as introductions to the images on pp11–13.

Example 1.
As an example of a picture taken spontaneously, see below. These Swedish train seats are covered with faux graffiti – the fabric has the handwritten names of the Swedish royal family (for example, Kristina, Viktoria, Sofia). (p11)

The section in bold above includes a passive structure: it says the picture was 'taken' rather than saying 'I took this picture'. The rest of the text makes statements about what the seats are like. Note that there is a mixture of verb **tenses**. While the picture 'was taken' in the past, in the descriptions of the features the present tense is used – the train seats 'are covered', the fabric 'has'. This fits with the idea of looking at the picture while it is being described. You may find that you need to mix tenses in this same way when you write your analysis. For example, you might want to say that texts 'were collected' but switch to the present tense when you describe their features.

Example 2.
Here is another example of something *seen* in passing, this time a piece of real graffiti, *photographed* on a public square in Paris. The writer *seems* to be playing with the traditional tag of 'X was here'. They claim to be nobody and in so doing, are creating a paradox because somebody must have written the language. (p11)

As with the first example, 'seen' and 'photographed' are passives, so there is no mention of who took the photograph. Then the features are pointed out again using the present tense – 'the writer seems', 'they claim', 'are creating'. Note that the interpretation of what the writer is doing is made with some tentativeness (using 'seems') as it's impossible to know what was really in the writer's mind.

Now compare these extracts with the examples of notes written for personal use on p14. How do the different styles of writing compare?

7.1 REVIEW YOUR SKILLS

- Do an audit of the areas covered in Part I. Which were new to you, and which were more familiar?
- Choose one activity where you can illustrate some of the skills you have learned and explain how you have put them into practice.
- Which of the skills covered do you feel you need to develop further, and how will you go about this?
- Choose a topic or area of study that you would like to take further. Why did this area interest you and how will you take it further?

7.2 COMMENTARIES FOR PART I

Activity 4.1

USING A CORPUS

The much more serious, topic-driven connotations of 'discussion' are clear. In 40 randomly chosen concordance lines, 'discussion' collocates with 'of' and 'about' (followed by name of subject matter) 13 times; the term is pre-modified by 'detailed', 'more serious', 'entire', 'challenging', 'round table', 'informed', 'theme for', 'topic of', 'level of' and 'a great deal of'; co-ordinated phrases include 'reading and discussion', 'discussion and debate' and 'thought and discussion'. In contrast, in the same number of concordance lines, 'chat' collocates with the prepositions 'to' and 'with' 9 times in total, followed by names of interlocutors, suggesting a focus on relationship with participants rather than subject matter; 'chat-up' occurs 3 times, 'sex chat' once, and 'chat shows' 9 times; informal vocabulary such as 'bevvy' and 'potboiler' occur in close proximity; and co-ordinated phrases include 'laugh and chat', 'drink and chat', 'visit and chat', implying social occasion and intimacy. In summary, while 'discussion' points us towards the idea of the content of the talk, 'chat' points us towards the interpersonal aspect of talk – the people themselves, and their relationship.

Activity 4.3

THINKING ABOUT TRANSCRIPTION

This shows several features typical of informal spoken language between people who know each other well:

- Informal terms of address – use of endearment 'sweetie'
- Informal opening and closing of routine – hi, bye
- **Vague language** – all that kind of thing, things like that, stuff
- Simple connectives – use of 'and'
- Informal simple vocabulary – eat, drink, walk, ok, lovely
- **Ellipsis – subject deletion** in 'hope you're ok', 'speak to you soon'
- **Pragmatics** of shared knowledge – use of first name only, reference to Ireland, particular sense of 'walk' to mean a hike
- Filler – 'um'

TRANSCRIPTION PRACTICE

This is the opening of the speech as written on the website:

> Thank you so much, Elaine…we are so grateful for your family's service and sacrifice…and we will always have your back.

This is what Michelle Obama actually said:

> (*Extensive cheering and applause*)
> Obama: **thank** you (2.0) **thank** you so **much** (1.0) heh heh (5.0) **thank** you (2.0) ah heh heh (2.0) oh goodness thank you so **much** [*cheering and chanting*] with your **help** (1.0) with your **help** (1.0) heh hehe lemme lemme **start** (.) I wanna wanna start by thanking Elaine, Elaine thank you so much, Elaine…we are are so grateful for your family's service and sacrifice (1.0) and we will **al**ways have your **back**.

Transcription key:

(.) normal pause
(1.0) numbers in brackets indicate length of pauses in seconds
bold indicates a stressed syllable
[*square brackets*] indicate contextual information in italics

Activity 4.4

TRANSCRIPTIONS OF INTERACTIVE WRITING

This activity asked specifically about the meaning of this line:

> Angela: coo lovely! we are having a chicken…oh!

Writing is linear – that is, one thing has to happen after another, rather than a group of things happening simultaneously. Try saying 'hello' to a group of people online, and see how long it takes for everyone to reply. Compare this to saying hello to a group of people in a real room – they can all answer at the same time. Writing takes a long time to produce and turns take a long time to conclude. If turns get missed, then catching up requires a kind of emergency strategy of cramming together the responses to several earlier comments or questions. The line above, then, responds to three previous issues – what Alice is having for dinner, what Angela is having for dinner, and what Alice's badge is ('a pirates in the carribean one'). Although writing online occurs in real time like speech, there are many ways in which it is nothing like speech at all. For example, if spoken language was this disordered in its turntaking and sequencing, we'd be in serious trouble.

Activity 4.5

Part II

Drilling down

How texts are structured

This part of the book focuses on the major internal aspects of text analysis, paying attention to the resources of language that writers and speakers can draw on in their meaning-making activities. Section A covers signs and sounds (graphological and phonological aspects). Section B deals with vocabulary (lexis) and semantics, and Section C with aspects of grammar. Each section is divided into smaller units in order to offer accessible steps to learning.

Section A

Graphological and Phonological Levels

Aim: Section A will increase your awareness of how signs and sounds help to shape meanings in texts. This will enrich and deepen the level of detail you are able to offer in any text analysis.

CONTENTS: PART II, SECTION A

8   Definitions
9   Language as a semiotic system
10 What are the rules?
11 Signs and symbols
12 Sounds and symbols
13 Speech, writing and multimodality
    Review your skills
    Ideas for assignments

CHAPTER 8

Definitions

The term **graphology** refers to the visual aspects of language, and for that reason it is more closely associated with writing than with speech. There is a specialist use of the term which refers narrowly to the study of handwriting, but the broader use of the term within language study refers to all the aspects of visual appearance that affect how we interpret written communication. This can range from the nature of the medium of production – such as the quality of the paper or brightness of the screen – to aspects such as typeface, font, the use of colour, and the effects of different layouts.

The term **phonology** refers to the study of the sound system of a language, which can form the basis for understanding how different languages (and different **dialects** of the same language) can have different numbers of phonemes, or individual sounds. To speak of a sound system of any language is to refer to the way a particular language classifies which sounds are seen as similar to each other and which sounds are seen as different from one another. This might seem rather an abstract area, but in fact phonological classifications can help us not only to understand some significant aspects of language learning, but also to analyse how representation and stereotyping work. For example, if speakers want to imitate a particular accent, they will emphasise one or two sounds that are distinctive in that language variety. This might seem convincing to a listener, but a narrow focus on a small number of features can stereotype the speakers of that variety. Representations of speakers can, of course, also occur in written form.

The term **phonetics** refers to a more detailed focus on how sounds are produced, and on the subtle variations that can occur between different articulations of the same sound.

CHAPTER 9

Language as a semiotic system

Language is sometimes referred to as a **semiotic** system. This means that it is thought of as a system where the individual elements – **signs** – take their overall meaning from how they are combined with other elements. The analogy that is often used to illustrate this principle is the system of road traffic lights: the red, amber and green lights seen in many countries work as a system, and the whole system has meaning which is not carried by any one of the lights alone, but by the lights in a certain combination and sequence. In the same way, written letters of a language are signs that have to be in a certain order to make sense to the user of a language, and the sounds of a language are signs that only have meaning to a hearer when they occur in predictable groups. It is clearly possible for the elements mentioned to occur in unpredictable ways – such as red and green lights occurring simultaneously, or written words or spoken utterances looking or sounding unnatural – but then these occurrences would be classified as 'mistakes', 'breakdowns' or 'creative innovations', depending on the context. The fact that occurrences are seen as rule-breaking demonstrates the fact that rules are operating.

Ferdinand de Saussure (1857–1913), a Swiss linguist who is often credited by Western scholars with founding the study of European linguistics, saw language as one of many signing systems that worked alongside each other. Working at the turn of the twentieth century, he coined the term **semiology** to describe 'the science of signs', believing that it was important to go beyond language in the narrowest sense and develop theories about how other signing systems worked.

In modern times scholars from many different fields, including language, use semiotics as an analytical method for exploring cultural rules of all kinds (see Chandler, 2004 for a useful introduction to this area). Analysts who are interested in seeing language as a cultural phenomenon would look at society as a whole as a system of signs: for example, films as a system where different signs are combined in patterned ways; dress codes as embodying rules where different elements can occur in many varied combinations; or food as rule-governed around what can be combined with what, when food can be taken, and what it is called. In all such aspects of culture, conventions are seen as highly culture-bound – in other words, different cultures have different semiotic systems.

The starting point of this book is a focus on language and the way it operates. However, 'the way it operates' is not easy to separate from the culture that produces it. While much of the focus in this book is on language in the verbal sense, we also consider the other signing systems that work alongside it, believing that all signs count towards the meaning of messages. Other subject areas – for example, media studies, cultural studies or sociology – may reverse this focus, concentrating more on the cultural rules and less on language use. In analysing texts, all analysts will prioritise and emphasise some aspects at the expense of others.

For students of language, semiotics has strong connections with both **semantics** and **pragmatics.** There are connections with semantics in the sense of the overall meaning of a text, and the way in which any text is part of a larger system of significance. There are also connections with pragmatics because pragmatics is all about assumed knowledge – what is implied and inferred, rather than directly said. Levels of acceptable directness or levels of required indirectness in constructing texts are important pragmatic considerations that need to be carefully judged. For any text to be effective, the producer has to understand the unspoken rules that operate within any society.

CHAPTER 10

What are the rules?

The sociologist Harold Garfinkel (1857–1913) designed a specific research method in order to test whether a rule operated in a culture. His advice to researchers who thought they had identified a rule was that they should deliberately break the rule. He claimed that if this provoked a reaction from the members of the culture, it was proof that a rule was indeed in operation.

Contemporary researchers still employ this method. For example, the anthropologist Kate Fox in *Watching the English* (2005) believes that people in the UK have a strong sense of fairness in everyday interactions such as queuing at the supermarket checkout or for public transport. She deliberately breaks some queuing rules and provokes, if not direct challenges, then certainly hostile stares and loud mutterings of complaint within her earshot. She concludes that there is a rule in UK culture about queuing, but there is also another rule about the need for indirectness and politeness in formulating complaints and challenges. In this example, you can see how a set of cultural rules about behaviour interconnect with language use: the people in the queues used non-verbal communication and verbal language designed to be overheard by the rule-breaker, but not addressed to her directly.

Of course, rules are not static. Societies change and evolve new social practices for a variety of reasons, including technological developments. A recent example of the latter was a case of a UK supermarket checkout worker who refused to process the groceries of a customer who was talking on her mobile phone. Initially the supermarket apologised to the customer and chastised the worker, but then a public outcry followed, supporting the checkout assistant and criticising the customer for rudeness. This example shows an airing of new practices involving language use, with attitudes being expressed about what is thought to be polite and acceptable in public interactions.

http://www.independent.co.uk/news/uk/home-news/is-it-rude-to-pay-up-while-talking-on-your-phone-dont-all-call-at-once-8683927.html

The activity that follows is designed to get you thinking about the cultural rules that operate in your community, with a focus on how those rules might produce or constrain certain kinds of language.

48 WHAT ARE THE RULES?

Activity 10.1

Think about (and discuss with others if possible) some of the social rules about language use in your community. One way to reveal some of the hidden rules is to imagine you are giving advice to a tourist coming to your community. How might they inadvertently break some of your rules and cause problems for themselves in the contexts below?

- Rules about talk — for example, loudness, or talking to strangers — on and around public transport
- Speaking on a phone while driving a car
- Talking to salespeople or checkout staff in shops and markets
- Language use in places of worship
- Language conventions for ordering in bars or cafés
- Telephone opening and closing routines
- Face to face greetings and farewells

There is no commentary on this activity as the possible dimensions of variation are so wide-ranging.

CHAPTER 11

Signs and symbols

This unit focuses more specifically on aspects of visual communication and the writing system.

In semiotic studies the idea of signs is divided into different categories, two major categories being signs that are **iconic** and those that are **symbolic**.

An iconic sign tries to be a direct picture of what it refers to (although this may consist of a generalised line drawing rather than a picture in the photographic, literal sense). A symbolic sign is not a picture of what is being referred to (the **referent**), but a picture of something that we associate with the referent. Examples of iconic signs can often be seen around road hazards, with warning pictures of falling rocks indicating unstable land, or pictures of wildlife indicating that animals may be seen near the road. Examples of symbolic signs include those, such as a rose or a heart to represent romance, where the only relationship between the sign and its referent is one based on cultural convention.

DOVE

This card humorously explores the random nature of the dove symbol to stand for peace, a connection dating back to the story of Noah's Ark in the Bible.

Text 11.1

It tends to be assumed that iconic signs are much more transparent and neutral than symbolic signs, where there are powerful cultural connotations at work. However, as is usually the case with human communication, the differences are not so clear-cut. An example of a sign which, in theory, is iconic is given below.

Text 11.2

CALL BUTTON

This was a call button sited in a UK hospital in 2013. It is certainly iconic in that it depicts a nurse, but even this simple line drawing carries certain connotations. For a start, the image is female, and so only depicts one group of workers. Also, even female British nurses do not look like this nowadays – if they ever did. The headdress dates from Victorian times and had its origins in the headdresses worn by nuns; the rest of the outfit seems more consistent with later twentieth century skirts and aprons. It is quite a sexualised drawing, depicting a curvaceous figure with a tiny waist. The figure is also carrying a drink, but the uniform and the whole context of the sign links this with a nurturing role rather than that of a waitress. So even this supposedly simple line drawing suggests some powerful values – invoking the history of a caring profession but also representing ideas about gender and sexuality.

A more recent trend in the iconic depiction of workers is via photographic images. For example, while older 'road works' signs often used a line drawing of a figure digging, a more contemporary approach is to personalise the image of the road engineer by using a photograph of a real person. Sometimes, this person is pictured with a child who addresses us by saying, 'Slow down, my daddy works here'. So while the image is iconic and generic (in that although it depicts an individual, that person stands for the whole workforce), it edges towards symbolism in focusing us on the love shared in families and on a child who will be robbed of a parent if we are not careful. Sometimes an image of a child, or a child's drawing of a parent figure, is used on its own. The effect can be very powerful. Google the phrase 'slow down my daddy works here' and see how you respond.

As well as being difficult to categorise simply as iconic or symbolic, signs can be clear mixtures of the two approaches. For example, in the Canadian example opposite, the message is that people trespassing on the riverbank will be fined at least $75.

CANADIAN RIVER SIGN

The picture of the trespasser is iconic. The gavel, used by judges in courtrooms, is symbolic of the whole process of law enforcement. The relationship between the gavel and the idea of the law can be described as **metonymic**, meaning that the gavel is a small part of the larger scene it refers to.

As we have already seen, signs are extremely culturally specific. To understand the Canadian sign requires not only an understanding of the object pictured and the currency being referred to, but also the meaning of the circle and bar printed around and over the figure, which draws intertextually on the system of road signs used in many countries.

The sign also relies heavily on the context of its siting, and a cultural recognition that some areas can be designated forbidden, with consequences for individuals who break the law. If the sign had been outside an auction house (where gavels are also used to conclude a bidding process) the sign might have been read differently, perhaps to indicate that anyone with less than $75 in their possession would not be admitted! The importance of place (and time) in textual interpretations will be discussed again in Part III.

SIGNS AND MEANINGS

Look at Text 'CCTV' overleaf, which was on the front of a building being renovated. How does this text work? Describe the various aspects of the image and explain how you interpret the overall message.

  Do you see the text as culturally specific and, if so, how?
  Do you have anything similar to this in your neighbourhood?

There is a commentary on this activity at the end of Part II.

CCTV

Graphology is not simply about pictures in the sense of photographs or drawings, however. Written language itself can also be used to produce pictures. For example, some Chinese characters are **ideographs**, where a written symbol stands not for a letter or sound, but for a whole idea. Beyond the alphabetic symbols of English, which themselves can appear in very different ways, other keyboard symbols have traditionally helped to shape the way texts look. Even the space bar is important in creating spaces which define where texts begin and end.

Digital communication – computer-based language used on smartphones as well as other devices – has found new ways to connect writing with pictures. While Western users of digital tools have been deploying non-alphabetic symbols such as punctuation marks to make pictures such as the 'smiley' :-) Japanese communicators have had their own traditions of images taken from manga art and from the Kanji characters in the Japanese writing system. Calling them 'emoji' ('e' meaning picture and 'moji' meaning character), symbols such as those opposite began being used in the 1990s in Japan. They have now become widely used in many other parts of the world as a result of agreement between large corporations such as the Japanese DoCoMo and the US-based Apple and Google to make their codes compatible.

EMOJI

Beginner
The Japanese equivalent of our P-plates for new drivers, the Shoshinsha mark, must be displayed for a year after the driver has passed their test. Introduced in 1972, the mark has become more generally used in Japan to mean 'for beginners' or 'beginners welcome'.

Bank
One of 17 symbols denoting buildings, an emoji bank is signfied by the letters 'BK'. But the symbol has come to have a secondary meaning in Japan; BK can also be interpreted as 'bakkureru', meaning 'to evade one's responsibilities' or 'to feign ignorance'.

Squared NG
A number of emoji display English words, including 'Up', 'Cool' and 'Free'. But 'NG' is more puzzling. It turns out that Asian variety shows sometime air blooper reels called NGs, meaning 'no good'. or 'not good'. As a consequence, 'NG' is now used when something's not quite to one's liking.

Tanabata tree
The Japanese Tanabata festival celebrates the legend of Hikiboshi and his lover Orihime, the Emperor's daughter, who were permitted to meet only once a year. This Tanabata tree emoji depicts a bamboo stalk hung with a piece of paper on which wishes for the future are written.

Dango
These sweet dumplings conceal a deeper meaning. "We have a saying in Japan, 'Hana yori dango'," says Motoko Tamamuro, "which means 'bread is better than song of birds'. It's a sarcastic comment on people who are more interested in food than their surroundings."

Tengu
The tengu features widely in Japanese folk religion – a goblin with a big nose and a red face. Because the idea of big-headedness is expressed in Japan as big-nosedness, to 'become a tengu' means to get too big for your boots. So the tengu emoji can be used to symbolise arrogance.

Text 11.5

Regardless of whether users are typing punctuation symbols on a computer keyboard in the UK, or choosing a ready-made emoji on a phone in Japan, the motivations are similar – to convey something of the feelings and attitudes that are normally expressed via non-verbal behaviour in spoken contexts, or to use a picture to communicate an idea that would have taken a long time to write in words. The symbols are also fun, of course, and can act as playful conundrums in the same way as **rebus** puzzles. In the process, though, as you can see from the explanations of the emoji characters, there are interesting original references that may or may not be understood by users from different cultures. However, that doesn't stop anyone from any part of the world giving characters new meanings within their own communities of shared practice.

Of course, the graphological features that formed the original ingredients for building emoticons from punctuation had an existence before the advent of digital communication. In this textbook you've already seen full stops, brackets, dashes, commas, colons and semi-colons, inverted commas, questions marks and an exclamation mark – and that's aside from some of the bigger design features such as bold type, italics, headings and the use of numbering systems.

Writers of fiction use aspects of textual design too. In fact, an American data engineer called Fred Benenson has 'translated' Melville's famous novel *Moby Dick* into emoji, calling the new version *Emoji Dick*. The book has been accepted into the Library of Congress:

http://www.smithsonianmag.com/arts-culture/text-me-ishmael-reading-moby-dick-emoji-180949825/?no-ist

This is clearly an extreme and playful departure from the norm of writing prose fiction. Even so, books do pay attention to many aspects of textual design that contribute to how we understand them. For example, they are regularly split into chapters and consideration is given to aspects of typeface, font, page size and line spacing, as well as the number of pages overall. At a more micro level, writers also use all the resources that are available in the expressive toolkit we term 'punctuation' in order to help readers create dramatic scenes for themselves, where characters speak to each other and have inner thoughts about the people and events around them.

LITERARY TECHNIQUES

Read the extract below, which is the opening of the novel *Ladder of Years*, and identify how the writer uses graphological features – in particular, punctuation and typographical variations – to suggest aspects of speech, thought and action.

There is a commentary on this activity at the end of Part II.

LADDER OF YEARS

This all started on a Saturday morning in May, one of those warm spring days that smell like clean linen. Delia had gone to the supermarket to shop for the week's meals. She was standing in the produce section, languidly choosing a bunch of celery. Grocery stores always made her reflective. Why was it, she was wondering, that celery was not called 'corduroy plant'? That would be much more colourful. And garlic bulbs should be 'moneybags,' because their shape reminded her of the sacks of gold coins in folktales.

A customer on her right was sorting through the green onions. It was early enough so the store was nearly empty, and yet this person seemed to be edging in on her a bit. Once or twice the fabric of his shirt sleeve brushed her dress sleeve. Also, he was really no more than stirring those onions around. He would lift one rubber-banded clump and then drop it and alight on another. His fingers were very long and agile, almost spidery. His cuffs were yellow oxford cloth.

He said, 'Would you know if these are called scallions?'

'Well, sometimes,' Delia said. She seized the nearest bunch of celery and stepped toward the plastic bags.

'Or would they be shallots?'

'No, they're scallions,' she told him.

Needlessly, he steadied the roll of bags overhead while she peeled one off. (He towered a good foot above her.) She dropped the celery into the bag and reached toward the cup of twist ties, but he had already plucked one out for her. 'What are shallots, anyway?' he asked.

LADDER OF YEARS (continued)

She would have feared that he was trying to pick her up, except that when she turned she saw he was surely ten years her junior, and very good-looking besides. He had straight, dark-yellow hair and milky blue eyes that made him seem dreamy and peaceful.

He was smiling down at her, standing a little closer than strangers ordinarily stand.

'Um…' she said, flustered.

'Shallots,' he reminded her.

'Shallots are fatter,' she said. She set the celery in her grocery cart. 'I believe they're above the parsley,' she called over her shoulder, but she found him next to her, keeping step with her as she wheeled her cart toward the citrus fruits. He wore blue jeans, very faded, and soft moccasins that couldn't be heard above 'King of the Road' on the public sound system.

'I also need lemons,' he told her. She slid another glance at him.

'Look,' he said suddenly. He lowered his voice. 'Could I ask you a big favour?'

'Um…'

'My ex-wife is up ahead in potatoes. Or not ex I guess but … estranged, let's say, and she's got her boyfriend with her. Could you just pretend we're together? Just till I can duck out of here?'

'Well, of course,' Delia said.

And without even taking a deep breath first, she plunged happily back into the old high-school atmosphere of romantic intrigue and deception. She narrowed her eyes and lifted her chin and said, 'We'll *show* her!' and sailed past the fruits and made a U-turn into root vegetables. 'Which one is she?' she murmured through ventriloquist lips.

'Tan shirt,' he whispered. Then he startled her with a sudden burst of laughter. 'Ha, ha!' he told her too loudly. 'Aren't you clever to say so!'

But 'tan shirt' was nowhere near an adequate description. The woman who turned at the sound of his voice wore an ecru raw-silk tunic over black silk trousers as slim as two pencils. Her hair was absolutely black, cut shorter on one side, and her face was a perfect oval. 'Why, Adrian,' she said. Whoever was with her – some man or other – turned too, still gripping a potato. A dark, thick man with rough skin like stucco and eyebrows that met in the middle.

Not up to the woman's standard at all; but how many people were?

In thinking about language as a semiotic system, it was suggested that where there is a system, then any departure from that system has to be accounted for in some way – for example, either as a 'mistake' or as a conscious piece of rule-breaking for deliberate effect. In Text 11.7: art'otel, overleaf, you can see some deliberate rule-breaking in action. The text is a 'welcome' letter from a hotel in Berlin which is left in every room for guests to read.

56 SIGNS AND SYMBOLS

Activity 11.3

BREAKING THE RULES

- In what ways does the letter follow a conventional format, and in what ways does it break those conventions?
- Are there different types of rule-breaking in evidence?
- Why do you think the hotel wants to break rules? What kind of identity is created by the language choices made?

There is a commentary on this activity at the end of Part II.

Text 11.7

ART'OTEL

berlin kudamm
w. vostell exhibition

dear ▮▮▮▮,

a very warm welcome at **art'otel berlin kudamm**, the probably largest hotel gallery in europe, showing 578 pieces of art on seven floors by the well known fluxus artist wolf vostell, who was born in leverkusen in 1932 and his art was strongly influenced by the post world war II period and the separation of berlin.

we do not see ourselves just as an ordinary city-hotel. we rather want to present you a hotel where art and individual service is especially and shown to you as a valued customer.

your room was thoughtfully checked by our housekeeping manager. but should there be anything missing or not in the proper way, please contact us by dialling #851.

our rich **breakfast** buffet is available to you every day from 6:30 am to 11:00 am at our restaurant "gartensaal" on the ground floor.

so if you return after a day on the exhibition or a trip through our amazing city take the time to relay at our **bar vostell's**. as a special valued customer we are happy to invite you to an **open drink** at our bar. please be so kind and present that to the bartender when placing your order.

our **bar vostell** is also located on the ground floor and we are glad to welcome you there from 6pm. please hand over this welcome letter to the bar tender and get one **drink complimentary** (beer, wine or non-alcoholic drink) for yourself and if present the person sharing the room with you.

dear ▮▮▮▮, we hope that you will have an art'rageous and wonderful stay at the **art'otel berlin kudamm**.

if you have questions, then please do not hesitate to contact us at any time.

with warm regards,
art'otel berlin kudamm

▮▮▮▮
hotel manager

CHAPTER 12

Sounds and symbols

Why might a text analyst want to know about sound? On the face of it, sound appears to be the rather exclusive property of spoken language and have little to do with written texts. However, there is a relationship between spoken and written language. It is a complex relationship, and this will be returned to throughout the book. The main insight to have at this point is that, although speech and writing are related to each other, they are not simply different versions of the same thing.

It is important to stress that even if you have already studied phonetics and phonology, you may well not have approached the topic in the way this book does. That is because you may have stayed with sound as a single system – there is much to say about sound in its own right – but you may not have thought about how we all represent sound in the everyday writing that we do, or how this is done in highly-worked texts such as advertising or literature. You may not have thought about how children inter-relate speech and writing, or how knowing about sounds can help us understand processes of stereotyping. In short, there is more to say about sound than simply learning about what sounds are in a particular language and how they are pronounced.

A useful starting point for everyone is to realise that as well as engaging in the act of speaking itself, we also find ways to write speech down. Written representations of speech come in varying degrees of closeness to the actual speech event, ranging from scholarly representations in the form of transcripts and phonetic symbols, all the way through literary dialogue to web-based reports of speeches and interviews. While no type of static writing can exactly mirror the real-time unfolding and articulation of spoken language, linguists try to create representations that allow us to recapture something of the original.

One of the written systems that tries to do this is called the IPA, or International Phonetic Alphabet, which uses symbols designed specifically to represent the sounds of language. Even if you have never heard its official name, you will have come across the IPA in dictionaries, where the pronunciation of a word is often given in brackets before the definition. If you have a voice app in a digital dictionary, the phonetic symbol may be linked to a pronunciation. The IPA is a working tool not just for lexicographers, but for speech and language therapists, drama voice coaches, tutors of those who need to produce some words in a foreign language without knowing the whole language (such as politicians and musicians), and anyone who has a professional interest in approximating to a set of sounds.

The IPA covers the sounds of all the world's known languages. This book will only be using that part of it that describes the sounds of the English language. Some of the symbols will already be familiar to you because they exist in the Roman alphabet; others won't be, but they will be explained later. When you work with the symbols that follow, remember that the underlined part of the word given as an example of each sound refers to how that sound would be produced by someone with a **Received Pronunciation (RP)** accent. This accent does not indicate the region a speaker comes from, but rather their social class, as historically it was the voice of educated people from privileged backgrounds. If a speaker has a different accent from RP, their list of phonemes (termed a **phoneme inventory**) might well be different from the one opposite.

Phonetic transcriptions have come into their own because the spelling system that we use every day to read and write is by no means a faithful representation of the sounds that we use in language. There is no one-to-one relationship between the letters that we use to write our language down and the sounds that we make. Although it is a bit of a simplification, there are forty-four sounds in English and yet there are only 26 letters that we can use to represent them. It is immediately obvious that 26 letters can't individually represent 44 sounds. However, that's not to say that we can't use combinations of more than one letter to represent a particular sound. This does happen, but because English has absorbed many words from other languages over the years, there are many varied and unusual spellings. You will be looking at the **etymologies** of different English words in Section B: Lexical and Semantic Level. Although this means that the lexical system has many interesting word histories to tell, spelling can be frustratingly unpredictable. Here is a rather extreme example of the mismatch between sound and spelling in English:

> A rough-coated, dough-faced, thoughtful ploughman strode through the streets of Scarborough; he coughed and hiccoughed.

If we compare the pronunciation of all of the sounds that are represented by the string of letters 'ough' here, we find that they are not the same; they don't rhyme. Even if we just look at the first four, they're all different:

> rough
> dough
> thoughtful
> ploughman

While the same string of letters can represent different pronunciations, conversely one sound can be represented by different written symbols ('meat', 'meet' and 'metre' all contain the same vowel sound, but this sound is spelled in different ways in each word).

Perhaps you can now see why an alphabet for sound is a useful piece of kit for linguists.

USING THE PHONEMIC ALPHABET

To get you familiar with the phonemic alphabet, and in order to show you some of the differences between sounds and spellings, transcribe the words containing 'ough' in the made-up sentence above by using the phonemic alphabet below. Answers are at the end of Part II.

The symbols below are available online, in clickable format. That means that you can go online and hear the symbols being pronounced.

http://www.phonemicchart.com

Activity 12.1

single vowels				diphthongs			
iː sheep	ɪ ship	ʊ book	uː shoot	ɪə here	eɪ wait	/	
e left	ə teacher	ɜː her	ɔː door	ʊə tourist	ɔɪ coin	əʊ show	
æ hat	ʌ up	ɑː far	ɒ on	eə hair	aɪ like	aʊ mouth	

consonants							
p pea	b boat	t tree	d dog	tʃ cheese	dʒ joke	k coin	g go
f free	v video	θ thing	ð this	s see	z zoo	ʃ sheep	ʒ television
m mouse	n now	ŋ thing	h hope	l love	r run	w we	j you

Speech production and description can involve detailed scientific, lab-based work. For example, speech and language therapists may need to consider how a particular physical impairment or brain dysfunction is connected to an individual's speech capacity, so at the very least they will need to know about anatomy and physiology. A forensics expert specialising in accent identification for a court case will also need to use scientific techniques, most likely computer-based acoustic software, to support their analysis. If you are interested in the more scientific applications of phonetics, you should supplement the basic introduction that follows by consulting the further reading suggestions at the end of the section.

12.1 THE VOCAL TRACT

Speech sounds are produced in the vocal tract, using air pushed out from the lungs. Different speech sounds are made by changing the shape of the vocal tract. This can be done by moving the lips and tongue to touch different parts of the vocal tract (place of articulation). Sounds can be further modified

60 SOUNDS AND SYMBOLS

by placing the articulators different distances from one another (manner of articulation). We can make an even wider variety of sounds by vibrating the vocal folds (**voiced** sounds) or not vibrating them (**voiceless** sounds).

VOCAL TRACT

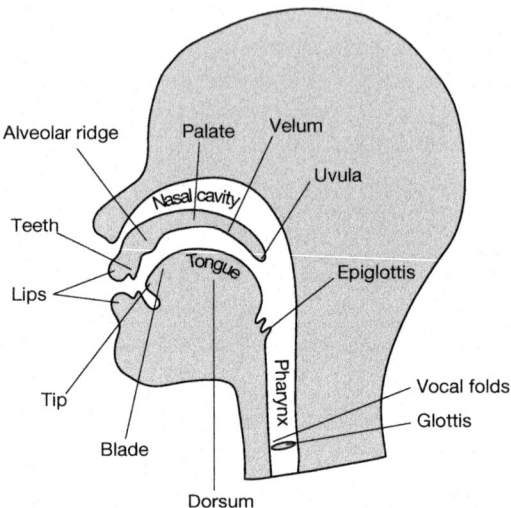

12.2 PLOSIVES: p b t d k g

These sounds are all explosions: they are created by obstructing the flow of air by bringing parts of the mouth together, then letting go suddenly. To explore this, place the palm of your hand in front of your mouth and, one by one, make each of these sounds in an exaggerated way. You should be able to feel the air from your mouth hitting your palm. English plosives (also called 'stops') are differentiated from each other in two ways: they are made in different places in the mouth (place of articulation), and they use different amounts of voice (voiced or voiceless sound). While /p/ and /b/ are produced using the two lips (bilabial), /t/ and /d/ involve contact between the tongue and the teeth ridge (alveolar); /k/ and /g/ are made by closing off air at the back of the mouth (velar). Refer to the diagram to see these locations.

Each of these pairs of sounds has one voiced and one voiceless phoneme, as follows:

Voiceless
p t k
Voiced
b d g

To understand the idea of voice, put your fingers on your 'Adam's apple' and alternate between the voiceless and voiced phonemes several times. You should be aware that your vocal cords are vibrating when you say the voiced sounds. If all the plosives sound voiced to you, this will be because you are adding a vowel (which are all voiced) and your voiceless plosives are picking up some of the vowel's voiced quality. If you are doing this, make the voiceless sounds as if you were whispering them.

12.3 FRICATIVES: f v θ ð s z ʃ ʒ h

While plosives are produced by completely obstructing the airflow, fricatives involve a lesser obstruction where air is forced through in a steady stream, resulting in friction rather than explosion. Plosives cannot be kept going in the way fricatives can. To illustrate this idea, say an /s/ until you run out of breath; now try to keep a /p/ sound going. You will find that all you can do for the latter is to produce a number of separate /p/ sounds, one after the other.

Fricatives, like plosives, are distinguished from each other by their place of articulation and by voice, each pair below being made up of a voiceless and voiced phoneme – apart from /h/, which is voiceless but has no voiced partner in English:

Voiceless
f θ s ʃ h

Voiced
v ð z ʒ

As with plosives, go through these phonemes, exploring where they are made in the mouth and sounding out their differences in terms of voice. (If your version of 'h' sounds voiced, this is because you are adding a vowel again, and saying something like 'huh'. The 'h' sound above is the sound that you would make if you were whispering.)

12.4 AFFRICATES: tʃ dʒ

There are only two of these consonant sounds in English. They have double symbols to represent the fact that each one is a plosive followed by a fricative. If you make these sounds at very slow speed you may be able to hear this sequence. /tʃ/ is voiceless and /dʒ/ is its voiced partner.

12.5 NASALS: m n ŋ

The distinctive feature of these sounds is that they are produced in a particular manner: the airstream comes out through the nose rather than the mouth. They differ from each other in being made in different places: /m/ is bilabial, /n/ is alveolar, and /ŋ/ is velar. When you have a cold and air cannot escape from the nose, nasals become plosives, as in the second version of 'good morning' below:

/gʊd mɔːnɪŋ/
/gʊd bɔːdɪg/

12.6 LATERALS: l

This sound is sometimes referred to as a 'liquid' sound, and is made by placing the tip of the tongue on the teeth ridge and sending air down the sides of the mouth. The easiest way to experience this airflow is to put the tongue in the right position to say an /l/, then breathe in instead of out: you should be able to feel the air flowing along the sides of your tongue. This is the reverse of what happens when an RP speaker says an English /l/.

12.7 APPROXIMANTS: r w j

The final three consonants are usually grouped together because they share the property of being mid-way between consonants and vowels; in some linguistic descriptions you will see them called 'semi-vowels'. They all involve less contact between the organs of speech than many of the other consonants: compare /r/ with /p/, for example. While /r/ and /j/ are produced in the palatal area (the roof of the mouth), /w/ is a bilabial.

12.8 GLOTTAL: ʔ

This does not appear on the list of symbols because it does not represent a sound as such. It is a closure of the vocal cords, resulting in shutting off the airstream, and it is sometimes produced as an alternative to certain plosive sounds. To explore this, say the words 'butter' and 'water', but 'swallow' the /t/ in the middle of each word. The glottal stop is a strong feature of some English regional accents.

/bʌʔə/
/wɔːʔə/

Overleaf is a summary of the consonant system in English. The chart shows place and manner of articulation. Where there is a pair of sounds contrasted by voice, this is marked by a colon, with voiceless sounds being to the left and voiced to the right. /r/ and /j/ are together because they are both palatal sounds, but they are not separated by a colon because they are not a voiceless/voiced pair.

Manner of articulation	Place of articulation							
	Bilabial (two lips)	Labio-dental (lips and teeth)	Dental (teeth)	Alveolar (on the teeth ridge)	Post-alveolar (behind the teeth ridge)	Palatal (roof of the mouth)	Velar (back of the mouth)	Glottal (the glottis, or vocal folds)
Plosive	p : b			t : d			k : g	
Nasal	m			n			ŋ	
Fricative		f : v	θ : ð	s : z	ʃ : ʒ			h
Affricate					tʃ : dʒ			
Approximant	w					r j		
Lateral approximant				l				

*The voiced sounds are on the right and the voiceless ones are on the left.

Aside from the more scientific uses for phonemic symbols, there are important insights about social attitudes that can be drawn from studying sound variations. Some of the sounds you have been studying vary considerably on a regional and ethnic basis: for example, speakers with strong London ('Cockney') accents and Afro-Caribbean Patwa speakers have no /h/ phoneme, while glottal stops are a common feature in many accents of English in the UK and beyond. The use or absence of particular phonemes can be the subject of stigma, and regarded as 'bad', 'sloppy' or 'lazy' speech by some people. It's important to realise that these judgements are social rather than linguistic: they are examples of how language can be used as a **shibboleth** – a way in which more powerful groups mark out their own forms of language as prestigious and 'correct' in order to defend their positions in society. The sociologist Pierre Bourdieu (1991) called such displays of symbolic power 'symbolic capital' in order to emphasise the real financial rewards that result from assumed status and claims of superiority.

Being able to describe aspects of language phonetically can help you to understand and explain the differences between linguistic facts and social attitudes. One aspect that should be apparent, if you work further on accent variation using a phonemic alphabet, is that quite extensive and complex sets of attitudes are based on rather small features of language – for example, that a speaker has specific character traits, a certain degree of social status, or a particular level of intelligence as a result of whether s/he uses one phoneme or another.

One clear example of how arbitrary social attitudes are – and how a sound in itself cannot be valued in any objective way – is the pronunciation of /r/ in the UK and the USA. In the UK, pronouncing an /r/ where it occurs in the spelling of a word after a vowel (called **postvocalic r**) is characteristic of some rural UK accents, which have historically had lower status than RP. Some examples of words are 'car', 'hurt', 'farm', 'port' ; in RP, the /r/ in these words would not be pronounced. In the USA, the situation is the reverse: pronouncing an /r/ in these contexts is higher status than not pronouncing it.

Some knowledge of phonetics can also help us understand how cross-cultural stereotyping works. For example, some Chinese speakers of English don't hear the difference between /l/ and /r/ in English because in their own first language, these sounds are heard as variants of the same sound. This difference between how speakers of different languages divide up their sound systems can produce distinctive speech habits which can then be exaggerated in stereotypes – in this case, saying 'velly' for 'very', or 'yerrow' for 'yellow'. Of course, stereotypes in written texts will use the traditional written alphabet to create their versions, as in the examples just quoted. This is a world away from the accuracy of a phonetic transcription, relying on readers to pick up on one or two distinctive features and construct a voice inside their own heads.

Although novelists are not necessarily trying to create stereotyped speakers, they too use a small range of language features to depict their characters in dialogues, sometimes using variant spellings or aspects of punctuation such as apostrophes to suggest pronunciations. This is termed **eye dialect**, because it relies less on the transcription of sound and more on the idea of language as a set of visual impressions. Here are some examples of eye dialect from American detective novels. These depict casual speech rather than particular accents:

Whaddya mean?
Whaddyacallit?
Is that 'cuz a me?
What's the frickin' point o' that?
Yeah, you 'n me both, pal.

The fact that we regularly make social judgements about people by characterising their language as 'good' or 'bad', as 'beautiful' or 'ugly', shows how sounds can be used in a symbolic way just as images can be. The relationship between the sounds that we make and the people or things being referred to could be just as **arbitrary** as using a rose to symbolise love, or a lightbulb to suggest an idea dawning (and note that even the term 'dawning' is **metaphorical**).

However, there is one area where there is some debate about whether language is totally symbolic and arbitrary. This is an area that is sometimes termed **expressive** – language that appears to connect with our physical senses and imitate the sensations that surround us. The most obvious example of this is **onomatopoeia** – words that seem to impersonate the sounds they describe, like 'bang', 'crash' and 'thud'. But is there any real connection between the sound of a word such as 'crash' and the sound of an actual crash?

One of the difficulties we have in answering the question above is that we rarely if ever experience onomatopoeic terms in isolation from their contexts. Many terms for noises are experienced early in our lives in the form of comics and playful stories. Human characters blurt out 'eek', 'aargh' and 'aaahhh' in the speech bubbles in comics, while cows 'moo' and sheep 'baa' in early reading books. Because of the strong associations we have for how such terms are used, it is very difficult to determine whether they have any meaning in their own right.

ARRRGGGGH!!

Here is an example of an expressive term, again from the art'otel, in the context of what happens if a guest forgets to pack an essential item. Goffman (1981) calls such terms 'response cries', saying that in speech we utter such cries when we have recovered our composure following a problem or mishap. This written form, then, is a kind of dramatic performance of such a cry.

One piece of evidence which appears to reinforce the idea of arbitrariness is that different languages have different words for noises, when in theory we should all hear and simulate noises in the same way. For example, while English dogs go 'woof woof' or 'bow wow', French ones go 'oua oua' and Greek ones 'gav gav'; Japanese cats purr by going 'goro goro'; and the Spanish for 'bang' or 'crack' is 'pum' or 'paf'.

There is a collection of animal noises from different languages on the website of Derek Abbott at the university of Adelaide, below:

http://www.eleceng.adelaide.edu.au/personal/dabbott/animal.html

The website of animal sounds contains plenty of evidence for the arbitrariness of language, and yet there does seem to be a correlation between some particular sound patterns and certain ideas. For example, several English words starting with 'sl', such as 'slime', 'slug', 'slippery', 'slick', 'slush', and 'slurp', suggest unpleasant sensations of cloying wetness, while words starting with 'gl', like 'glitter', 'glimmer', 'glow', 'glare', 'gleam', 'glisten' and 'glass', seem to share associations with light or suggest brittle qualities.

Of course, there will be exceptions to the connections suggested above. 'Sleep' and 'glad' don't fit the pattern, nor do 'slim' or 'glide'. But it may be the case that through a certain force of numbers, groups of sounds do gather a habitual set of associations that are added to as new words – for example, new inventions, or advertising brand names – join the lexicon.

Activity 12.2

EXPLORING THE REPRESENTATION OF SOUNDS

In both the activities below it will help if you read the words aloud, in order to gain physical sensations of how the sounds in them are produced.

1. Look at the two 'starter' words in the list below. Do you think the sounds in any of these words have group associations with certain ideas or sensations? See if you can continue the list if you believe so, in order to offer more evidence.

   flip, flutter …
   twist, twiddle …
   bump, lump …
   puff, huff …

2. Poetry uses sound effects, sometimes in quite concentrated ways, to help us create interpretations of ideas and scenes. Read the lines below, which have all been extracted from longer poems. Are the sounds involved suggestive of particular ideas in each case? If so, are there any physical connections between what the sounds represent, and how the sounds are produced physically?

There is a commentary on this activity at the end of Part II.

a) From a poem by Wilfred Owen (1893–1918) describing a battle in progress:

   Only the stuttering rifles rapid rattle

b) From a poem by Geoffrey Hill (1932–) about the Crucifixion:

   …while the dulled wood
   Spat on the stones each drop
   Of deliberate blood.

c) From a poem by Peter Redgrove (1932–2003) describing wind around a house:

   Limped up the stairs and puffed on the landings
   Snuffled through floorboards from the foundations

d) From a poem by Sylvia Plath (1932–1963) addressing a sleeping baby:

   All night your moth breath
   Flickers among the flat pink roses

EXPLORING THE REPRESENTATION OF SOUNDS
(continued)

e) From a poem by Tennyson (1809–1892) describing the sounds of doves and bees:

The moan of doves in immemorial elms
And murmuring of innumerable bees

f) The first verse of a poem called *The Bells* by Edgar Allan Poe (1809–1849):

Hear the sledges with the bells—
Silver bells!
What a world of merriment their melody foretells!
How they tinkle, tinkle, tinkle,
In the icy air of night!
While the stars that oversprinkle
All the heavens, seem to twinkle
With a crystalline delight;
Keeping time, time, time,
In a sort of Runic rhyme,
To the tintinnabulation that so musically wells
From the bells, bells, bells, bells,
Bells, bells, bells—
From the jingling and the tinkling of the bells.

Activity 12.2

So far the focus has been on consonants in English, but vowels can also have a role in **sound symbolism**. They also vary in the phoneme inventory of people from different regions and social class backgrounds. For example, the headline below, from a UK tabloid newspaper, announced that Prince William of Cambridge was to take a year to decide what royal duties to take on:

"Wills' year orf"
(*The Sun*, 12.9.13)

The word 'orf' is eye dialect for a vowel sound that used to feature in older forms of RP – the type of voice heard on older newsreels. The transcription of this sound would be /ɔː/ In contrast, modern RP-accented English speakers would say /ɒ/.

The prince probably doesn't say 'orf' at all, but this sound is being imitated to suggest that the privileged lifestyle of the royal family has not gone away. The term 'Wills' as a nickname for the prince also shows that the paper wants to cut him down to size. It's saying that for anybody else, this year would be seen as a holiday.

SOUNDS AND SYMBOLS

As with consonants, vowels seem to be able to be used to suggest certain ideas. For example, /i:/ is often associated with diminutive size, as in the words 'teeny', 'weeny', 'wee'. /i:/ also features on the ends of words in 'baby talk' – for example, 'cardies' for 'cardigans', 'jarmies' for 'pyjamas', 'drinky' for 'drink', 'walkies' for 'walk' and so on. As well as individual sounds appearing to have some symbolic value, vowels can also have cumulative force, either in repetition or in contrast. For example, 'teeny weeny' as a phrase is more effective for the repetitions in it.

Activity 12.3

VOWEL PATTERNS

English has many expressions that exploit vowel sounds by using either repetition or contrast. Below is a list of some of them. Sort them into categories by deciding which of these use repetition and which use contrast, then identify which vowels are being used. When you have finished, think about the nature of these terms: what type of language do they represent? Where might they be used – by whom, and in which contexts? If you are unfamiliar with any of them, look them up in a dictionary or phrase finder – there are many online – to check their meanings and possible contexts of use.

helter skelter   flip flop   topsy turvey   wishy washy   fat cat
hoity toity   lovey dovey   hip hop   see saw   mishmash
ding dong   spick and span   big wig   knick knack
harum scarum   tick tock   tit for tat   jet set   heebie jeebies
hanky panky   sing song   willy nilly   shilly shally   nitty gritty
ping pong   hotchpotch   pitter patter   namby pamby
hugger mugger   collywobbles   hoi polloi   jim jams (for pyjamas)
airy fairy   arty farty   roly poly

There is a commentary on this activity at the end of Part II.

Vowels can also play a part in a range of sound patterns, including **rhyme**, which involves the repetition of sounds. There are various degrees and types of rhyme, including **pararhyme**, **assonance** and **reverse rhyme**. You can see the operation of full rhyme in some of the expressions above, where the ending of the word is repeated but there is a change at the beginning of it – for example, willy nilly, nitty gritty. This aspect of patterning is learned early as part of our childhood experience of language, via songs, nursery rhymes and the chants that accompany play.

As well as full rhyme, there are other types of near-rhyme that set up relationships between sounds, and these can be used where full rhyme may seem too neat and tidy or childlike (although sometimes full rhyme can be very effective in serious texts, as a deliberate device).

First, it's important to realise that rhyme of all kinds is based on the sounds of words rather than the spelling. Here, the operation of homophones (words that are spelled differently but have the same sound) can have an important role. To get your ear tuned in to relationships between writing and sounds (**grapho-phonemics**), try the activities below.

HOMOPHONES

1. The following are homophones in RP. How many different words can be represented by these sounds?

   a) niːdz
   b) ɑːmz
   c) bruːz
   d) kɔːs
   e) səʊl
   f) kɔːt
   g) lesən
   h) kwɔːts
   i) kɔːz
   j) rəʊz
   k) sent

Answers are at the end of Part II.

There are many forms of language play that adults engage in, involving sound patterns. For example, the following words are from a daily newspaper crossword puzzle, where each day the words that form the answers to the two first clues in the puzzle can become a further, single word. Guess the single word or alternative phrase that each pair can produce by saying them aloud. This exercise plays off the boundaries of written words against sound patterns.

   a) heir male
   b) flay quay
   c) conned oar
   d) pyre nears
   e) infer know
   f) mill inner
   g) bling curd
   h) clap tout
   i) anna kissed
   j) bone apart

Answers are at the end of Part II.

Activity 12.4

Some of the expressions you sorted earlier used contrasting vowels within the framework of the same consonants, setting up a **half-rhyme** or pararhyme – for example, 'sing song', 'shilly shally'. These examples are playful and light-hearted, but the same strategy can also be used to help communicate very serious messages. For example, it is used in the poem 'Strange Meeting' (1918) by Wilfred Owen (1893–1918) in order to set up echoes between words, without providing the sense of completeness that would come with full rhyme. The narrator describes an imaginary journey down into hollow spaces in the earth where he encounters a dead enemy soldier who was one of his victims during the battle. Printed below are the first few lines of this poem.

STRANGE MEETING

It seemed that out of battle I escaped
Down some profound dull tunnel, long since scooped
Through granites which titanic wars had grained.
Yet also there encumbered sleepers groaned,
Too fast in thought or death to be bestirred.
Then, as I probed them, one sprang up, and stared
With piteous recognition in fixed eyes,
Lifting distressful hands as if to bless.

Pararhyme can be seen in escaped/scooped, grained/groaned, and bestirred/stared. These lines also use assonance (the repetition of vowels, without the other components that entail full rhyme): for example, the vowel sounds in 'down' and 'profound', and in 'dull tunnel'. The term 'collywobbles' in the list on page 68 was also an example of assonance. Seeing the same strategy used in both serious and playful contexts shows that there is no one-to-one correlation between a language feature and an effect.

CHAPTER 13

Speech, writing, and multimodality

The fact that speech and writing are inter-related, but are not different versions of the same thing, should have become clear by now. We use various forms of writing in order to represent speech, but they are all representations rather than the real thing. At the same time, although writing can look as though it's just designed for the page, it often requires an 'inner ear' to make it come alive. More often than not, we need to experience something in speech before we can understand it in writing. There is an example of this below.

SSSHHH!!

If we hadn't heard people say SSSHHH! to get others to be quiet, when it was used on the notice the word would just look like a random assortment of letters.

Text 13.1

New technologies have brought to the fore some of the ways in which speech and writing are intertwined. Previous scholarship on speech and writing sometimes made it seem as though these modes were very different – for example, by suggesting that speech was a here-and-now, fleeting form of communication while writing was more removed, spatially distant and permanent. In the many forms of digital communication now embedded in our everyday lives, we can write in real time in some very spontaneous ways, while being able to record speech and video its context for permanent display to the world on YouTube. Also, the communication environments we use often allow us to use multiple forms of interaction alongside one another, with webcams, voice tools and screens for real-time writing all on offer. We can also choose to translate one type of communication into another – for example, by speaking into a voice tool and having it write the result, or vice versa. All this adds up to a complex picture, but one where there are many fascinating new aspects of language to explore. **Multimodality** – the quality of drawing on more than one system of communication at any one time – is clearly an aspect of many of the texts that surround us daily. However, there is an argument that it was always so, and that we simply chose to ignore the fact. For example, an article that uses images alongside written text is also multimodal, because we move back and forth between the two in order to interpret the communication. In reading this textbook, you are working multimodally.

But, there are some brand new aspects to the new forms of communication that we engage with, so they are not describable simply by adding notions of speech to those of writing and making a new sum of parts. New multimodal communication tools do things that none of the individual modes could do before, such as broadcasting a piece of writing to millions of people instantly (for example, on Twitter), or linking texts together that were previously in different contexts – for example, clicking through from a medical webpage of definitions to a video illustrating how to treat an illness. So rather than asking whether these tools are more like speech or more like writing, it is better to ask what they allow us to do (their **affordances**) and what their limitations are.

Although the new tools we are constantly being offered allow us to do things we might not have tried before, the users of these new tools typically have some experience of language use in other mediated contexts. Therefore, one of the interesting questions in looking at new contexts is how users bring their existing knowledge to bear to help them learn afresh.

The examples of language use on the next page are from a group of students who were asked to work online in 2000 using a chat (real-time writing) tool (Goddard 2005). At this point most had never been online before, and none had ever used computer-based writing before for this kind of activity. The examples show how participants were calling on their knowledge of spoken language, particularly the kinds of 'response cries' described earlier when discussing the example from the art'otel. These little terms clearly carry a lot of meaning, but cannot be found in any normal dictionary of language use. However, in a medium where participants can't see or hear each other, squeezing every drop of expressive potential from written language is clearly important. The fact that the students in question were working online before anyone had access to the more sophisticated tools and icons we have today meant that they had to make their writing work extra hard.

RESPONSE CRIES

The cries below have been classified into different types, and an account is provided of how participants were using them.
    Try to answer the following questions:

- Have you used any of these yourself, in any written contexts? If so, which ones? How did you use them? Which environment were you in? (E.g. texting, email, social media site, chat tool, in a piece of dialogue when writing fiction, paper-based letter to a friend, etc.)
- There is no agreed written spelling for many of these expressions. Did you or would you spell these in the same way as below, or in a different way?
- Some of these occur in comics and other playful texts. Have you seen any of them written down before? If so, where?
- If you know another variety of English, or another language apart from English, do you have a version of any of these in that language?
- How far are expressions such as these now replaceable by emoticons?

There is no commentary on this activity because readers' experiences are likely to vary considerably.

13.1 EXAMPLES

Laughter

    ha ha
    ha ha ha
    he he he
    heh heh
    tee hee
    oh har har
    hee hee hee ha ha ha hooooo hoo

Registering a mistake or problem

    oops
    woops
    whoops
    uh-oh!
    duh

Frustration at not being able to achieve something

arhhhhh!!!!
aaarrrgghh!

Delight at achievement

WOOOOOPEEEEEE!!!!!
ta da!

Disgust

eeuuchhhh!
yuk!

Fear

eek
yikes

Registering something as 'naughty'

wey hey!
woo hoo!

Sympathy

ahhhh!
aaawww!

Prosodics: voice quality

(Begging, whining) don't go pleaseeeeeeeeeee

Variants of 'yes'

yaaa
yeh
yea
yeah

yep
yeahhh
yeay
yess

So far the focus has been on individual expressions in online contexts, but how can a whole environment such as a social media site be analysed? Because online writing is potentially readable by a mass audience, it's possible to see the phenomenon of social media as a form of instant publishing and instant self-promotion – a way of advertising oneself to the world. Some years ago Daniel Chandler (1998) talked of such texts as places where the writer's identity is permanently 'under construction', as writers change and adapt the elements that go to make up their site. Although the available tools of construction may change, this is undoubtedly still the case. Following the **metaphor** of site construction, Chandler saw online writers as 'bricoleurs', people who assemble varied elements into a shape or pattern. In his view, it followed that analysing such bricolages required consideration of a wide range of textual aspects, which he termed 'the Bricoleur's Web Kit', set out below. The webkit was designed originally with personal homepages in mind, but can be adapted to suit most of the social media sites that individuals use. However, a basic starting point will be the need to determine how much freedom an individual has for their own creative work, and how much is predetermined by the service provider or site owner. All the areas and questions below can only be covered by looking at the language choices that have been made, so language evidence needs to be provided at every stage to make this analytical approach effective.

13.2 THE BRICOLEUR'S WEB KIT

Types of activity:

- Inclusion – what different ideas and topics are included?
- Allusion – what different ideas are being referred to?
- Omission – what has been left out or remains unsaid?
- Adaptation – how have materials been added to or altered?
- Arrangement – how have things been organised on the pages(s)?

Types of content:

- Personal statistics, biographical information
- Interests, likes, dislikes
- Ideas, values, beliefs, causes
- Friends, acquaintances, other connections
- Material imposed by site owner – for example, advertising

Types of structure:

- Written text
- Graphics, including images
- Sound
- Video
- Links

13.3 REVIEW YOUR SKILLS

Complete two assignments from the list below. Choose assignments that enable you to focus on some of the different aspects of communication that have been covered in this section. For example, some of the assignment ideas have a graphological focus, some have a phonological focus, and some explore grapho-phonemic relationships.

13.4 IDEAS FOR ASSIGNMENTS

1. Collect and analyse some advertising logos and explore how the symbols connect with other aspects of the texts, for example the brand names, slogans, images and writing.
2. Collect some logos from institutions, for example schools, universities and other public bodies. Do these tend to rely on certain themes and ideas?
3. Choose a literary extract and analyse the way the writer uses punctuation and other graphological effects to create meaning.
4. Go to a collection of poetry online, such as poetrysoup.com, and search for examples of concrete poetry. How are the writers using visual designs to help them create their message?
5. Collect some examples of rule-breaking or unusual visual effects in other written texts and discuss the motives of the writer or designer.
6. Transcribe some differently-accented speakers and analyse phonetically the way their accents vary.
7. Analyse the nature of sound symbolism by collecting some texts that are trying to create a particular impression. For example, plosives are often used in newspaper headlines to give a sense of energy and drama – for example, in words like 'probe', 'cut', 'hit', 'quit', 'scoop' and 'block'. (These words are also monosyllabic, giving them extra bluntness.)
8. Advertising brand names are carefully chosen by manufacturers to have a certain 'ring'. Choose some different products and analyse their brand names. Do certain sounds recur, or are certain sounds associated with particular types of product? For example, the names 'Twix', 'Crunchie', 'Snickers', 'Kit Kat' and 'Picnic' all contain plosives, perhaps because the manufacturers want to suggest a crisp, cracking noise. Are fricatives used for scouring creams and liquids, or air fresheners?

9. Slogans can often use sound patterning, too: for example, alliteration can make slogans memorable. This isn't just a feature of advertising: political slogans are intended to have staying power. Collect some slogans and look at the sounds they use.
10. Collect some poetry and analyse how the sound patterns used contribute to the meaning.
11. Collect some puzzles and games that use aspects of language play, and analyse how they work.
12. Apply Chandler's Web Kit in analysing a social media site. Amend Chandler's sections and questions to suit the type of site under scrutiny.
13. Children spend the early years of their lives acquiring an understanding of the spoken and written patterns that occur in the language(s) around them. Analyse Hedy's pronunciation overleaf, answering the questions attached. Then collect your own examples of children's speech and analyse what you find.
14. Analyse Omar's writing (on p79), then collect and analyse some further examples of children's writing.
15. Children are now early users of online environments, where spoken and written forms can often co-exist; or where the types of language used are **hybrid** forms that mix qualities of speech and writing together. Collect some examples of children's use of digital communication and analyse their language choices and skills.
16. Children's toys now include simulations of new technologies – for example, there are imitation mobile phones, tablets and computers. Investigate any 'new technology' toys that are being sold in shops or online, focusing on how the toys are being sold and what the advertisers claim for the toys as learning tools.

Text 13.2

HEDY'S SPEECH

Hedy was one year eleven months old at the time she was recorded. Look at the transcriptions of her speech and compare them to the transcriptions provided of how you might expect an adult to pronounce the same word. Square brackets have been used for Hedy's pronunciations of the adult sounds.

Word	Hedy's pronunciation	Adult pronunciation
sun	[dʌn]	/sʌn/
circle	[dɜːkʊ]	/sɜːkl/
stripy	[daɪpiː]	/straɪpiː/
sky	[gaɪ]	/skaɪ/
drums	[dʌms]	/drʌmz/
green	[giːn]	/griːn/
fish	[bəs]	/fɪʃ/
phone	[bəʊn]	/fəʊn/
flower	[baʊə]	/flaʊə/
brush	[bəs]	/brʌʃ/
yellow	[jejəʊ]	/jeləʊ/
red	[wed]	/red/

Does Hedy always pronounce /s/ the same way?

What are the variants?

Does there seem to be any pattern governing when she uses one pronunciation rather than another?

If you look at the place and manner of articulation, can you notice what the similarities and differences are between Hedy's pronunciations of /s/ and the adult pronunciation?

Now have a look at the words that begin with a consonant cluster. Does Hedy pronounce both sounds where a word begins with two consonants together in the adult pronunciation? Which of the two consonants tends to be pronounced? Are there any exceptions to this, and if so, why do you think that is?

There is a commentary on this activity at the end of Part II.

OMAR'S WRITING

Omar was five years old when he wrote this ghost story.

How does he draw on his knowledge of spoken language and on **genre** conventions in order to make his writing dramatic?

ones a pone tieem therer
wes a hntb hous no one
went to the casel be cos The
Spereit The Spereit
meycs peepel ther in to
goost

(Once upon a time there
was a haunted house. No one
went to the castle because "The
Spirit!" "The Spirit!"
makes people there into
ghosts.)

There is a commentary on this activity at the end of Part II.

Section B

Lexical and Semantic Level

Aim: Section B will increase your awareness of how words and expressions help to shape meanings in texts. This will enrich and deepen the level of detail you are able to offer in any text analysis.

CONTENTS: PART II, SECTION B

- 14 Introduction
- 15 Frequent words
- 16 Words and morphemes
- 17 Forming words
- 18 Words and semantic fields
- 19 Words and word families
- 20 Words and multiple meanings
- 21 Connotation and collocation
- 22 Words and metaphors
- 23 Lexical cohesion
-    Review your skills
-    Ideas for assignments

CHAPTER 14

Introduction

In this section the focus will be on words. The analysis of words may seem straightforward, and in one sense, of course, it is. Words are a sequence of letters that can't be split up and are surrounded by a space.

However, as soon as we make this perfectly sensible definition, we see that there is a lot that it fails to capture. For example, can it apply to spoken language where we can't see spaces around the words? What about phrases which you can't easily break up, such as *I'm going to have forty winks* (forty winks = a short sleep)? You can't say 'fifty winks' or 'thirty-nine winks'; it has to be *forty winks* to be correct, and the two words 'forty' and 'winks' are inseparable as a combination in this context. The same problems of definition apply even more when the unit is longer, as in the case of *to give somebody the cold shoulder* (to ignore somebody). So we can't simply say either that a word is an item listed separately in a dictionary. What is the separate item? *Cold* or *shoulder*? *Forty* or *winks*? And what about words in which individual letters change? Are *run*, *running*, *runs*, *ran* all separate words, or are they the same word? Is *running a race* the same as *running a business*? It is clearly better to talk about patterns of words and meaning, rather than about words as individual items.

Patterns of vocabulary are a key element in the way language is organised and in the way meanings are made. A better understanding of how lexical patterns work can illuminate all kinds of texts, and in this section we look at a range of different texts including holiday brochures, literary texts, advertisements and other promotional material. Computers can help us analyse patterns, using large multi-million word collections of text (corpora) to do this. Corpus material will be used in some of the units in this section to illustrate nuances of meaning associated with particular lexical patterns and structures, and also to point up some of the specific structures that are characteristic of some types of spoken language and informal writing.

It is not our aim to say everything there is to say about lexis and semantics, but we do aim to look at those features of vocabulary which will enable you to analyse texts better. By learning about the topics in this section you will develop the key skill of noticing structures and patterns in texts, making any analysis you do far more detailed, rigorous and convincing.

CHAPTER 15

Frequent words

The list of words below is collated from the 100 million-word British National Corpus and the two-billion word Cambridge English Corpus. The sample is a corpus of five million of the most frequent words in written English.

Text 15.1

FREQUENT WORDS

What do you notice about this list? Are there any words which surprise you? Are there words which you would have expected to be in the top forty list, but which are not? How much meaning do these words have?

Top 40 most frequent words: 5m written

1	THE	21	AS
2	TO	22	AT
3	AND	23	BUT
4	OF	24	BE
5	A	25	HAVE
6	IN	26	FROM
7	WAS	27	NOT
8	IT	28	THEY
9	I	29	BY
10	HE	30	THIS
11	THAT	31	ARE
12	SHE	32	WERE
13	FOR	33	ALL
14	ON	34	HIM
15	HER	35	UP
16	YOU	36	AN
17	IS	37	SAID
18	WITH	38	THERE
19	HIS	39	ONE
20	HAD	40	BEEN

These words occur hundreds of times a day in English. They are vital to everyday communication and provide the glue that holds language together. Without these words we could not make sense. Here are some of the functions and meanings these words have.

15.1 REFERENCE FUNCTION

The reference function for language is crucial, both in speech and writing. Reference means pointing things out. If you think about our everyday communicative needs, being able to point things out is fundamental in our interactions with others. We often need to refer to people, places and events in the immediate environment, as well as to things both in the past and the future. Being able to point and name the world around them is an important stage in young children's acquisition of language. Written texts need to create a world that makes sense on its own terms. Asynchronous writing doesn't offer the affordance that we have in spontaneous speech to re-run and reformulate unclear aspects, so reference in writing plays an important role in pointing to places, times, people and events.

15.2 'A' AND 'THE'

The words 'a' and 'the' are termed '**articles**'; 'a' is an **indefinite article** and 'the' is a **definite article**. We can use these words to refer to many different phenomena, with 'the' being used to refer to something specific, possibly even unique, while 'a' can refer to a single item, possibly among many.

Advertising and other promotional texts are fond of using the meaning of individuality that the word 'the' can carry, in order to suggest that a product or experience is distinctive and therefore superior, or the only one worth having. Here are some examples:

> *Hipster bar, the place to be seen* (from a tripadvisor review of a café in Marrakech)
> *THE BEST. REST ASSURED* (from Premier Lodge, a UK hotel chain)

Book, newspaper and magazine titles, as well as institutions of different kinds, also often use 'the' to suggest the authority that comes with the idea of being 'the one and only':

> *The Big New Yorker Book of Dogs* (collection of cartoons from the *New Yorker* magazine)
> *The Incredible Spice Men* (cookery book of curry recipes)
> *The Chambers Dictionary*
> *The University of Manchester*

The word 'a', on the other hand, can suggest repeated or common occurrences as well as a single item, for example in the following slogans:

> *A Mars a day helps you work, rest and play* (advertising a chocolate bar called Mars)
> *We won't make a drama out of a crisis* (Commercial Union insurance company advert)

You can sometimes see the difference between the terms 'a' and 'the' if you substitute one for the other. For example, the slogan below was used by a former UK bank, The Midland Bank (now part of HSBC):

The Listening Bank

This was intended to suggest that the bank was different from others in listening to customers. But if the bank had used this slogan instead:

A Listening Bank

it would not have suggested the same distinctive difference from other banks, perhaps suggesting instead that it was listening rather than doing other things (such as making money!).

The articles 'a' and 'the' are not the only items from the corpus list that have a reference function.

15.3 PRONOUN REFERENCE

Pronouns allow us to refer easily to people, by replacing their names (proper nouns) with items that stand in their place (hence pro-nouns). The corpus list includes the following personal pronouns: I, he, she, it, you, they. The only pronouns missing are 'we' and 'one', the latter being an indirect way of saying 'I' which sounds somewhat archaic nowadays. (The word 'one' is on the list, but this is because the number 'one' is so frequent rather than as a result of its frequency as a pronoun.)

Variants of the pronoun forms above – me, him, her, them – are used when the pronouns are the object in a sentence. Of these, the list features 'him' and 'her'. It also features the possessive pronoun, 'his'.

Like articles, pronouns are seemingly small words that can have great significance. They can identify participants and specify both their number (a single person or a group) and their gender (male or female, plus a sort of neuter in the term 'it'). They can provide a sense of intimacy, for example where someone uses 'I' to bring themselves into the frame. However, they can also operate at a level of generality that allows references to remain unspecified. For example, if someone says 'they say it will rain tomorrow', there is no way of knowing who 'they' are. Similarly, in the Mars and Commercial Union advertising slogans above, the pronouns 'you' and 'we' are usefully vague from the advertisers' point of view.

15.4 DEICTICS

Although 'a' and 'the' can have a pointing (**deictic**) function, there are some terms on the list of corpus items that are perhaps more easily seen in that way. 'This', 'that' and 'there' are examples of terms that can have a very direct pointing function in face to face communication, to identify and delineate shared space. Much more will be said about these terms in Part III, where we look more closely at context as a shaping factor for language use.

However, the corpus list relates primarily to written, rather than spoken language, and 'this', 'that', 'here' and 'there' don't have to apply simply to immediate physical environments. They often have a pointing function of a different kind in writing, where they can be used to connect with different parts of a text. For example, re-read the last sentence in the previous paragraph. It says 'much more will be said about *these* terms' – the word *these* points backwards to the sentence before, where the terms are listed. Where terms point backwards, they are called **anaphoric** references; where they point forwards, they are called **cataphoric**. Further examples of terms that point to spatial dimensions include 'up', 'on' and 'to'.

15.5 TIME

Further words or parts of words on the corpus list help us to understand which time period is being referred to. For example, while 'is', 'are' and 'have' refer to present time, 'was', 'been', 'had' and 'said' all refer to past events. We can begin to see references to a time long ago (*had/been/said*).

15.6 CONJUNCTION

A different kind of function from reference is **conjunction**, or linking elements together. Some words – for example, 'and' and 'but' – have this connecting function, helping us to understand how one part of a text relates to another.

15.7 LEXICAL AND GRAMMATICAL WORDS

The main point to grasp in what has been said so far about the corpus list is that many of our most frequently used words may be tiny and seem insignificant, but in fact they serve to help convey some powerful meanings. However, they do not make sense collectively. Try putting them together to create a text, and you soon make nonsense (which is great if your aim is to write nonsense poetry):

I had a said were from not….

Conventionally, words also refer to specific things, places, ideas and processes, but none of these words do that. The words in the list are also all very small words, most only consisting of one syllable. Most words consist of many more syllables than this. So, these words are very important in a language, but they don't appear to mean very much on their own, as would be the case with individual words such as *love* or *school* or *football* or *mountain*.

Look at the sentence below. Does it make any sense to you?

The crans sligged bibily.

All the words in the frequency list make sense, but they do not make sense when put together. The words in the made-up sentence above make no sense as individual words, but the more we read the sentence, the more they might begin to have a particular kind of meaning. Can you, for example, answer these questions?

Was there one *cran* or more than one *cran*?
What were they doing?
Were they doing it now or at some point in the past?
How or in what manner were they doing it?

Most speakers of English will have very little trouble answering these questions. There was more than one *cran*, because this word carries the **plural** marker 's'. '*Sligged*' is marked as a verb as a result of the presence of a past tense marker 'ed'; we can therefore (if we knew the meaning of *slig*) work out what the *crans* were doing, and the fact that they were doing it in the past. Finally, we can tell how or in what manner the *crans* were *sligging*, because the word *bib* carries with it the adverb marker '*ily*' (as in the word happ***ily***).

We can see therefore that grammar is important in helping us to create and decipher the meanings of words. We can also see that a language needs both **grammatical words** and **lexical words**. The words we have been discussing in the frequency list are almost all grammatical words, whereas words such as *school* or *football* are lexical words. The grammatical words more or less provide the structures within which the lexical words make their meanings; the function of the grammatical words is largely to structure the lexical words which carry a higher informational content than the individual grammatical words. Grammatical words are generally finite and do not change much over time in either structure or meaning; however, the number of lexical words is potentially infinite, with new words entering and disappearing from the language all the time. For example, in 2013 the Oxford English Dictionary recorded over a thousand new lexical words with many influenced by new technology, such as:

selfie and *phablet*

That is, if someone wants to show you a *selfie* they took with their *phablet*, this is a particular kind of photograph they took of themselves on their tablet-phone.

Lexical words are therefore in theory an *open* class of words; grammatical words are correspondingly a *closed* class.

CHAPTER 16

Words and morphemes

16.1 WHAT IS A MORPHEME?

The focus in this section so far has been on very small words. However, not all words are small and monosyllabic. Look at words like *deforestation* or *parliamentarian*, for example. Instead of defining words as groups of letters surrounded by a space, it might therefore be more accurate to say that words are simply the smallest units of language that carry meaning.

However, our made-up examples of the noun *cran* and the verb *slig* underline that there are other even smaller units of language which help to structure and convey meanings. For example, *cran* was used in the form *crans* and *slig* was used in the form *sligged*. These units are **morphemes** and the study of the structure of words is called **morphology**.

16.2 HOW MANY MORPHEMES CAN THERE BE?

Words may be made up of one or more morphemes. For example, the word *inexpensive* consists of three morphemes *in*, *expens(e)* and *ive*, with the addition of *in* adding a sense of not expensive. Similarly, the *ed* in the word *laughed* underlines that the action took place in the past. Morphemes can also be a single letter, and the letter can still change meaning. The *s* in the word *gardens* tells us that there is more than one garden. There are exceptions found in highly specialised areas of language; for example, terms used in some fields of organic chemistry or law or medicine can have several morphemes, and in theory there is no limit to the number of morphemes a word can have, but logic and comprehensibility mean that there tends to be an upper limit, and six morphemes is about the normal limit for English:

   anti dis establish ment arian ism

is often as long a combination of morphemes to make a word as we can expect to find.

16.3 DIFFERENT CLASSES OF MORPHEME

There are two main classes of morpheme. There are those morphemes which are independent and free-standing as words (**free morphemes**), e.g. *laugh*, *city*, *money*, and those morphemes which cannot stand on their own (**bound morphemes**) because their meaning depends on being attached to a free morpheme. Examples of bound morphemes are *in-*, *-s*, *-ed*, *-ly*, *anti-*, *-ism*, *dis-*, *-hood*.

It is easy to confuse some bound morphemes with free morphemes that have an identical sound and structure. For example, English has free morphemes 'hood' (a head covering) and 'ship' (a seagoing vessel). It also has the bound morphemes '-ship' and '-hood', that are both used to form nouns. 'Hardship' means a state of deprivation or difficulty, but 'hard ship' means something different – a vessel that is difficult to sail, perhaps. 'Motherhood' means the state of being a mother, not the head covering that a mother might wear. Having said this, there's always room for creative rule-breaking: it's not hard to imagine a hoodie designed as part of a maternity wear range being called a 'motherhood'.

It is also easy to confuse part of a word that is a single morpheme, like 'hammer', with a bound morpheme, in this case '-er', that is used to create nouns of agency (as in 'play', 'player') or adjectives of comparison or degree ('tall', 'taller').

Bound morphemes have two functions. One is to act as a grammatical marker, giving information about number, verb tense, aspect and other grammatical functions. These are **inflectional morphemes**. Examples are *-s*, *-ed*, *-er* (comparative). The second function is to form new words. These are called **derivational morphemes**. Examples are *un-*, *-ly*, *-hood*, *-y*, *dis-*, *-ship*.

CHAPTER 17

Forming words

The way morphemes can form words and meanings is a distinctive feature of English as a language. However, words can be formed in a number of other ways too, and this range of options often makes for creativity in the ways words are made. Some of the main features of word formation in English are:

Affixation
Compounding
Conversion

Affixation involves the addition of **prefixes** and **suffixes** to words. Suffixes are a key class of the derivational morphemes discussed above, and they commonly enable different word classes to be recognised.

17.1 SOME COMMON SUFFIXES

examples	suffixes
terrorism, sexism, kingdom	-ism, -dom are commonly used to form nouns
actor, employer	-er, -or are commonly used to describe people who do things
widen, simplify	-en, -ify are commonly used to form verbs
reasonable, irritable	-able is commonly used to form **adjectives**
naturally, steadily	-ly, -ily are commonly used to form **adverbs**

Some suffixes, such as -ism and –ology, are also sometimes used as words in their own right.

Prefixes are more common and often have independent meanings. They are added to the base form of words to create extra meanings.

17.2 SOME COMMON PREFIXES

examples	prefixes
monorail, monolingual	*mono-* means 'one'
multipurpose, multicultural	*multi-* means 'many'
post-war, postgraduate	*post* means 'after'
unnecessary, undemocratic	*un-* means 'not'
regrade, recycle	*re-* means 'again'

Very recent prefixes include *nano-*, *mega-* and *e-*.

MORPHEMES

1. Look at the text below, which is a two-part advertisement promoting the credentials of a shop called Matalan as an ecologically aware retailer.

How is the prefix 're' being used in the hooklines of this advertisement?

MATALAN

There is a commentary on this activity at the end of Part II.

2. Look at the text below, which is an advertisement for a new kind of toilet roll.

Explore how the vocabulary and images in this text connect with the term 'cycle' and its related terms.

There is a commentary on this activity at the end of Part II.

ANDREX ECO ROLL

The text reads 'Recycled loo rolls can be a little rough. Ours is made with 90% recycled paper but, unlike other eco rolls, we've added 10% sustainable bamboo pulp. It's that combination which makes it soft. That's why Andrex Eco is more than a recycled roll; it's an upcycled roll. Find out more at andrex.co.uk'

At last, an eco roll that's actually soft.

Text 17.2

Compounding refers to the process by which two or more existing words (free morphemes) are combined to form new words. Compounds can result in verbs, nouns, adjectives and adverbs. Some of these combinations involve hyphens between the words.

Some examples are: *old-fashioned*; *sugar-free*; *chain-smoke*; *car park*; *good-naturedly*; *fanzine*. Compounds occur very commonly around new technologies, and sometimes these start by being hyphenated but then lose their hyphens as the terms become more familiar. The examples below (common in the 1990s) are now rarely seen in these originally hyphenated forms when used in relation to technologies: *desk-top*; *e-mail*; *web-site*; *log-in*; *start-up*; *chat-room*.

Noun compounds such as 'desktop', above, are especially common, with many nouns joining with other nouns to create new meanings. Further examples include: *footprint*; *computer virus*; *quality time*; *letterbox*. As is shown here, some compounds are formed by joining the words, some by keeping the words separate, and some are linked by a hyphen.

Conversion is a process by which different words are changed from one word class to another.

For example:

jet, text (verb from noun);
download (noun from verb)
definite (as in 'We'll meet at six. That's a definite') (noun from adjective)
ups and downs (nouns from **prepositions**)

Here, again, terms for new technological processes are a rich source. We now talk freely about 'texting' people, but this term was a noun before its use as a verb in SMS contexts. In the early years of its usage as a verb, people were unsure what the past tense should be – 'texted', or 'text'? If in doubt, people could return 'text' to its status as a noun – 'I sent you a text yesterday'.

Words can also be created by other means such as *abbreviations*, **blends**, *acronyms* and *initialisms*. For example:

Abbreviations: *ad* (advertisement); *app* (application)
Blends: *blog* (web and log); *smog* (smoke and fog); *chillax* (chill and relax); *broga* (male yoga); *duffin* (doughnut and muffin); *cronut* (croissant and doughnut); *labradoodle* (new sort of dog breed, mixing a labrador with a poodle)
Acronyms (initials said as words): *NATO* (North Atlantic Treaty Organisation); *scuba* (self-contained underwater breathing apparatus); *radar* (radio detection and ranging)
Initialisms (said as letters): *FAQ* (frequently asked question); *SMS* (short messaging service); *GPS* (global positioning system); *FBI* (Federal Bureau of Investigation)

Some terms are mixtures of the two: for example, *jpeg, CD-ROM*. There are also terms that exist in both categories: for example, *lol* is an online abbreviation for 'laugh out loud', but some people now also say 'lol' as a word in face to face contexts, indicating that they are amused. This is not as a replacement for spontaneous laughter, but 'laughter with attitude' – an expression of ironic or knowing amusement.

The processes of affixation, compounding and conversion are regularly applied to English words, regardless of the languages they came from originally. English has absorbed many words from different languages over the years, during many periods of cultural contact and conquest. Writers often comment on the imperial history of English as that of ruling nations, but they forget that after the French invasion of the UK in 1066, English had only the status of a 'street language' and all official business had to be conducted in French. As a consequence, English has huge numbers of French-based terms, as well as words from many other languages in Europe, the Middle East and Asia.

An example of a problem in conversion and affixation can be seen with the term 'graffiti', originally from Italian. If you wanted to use this word as a verb – to graffiti – and you wanted to add an 'ing' ending to show that someone was doing this constantly, the result would be 'graffitiing'. English normally doesn't have more than one i in the spelling of words, so this word looks odd. A pragmatic solution would probably be to hyphenate it – 'graffiti-ing'. Similar problems occur with the word 'queue', from French, where adding 'ing' – 'queueing' – produces an unnaturally long sequence of five vowels in a row.

> ## ETYMOLOGY
>
> Look at the groups of English words below. Can you work out which languages these words came from originally? A good dictionary will give you all the help you need.
>
> For each cultural group represented by the language, find out what the nature of contact might have been that led to English speakers adopting their terms. If you recognise any of these terms from being a speaker of the original language yourself, do these words seem very different in their anglicised form from how you know them in their original language?
>
> | algebra | alcohol | alchemy | elixir |
> | --- | --- | --- | --- |
> | alligator | tomato | avocado | potato |
> | pecan | husky | toboggan | wigwam |
> | yacht | schooner | boom | hoist |
> | stiletto | volcano | umbrella | cello |
> | shampoo | pyjamas | kedgeree | gymkhana |
> | skyscraper | know-how | disc-jockey | tear-jerker |
> | try | stew | wash | clothes |
> | endeavour | casserole | launder | attire |
> | karaoke | manga | haiku | origami |
> | gung-ho | ketchup | typhoon | tycoon |
> | yogurt | bosh | kiosk | balaclava |
> | anorak | saga | fjord | troll |
> | ok | jukebox | hip | jazz |
>
> There is no commentary on this activity

Activity 17.2

But if you are working in a group situation, you could pool your findings and inform each other. First you will need to identify all the languages represented, and then each group could focus on a particular language, research the history of its connection with English-speaking communities, and present their results.

94 FORMING WORDS

Activity 17.3

WORD FORMATION

The text below was in the window of a large department store that was having a special promotion.

What is being sold here?

How would you describe the process of new **word formation** in this text?

What sociocultural knowledge does the text take for granted?

Looking at the text as a whole, what other features of language and image are noticeable?

There is a commentary on this activity at the end of Part II.

Text 17.3

COMFORT ON SALE

CHAPTER 18

Words and semantic fields

Words can be grouped together because they belong to a particular subject domain or **semantic field**.

Good examples would be the domain of medicine (*steroid, membrane, vaccinate*), academic research (*data, method, hypothesis*) or sport (*shoot, tackle, penalty*).

> **SEMANTIC FIELD**
>
> Look at the text overleaf, which is a recipe from a Peruvian cookery book called *Ceviche*. There are many terms in the text that can be seen as specific to the semantic field of cookery and recipes. Before we look at them, though, it's important to remember that we don't encounter texts in a vacuum. The language used in medicine, academic research, football or cookery will have a context: in the case of the recipe, this is the book as a whole, with its cover, introduction, colour photographs and distinctive layouts. These are all part of the **genre** of cookery books, and individual recipes also have specific genre characteristics. As a minimum, these include lists of ingredients and sets of instructions, features which link cookery books with other instruction manuals such as how to arrange flowers, plant shrubs, make furniture or design clothes. All these texts will have lists of 'ingredients' and 'how to' sets of instructions. This textbook has 'How To' in its title and uses a toolkit metaphor, so is claiming a similar genre identity as other manuals that teach productive skills.
>
> There are also larger cultural issues that surround any book: for example, the book's author, Martin Morales, makes the point of using Spanish initially for the recipe name as a way to underline his food's heritage. Part III of this book will enable you to think in more detail about such contextual factors.
>
> Here are some aspects of the semantic field of recipes that are in evidence in the text:
>
> - The names and listing of ingredients: scallops, limes, a pomegranate.
> - Numbers and quantities, both specific and approximate: 12, 1, a small handful, some.
> - Abbreviations: tbsp.
> - Imperative (command) verbs: arrange, sprinkle, drizzle, decorate.

Activity 18.1

Some of the other features are characteristic of a certain kind of modern cookery book. For example, the author shares a kind of 'work in progress' account of how he has developed the dish, and he gives readers a personal tip on how to serve the dish. This shows that while some aspects of recipes may have stayed the same for many years, there are some elements that change from age to age. Genres are not static, nor are they universal: they can vary widely from culture to culture, they can die out, new ones can be invented, and those that have a long shelf life can be subject to constant change.

Text 18.1

CONCHAS BORRACHAS

DRUNK SCALLOPS *I have always been a huge fan of scallop sashimi. After experimenting with various flavour combinations and some trial and error, this scallop dish was born. It's one of the prettiest, most delicate and most loved dishes on our menu.*

SERVES 4
12 large scallops, each cut unto 3 thin slices
2 limes, cut in half
Seeds from 1/2 a pomegranate
1 limo chilli, deseeded and finely chopped
2 tbsp pisco (or a good-quality vodka)
4 tbsp Coriander Oil (see here)
A small handful of freshly torn coriander leaves or micro coriander
Fine sea salt

Arrange the slices of scallop on serving plates. Don't worry if you have to overlap them slightly. Sprinkle some salt over them and squeeze half a lime over each plate.

Sprinkle with the pomegranate seeds and chilli and then drizzle over a few drops of pisco or vodka and the Coriander Oil. Decorate with coriander or micro coriander leaves and serve straight away.

NOTE
◊ Rather than serving straight on a plate you could also serve these scallops on clean scallop shells.

LANGUAGE CHANGE

Go back to the British Library 'Texts in Context' site that you were first introduced to in Part I of this book (p17). Go to the 'Books for Cooks' section and choose a recipe from a previous era. Compare the older recipe you have chosen with the modern recipe you have just been studying. What genre characteristics are shared, and what are different? Is the semantic field of the older text easy to understand?

The British Library site has many other themes and semantic fields for you to explore, offering a fascinating look back in time via texts of all kinds:

http://www.bl.uk/learning/langlit/texts/context.html

Activity 18.2

Not everyone will know about every semantic field. In fact, semantic fields are the basis of the different types of knowledge required for people to be considered 'experts', and we often talk about individuals being 'experts in their field'. The idea of an area of knowledge is strongly connected with knowing the vocabulary that expresses it. Occupational varieties of language are a specialist form of **register**, which refers to the way in which language choices reflect the context of the communication. Occupational registers do not have to be language that is used uniquely in that occupation, but simply language with a particular meaning for those people in that group. However, the fact that different groups of people might have their own in-group understandings of language means that language can function as a kind of badge of group membership. This is something that can be used by the producers of texts in order to construct ideas about who the text is aimed at.

COMPLEXITY

Of course, semantic fields don't have to exist on their own. You will often find a range of different semantic fields in a text, used either consciously or subconsciously. For example, the text that follows is a deliberate weaving together of two distinct semantic fields. The two semantic fields rely on the use of the same terms – 'techno' and 'metal' – but these terms exist in two different semantic fields, those of music and mechanics.

How does the use of the terms 'techno' and 'metal' construct ideas about who the text is aimed at? Also, think about why the copywriter has used a particular grammatical construction – 'bored of' – which has been gradually replacing the previous expression 'bored with' in spoken language.

Activity 18.3

98 WORDS AND SEMANTIC FIELDS

Text 18.2

TECHNO AND METAL

There is a commentary on this activity at the end of Part II.

CHAPTER 19

Words and word families

The place of **words** in particular semantic fields raises another question concerning the ways in which vocabulary is organised. Take a word such as *medicine* or a word such as *agree*, along with all the extensions we can have to each of these words. Are they all simply single words?

medicine, medicines, medic, medical, medicament, medicinal
agree, agreed, agreement, disagree, disagreed, agreeable, disagreeable

In these cases, is *medicine* one word or six words? Is *agree* one word or seven?

Here the idea of a **word family** is helpful. Most dictionaries operate on the basis that you cannot list all the words in a language; you have to arrange them in a dictionary according to a basic form or 'root' of a word (commonly called a **headword** or **lexeme**) and then group all the other words in the word family around it. A word family can be said to consist of the headword, its morphological inflections and its closely related derivations.

However, it is not always straightforward to decide which words belong in a family and which shade into different families of meaning. Can all the words in the word family of *agree* (above) be said to be related? For example, *house* is one of the most common words in English. It is in the top three hundred words in most multi-million-word corpus collections of English words. The *Cambridge English Dictionary* defines *house* as follows:

A building in which people, usually one family, live.

However, an examination of dictionary entries which have *house* as their main lexeme reveals a number of words that don't quite fit the core definition.

What about the verb *to house*? How many of the following words and phrases are close to the above definition?

lighthouse; greenhouse; hothouse
warehouse; house plant; houseboat
Houses of Parliament; The White House
housemate; housemistress; housemaster;

> housewife; doghouse; outhouse; treehouse
> house of correction; house music; house wine
> house-sit; house-trained; doll's house

Additionally, what about the following phrases?

> put your house in order;
> to go round the houses;
> on the house

As you can see, there are no clear-cut boundaries to tell us where word families begin and end. However, it is important to realise that we have a sense of connectedness between variants, as this is one of the ways in which we are able to both construct and detect patterns within texts.

CHAPTER 20

Words and multiple meanings

The previous unit saw how words can feature within a larger group of 'relatives', with the implication that we are cognitively aware of networks of relationships between words. However, a single word can also have multiple meanings, and this offers opportunities for us to create interesting puns and ambiguities.

> **MULTIPLE MEANINGS**
>
> In the text below, which was on a paper napkin in an American Oyster House called *Rodney's*, the term 'bed' has more than one meaning. Explain the possible meanings and say what part the ambiguity plays in the text as a whole.
>
> There is a commentary on this activity at the end of Part II.

Activity 20.1

RODNEY'S OYSTER HOUSE

Text 20.1

The fact that many English words have multiple meanings can be creatively exploited, as in the text above. The word *right* is an example of another ordinary term that has several meanings, outlined in the dictionary definitions immediately opposite:

1. *right* (as the opposite of wrong)
2. *right* (as the opposite of left)
3. *right* (in the sense of individual entitlements)

It also has a sound that is identical to *Wright*, a common surname in English, as well as the words *write* and *rite*.

However, *right* also has some quite distinctive functions in spoken English, and meanings that are different from those above.

In everyday conversations, *right* can have a **pragmatic** function, signalling that a stage in a conversation has been completed. For example, it is often used by speakers on the phone as a pre-closing signal, letting the listener know that the speaker is getting ready to conclude the conversation. In other real time contexts, *right* has also made an appearance with a similar function. For example, here are two students in a university-based online chat. Ben is anxious to do his assignment, but Rebecca wants him to stay online and play. At the point where Rebecca says 'right', Ben takes this as his permission to leave, suggesting that he understood the word as signalling Rebecca's agreement to end the interaction.

> Ben: I think the idea is for u 2 do an assessment too
> Rebecca: oh
> Rebecca: I see
> Rebecca: Right
> Ben: ok I'll go then
> Rebecca: see ya
>
> (Goddard 2005)

Real time communication, whether this is spoken or written in nature, requires strategies for signposting junction points in interactions, and words like *right* and *ok* (which are called **discourse markers**) facilitate this.

In the example below, from face to face speech, *right* has a different meaning again, this time acting as a tag question ('doesn't it?'):

> The film starts at 8.30, right?

This final spoken example shows speaker A using *right* as a response marker, indicating that B's answer has been understood.

> A: what did you do last weekend?
> B: not much but we went to the match on Saturday.
> A: right.

In thinking about multiple meanings, therefore, we need to remember that this area is not simply about the definitions of different written words. It is also about the fact that a single term can have very different functions and meanings depending on which mode of communication it appears in.

20.1 SUMMARY SO FAR

- The definition of a word is not straightforward, although *word* remains the most commonly used term in the study of vocabulary and semantics.
- Meaning exists in morphemes, units of language smaller than the word.
- The study of morphology is the identification, analysis and description of the structure of the linguistic units that make up words.
- The distinction between grammatical and lexical words is useful.
- The processes of word formation are very varied. The potential for creativity and innovation is rich.
- Many words belong to or are mainly associated with particular semantic fields.
- The notion of a headword and a word family can sometimes be useful in differentiating words that are closely related in form.
- The meanings of words are often not straightforward. Words can have multiple meanings. Some words can have pragmatic meanings rather than straightforward propositional or referential meanings.
- The same word can have a different meaning when used in a different mode of communication.
- Larger social contexts are also needed in order for some meanings to be deciphered.

CHAPTER 21

Connotation and collocation

HOUSE & HOME
Australia's magazine of home and style

Text 21.1

The word *house* was discussed earlier. The differences in meaning between the two words *house* and *home* illustrate the phenomenon of **connotation**, which refers to the associations we have for a particular term. In a strictly factual sense, there is little to choose between a house and a home – they both refer to places to live, although a home could be a flat or a boat or a palace.

However, the connotations of house and home are very different, with house much more associated with a particular type of structure, while home has powerful connotations of warmth and security. 'Turning your house into a home' is a frequent slogan used by companies advertising interior design services. It suggests turning a neutral structure into something personal and unique to you.

Connotations operate at a number of levels. They can have wide-ranging social and ideological associations because they encode the practices and values of a society. This can be seen in the history of the terms 'bachelor' and 'spinster', which, although referring in both cases to unmarried individuals, have had very different connotations. 'Bachelor' has been much more positive than 'spinster' because historically women had very few options beyond marriage, and so to be unmarried was, in effect, to be a failure: Baker's (2008) corpus research on the connotations of these two terms paints a picture of 'eligible' bachelors and 'frustrated' spinsters. As English expands its use as an additional language in many countries around the world, however, the connotations that derived originally from the customs and values of a particular group of English speakers are likely to change.

There are also connotations that operate at a much more local and personal level. No two individuals have exactly the same life experiences, and people may well attach strong feelings to certain items of language through associating them with particular events, people or emotions.

PAIRS AND CONNOTATIONS

Activity 21.1

Look at the pairs or groups of terms below, with their factual definitions in bold on the left. Explore the connotations of these terms, listing the associations you have for each.

A person who does not have a child	childless	childfree
To parent a child	to father a child	to mother a child
A system for managing a country	regime	government
Someone who makes war on a society for a political cause	terrorist	freedom fighter
Money to support someone who is out of work	unemployment benefit; jobseeker's allowance	
Reducing the number of employees in a company	firing people; rightsizing; making economies	
Increased use of temporary contracts	increased job insecurity; increased flexibility	
A person who is physically small	slim; slender; thin; skinny; scrawny; emaciated	

There is a commentary on this activity at the end of Part II.

A WORLD OF CONNOTATIONS

Activity 21.2

Opposite is a photograph taken in Pokhara, Nepal, of notices advertising hotels and guesthouses in the local town.

Explore the connotations of the different names. Which sound more attractive to you, and which sound less appealing? Where would you choose to stay and why?

There is no commentary on this activity.

Text 21.2

POKHARA HOTELS

The terms *house* and *home* have been discussed with reference to connotation, but they also illustrate **collocation**, or 'the company that words keep' (Firth, 1957, p.11). Collocation refers to the repeated co-occurrence of words – that is, the way in which some words seem to regularly occur in the same environment as others, in the same sentence or utterance, or even in exactly the same order. For example, the words in the phrase *house and home* can't occur in any order – it couldn't be *home and house*. Similarly, the phrase 'tall, dark and handsome', used to describe the stereotypical male hero in fantasy stories, wouldn't work if it was 'handsome, dark and tall'.

Collocation is often about looser relationships than those between the words in set phrases, however. Words can take on an association through their regular appearance in and around others, building into a whole set of representations about the seeming nature of things. For example, Herriman (1998) used the five-million-word Collins Cobuild corpus to search for collocations of the terms 'man' and 'woman'. She found that words for physical attractiveness (pretty, sexy, glamorous) collocated most frequently with 'woman', while terms describing height, abilities and personality collocated most frequently with 'man' (see Goddard and Mean (2009) for more discussion of connotation, collocation and gender).

Terms can take on a particular kind of flavour through their habitual use in certain contexts. While some terms are inherently evaluative, striking a specific attitude, there are other terms that don't come out in their true colours until corpus searches reveal a pattern of usage.

Here is an extract from a concordance from a ten-million-word corpus of English, once again sampled from a combination of the British National Corpus and the Cambridge English Corpus. (A concordance is produced by the computer software that helps us to explore the corpus.) The focus is on the word 'cause'. The extract here enables us to begin to see how the word *cause* is used when viewed across multiple occurrences.

CONCORDANCE OF 'CAUSE'

Text 21.3

'Cause' is a seemingly neutral word, but what kinds of pattern does it create with other words, and what meanings emerge from these patterns?

```
       have searched for a single  cause of aging – a critical gene, hor
         s in property lending will  cause a a serious credit crunch – compa
       lit second nobody moves?  Cause we're looking at the dolly-bird
          ith in the fas lane is no  cause for driving without due care and
         ion so far available gives  cause for concern about the circumstan
          of 70–90 mph expected to  cause structural damage. The forecaste
            aming. If untreated it can  cause permanent damage to heart. *
            urder came not from any  cause worth the name but from the very
             e in prison without good  cause, he says. The Foreign Office has
         es of martyrdom in a noble  cause. He said they had been granted *
             South West Water] did not  cause the problem is no defence at all
             obviously bleeding, could  cause blood to seep from veins and art
            justice is the Palestinian  cause and the right of the Palestinian
          d the relevant details may  cause an underpayment and perhaps resu
          onous toxins which could  cause kidneys to fail. This could happ
           e of information liable to  cause serious injury to the nation wi
            ity and its strength gives  cause for optimism for the prospects
         ng legislation which could  cause considerable problems for compan
           t in a situation likely to  cause unnecessary suffering, and permi
             on of schools is likely to  cause ministers more problems than it
           ffice staff, said the main  cause of recruitment problems was low
              inspectors as the biggest  cause of poor reading standards. "Some
         mmit criminal damage, and  cause public disorder, yesterday were
             dence in you is total. Our  cause is just. Now you must be the thu
             in 1987 for conspiracy to  cause explosions, was yesterday refuse
```

It's interesting to note here that *cause* isn't necessarily a 'neutral' word; it creates patterns that show that its meanings can often be negative (*cause explosions, cause disorder, cause suffering, cause injury*). The **semantic profile** of the word is only fully revealed in this extended context. (See the section *Corpus Resources and Projects* p222 for further ideas for investigating the **semantic** profiles of words and phrases.)

108 CONNOTATION AND COLLOCATION

Activity 21.3

CORPORA MEANINGS

Now look at the following advertisement taken from part of the United Nations website called UN Women, the United Nations Entity for Gender Equality and the Empowerment of Women. Their series of texts below reflect the results of corpus searches in Google databases from different regions of the world (all dated March 9, 2013). That is, the phrases

Women should…

and

Women shouldn't…

were entered into the Google search box with the most frequent patterns shown in the extended phrases and sentences that are placed across the mouths of the women in the ads. What do the searches reveal? How are the photographs and images used and for what purposes? What kinds of semantic profiles and meanings are found when such words and phrases are placed in the extended context of a longer sentence?

Text 21.4

UN WOMEN

The UN Women ads illustrate how corpus searches can also reveal patterns that extend beyond individual words and can reveal underlying ideologies.

women should
women should **stay at home**
women should **be slaves**
women should **be in the kitchen**
women should **not speak in church**
· · · · ·
women should **have the right to make their own decisions**

[UN comment]

CONNOTATION AND COLLOCATION   109

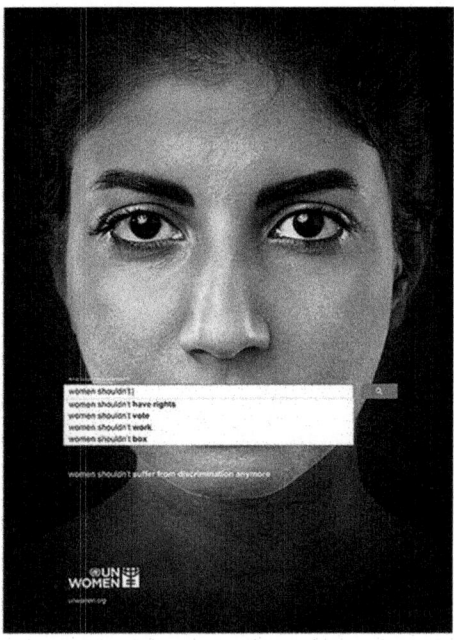

women shouldn't
women shouldn't **have rights**
women shouldn't **vote**
women shouldn't **work**
women shouldn't **box**
　· · · · ·
women shouldn't **suffer from discrimination anymore**
                              [UN comment]

See more at: http://www.unwomen.org/en/news/stories/2013/10/women-should-ads#sthash.25Smj67N.dpuf

There is no commentary on this activity.

> **CONNOTATION AND COLLOCATION**
>
> Connotation, the powerful associations that words can call up in our minds, is obviously an important aspect to explore in any text – but so is collocation, the way in which terms occur in habitual proximity to others.
>
> The text overleaf is from a brochure promoting the sale of short-break holidays 'for discerning travellers'. What ideas about the attitudes and values of 'discerning travellers' are given by the vocabulary choices made to describe Muscat in Oman? Are there specific connotations and collocations that stand out? What reassurance is given to potential tourists by the language of the brochure? What do you see when you 'see through' the language of the text – in other words, when you analyse the view of the world that is constructed by the language choices?

Activity 21.4

MUSCAT

MUSCAT, GULF OF OMAN

The Jewel of the Arabian peninsula and source of gold, frankincense and delicious fresh dates, this wonderful country has been nurtured by her proud people for centuries and is now a blissful oasis of calm in the heart of this fascinating part of the world. Ever since the Sultan took over from his father in 1970, the country has developed from being a key trading centre with close links to Britain and the Indian subcontinent, to becoming one of the most sophisticated and tolerant societies in the Middle East where they have preserved much of their heritage and Muslim traditions whilst offering warm hospitality to Western visitors. The Omanis have embraced many of the benefits that have come with their new found oil wealth, but they have resisted the worst excesses of consumer society and have much to offer the discerning traveller. Muscat itself is a highly civilised city with comfortable hotels, interesting architecture, the fabulous Grand Mosque, traditional markets and souks, sandy beaches and opportunities for dolphin and turtle watching in the shimmering turquoise sea of the Gulf of Oman.

Grand Mosque

There is a commentary on this activity at the end of Part II.

CHAPTER 22

Words and metaphors

Words can also act as metaphors. Metaphors are made when words are used to create an 'as if' world; that is, the word or words are compared to something to which they are not normally applicable in order to suggest a resemblance. The resulting comparison shows how two things that are not normally alike in most ways are similar in another important way. For example, in "All the world's a stage", a phrase from Shakespeare's play *As You Like It*, the comparison of 'world' to 'stage' suggests that the world is a place in which people perform parts and assume roles as if they were actors in a play. Another frequently quoted example is "argument is war". For example, in phrases such as "*he demolished* his argument by *attacking* every weak point at every stage in the debate", the metaphor shows how perceptions are constructed through language: argument is being seen as war or as a battle to be won. In turn, this thinking can connect with our behaviour: if we think arguments are like war, then aggressive behaviour can seem appropriate and 'normal'.

Other common metaphors draw on other similar analogies and comparisons. Many are rooted in everyday experience and concepts. For example:

22.1 ORIENTATIONAL METAPHORS

Happy is *up* (I'm in high spirits; things are looking up)
Sad is *down* (She was very low after the exams)
The future is *in front* (There are exciting times *ahead*)
The past is *behind* (We need to look *back* and learn from the match)

22.2 ONTOLOGICAL METAPHORS

Time is money (Don't waste your time; spend the time wisely; can you spare me ten minutes to discuss the meeting?)
Life is a journey (Some *travel* towards clear *destinations*; others seem to have no *direction*; many *lose their way*).

22.3 CONTAINER METAPHORS

Emotional states are both containers and fluids in containers.

Her heart *overflowed* with sympathy.

22.4 METAPHORS OF E-COMMUNICATION

The language in our digital environments is now so familiar to us that it's hard to see them as metaphors – but they are (or were, originally). For example, none of the terms below, when used in a virtual context, describes the physical items or activity they originally labelled:

desktop   chatroom   mail   folder   page
browsing   surfing   navigating

We also have metaphors that we have taken from mechanical worlds in order to describe our own human states and feelings; for example:

'I'm still processing that idea'; 'I can't cope, I'm in overload'; 'I need to switch off for a while',
'I need some downtime'; 'We have our wires crossed'.

Activity 22.1

METAPHOR

Collect and list some more examples of metaphors, to add to the lists above. We often use metaphors where we are trying to understand abstract ideas and emotions, so you could start by thinking about how we describe different moods such as anger and love, or different experiences such as being in a relationship or learning new ideas.

There is no commentary on this activity because many varied outcomes are possible. Different languages and cultures may well have distinctive sets of metaphors, so if you are in a situation where there is a mixture of people from different backgrounds, present your findings to each other and examine whether your metaphors show different ways of thinking.

WORDS AND METAPHORS

Activity 22.2

METAPHOR AT WORK

This activity focuses on how metaphors can work within texts and be threaded through them to create meanings. Look at the text below, which promotes an online dating service. How many multiple meanings can you detect? What is the central metaphor that is threaded through the text? Why do you think the writer has chosen that particular metaphor?

There is a commentary on this activity at the end of Part II.

Text 22.1

ENCOUNTERS DATING

encountersdating
because you go together

WHERE BUCKET MET SPADE

There are some things that just go together. But there was a time when Bucket didn't know Spade. They had never met.

Bucket had a load of boyfriends when she was younger but she hadn't met anyone for years and life just felt a little empty.

Spade was in a bit of a hole too, but had been digging around for a date when he discovered Encounters. He soon got hold of Bucket and scooped her up to go out with him.

They booked a holiday together to the seaside almost immediately, and it wasn't long before they were happily engaged.

The rest is history. They've been together ever since. (And still go back to that beach every summer to build sandcastles with their kids.) In fact it seems extraordinary they didn't come across each other sooner.

But that's how it is. And that's why more and more people turn to Encounters Dating as a way to meet someone they are just going to click with – other Times readers who share that attitude of living life to the full.

So log on, write your profile, and it shouldn't be long before you find someone you really dig.

Exclusively from
THE TIMES
THE SUNDAY TIMES

Find your perfect partner at
encountersdating.co.uk

CHAPTER 23

Lexical cohesion

In looking at lexis and semantics, the focus in this section has been more on words and on their individual properties than on the way words link together across a text. However, in the previous unit on metaphor, you were asked specifically to look across a text in order to see how metaphorical references were built up.

The study of connections across a text is called **cohesion.** It involves awareness of grammar as well as vocabulary, and the next section will focus on grammatical patterns, taking the idea of cohesion further.

Aspects of **lexical cohesion** don't have to be complex: the process of simple repetition is a basic way in which different parts of a text can echo each other. However, all the other areas that have been explored in this section – from word families to semantic fields – also play their part in knitting a text together. Cohesion is a resource for writers in their process of composition; it is also a resource for readers in their comprehension and textual interpretation.

Activity 23.1

COHESION

Opposite are some jumbled up sentences, which were originally six texts consisting of two lines each.

See if you can join the right sentences to each other. When you have finished, you should have created six texts, each from a different area of activity or context. Try to identify what these different contexts might be.

There is a commentary on this activity at the end of Part II.

JUMBLED SENTENCES

Text 23.1

You are entering a holy site.
Cover lightly with soil and keep moist.
Allow them to cook gently on a medium heat for about 15 minutes, or until they are soft and lightly browned.
Do not exceed the stated dose without consulting your doctor.
The playwright Harold Pinter was born in 1930.
A man is seriously ill in hospital today after exposure to extreme cold during a mountaineering expedition with friends in the Swiss Alps.
All shoes and socks must be removed before entering.
Sow between April and May in a prepared seed bed.
Add the butter and onions to the saucepan.
The author of over 25 plays and several books of poetry, he won the Nobel Prize for Literature in 2005.
Man critically ill after overnight mountain rescue.
Take two tablets every four hours.

COHESION AND SPEECH

Activity 23.2

Cohesion is not simply an aspect of written language. Spoken language has cohesion too, although it tends to work differently. In order to explore this, read through the transcript overleaf, which represents a conversation between two friends. They used to work together for a small clothing company called Dawson's when they left school, and they are reminiscing about their time at the company.

What are the main patterns of cohesion that you can detect across the individual speaking turns of the two friends?

There is a commentary on this activity at the end of Part II.

TWO FRIENDS

Transcription key:

(.) normal pause
(2.0) longer pause with duration indicated in seconds
bold type indicates speaker emphasis
? indicates a questioning intonation

Jill: I was amazed walking into Dawson's how it had changed (.) but of course it **had** changed but it **hadn't** changed (.) if you know what I mean

Carol: erm (.) yeah (.) I **do**

Jill: the desks were still in the same place (.) but everyone has **mo**biles now (.) so no big **tel**ephones

Carol: the **lights** were still the same (1.0) I remember then they were too bright and still are (.) give you a headache they do (1.0) and don't forget the curtains in the toilet (.) still those grey-green ones (.) **horr**ible

Jill: mm (.) all the same, the boss's office is a lot smarter (.) she's had leather chairs put in and nice blinds (1.0) did you see the reception area?

Carol: I think so (.) is it the glass area where the canteen used to be?

Jill: yes (.) much better and brighter (.) isn't it?

Carol: yeah (.) but I still wouldn't want to **work** there (.) would you?

Jill: I **might** (1.0) depends how much they'd **pay** me (1.0) what's **more** (.) the time they allow for holidays is three weeks now

Carol: that's not enough to make me want to go back (1.0) anyway (.) it's never good to go back.

Jill: I suppose so (.) cos you always have the old place and people in your mind.

COHESION AND POETRY

Cohesion is also a strategy in many literary texts, especially poetry, which is often densely patterned. Analyse the following poem by the Malaysian poet Hilary Tham (1946–2005) with particular reference to patterns of lexical cohesion.

There is a commentary on this activity at the end of Part II.

OFFERINGS

Offerings

I came to you at sunrise
With silvery dew on sleeping lotus
Sparkling in my gay hands;
You put my flowers in the sun.

I danced to you at midday
With bright raintree blooms
Flaming in my ardent arms;
You dropped my blossoms in the pond.

I crept to you at sunset
With pale lilac orchids
Trembling on my uncertain lips;
You shredded my petals in the sand.

I strode to you at midnight
With gravel hard and cold
Clenched in my bitter fists;
You offered me your hybrid orchids,
And I crushed them in my despair.

Hilary Tham, *Offerings*

23.1 REVIEW YOUR SKILLS

Write a substantial paragraph in your own words, explaining how at least three of the following can contribute to the meaning of a text:

- Semantic field
- Words with multiple meanings
- Connotation
- Collocation
- Metaphor
- Cohesion
- Genre
- Register

23.2 IDEAS FOR ASSIGNMENTS

23.2.1 Births and deaths

Paying particular attention to vocabulary choices, explore the way birth announcements or obituaries are written in different English language newspapers worldwide (e.g. Britain, Canada, USA, Singapore, South Africa). Many of these newspapers can be viewed online and many are also produced in countries in which English is a foreign language (e.g. China, Arabic-speaking countries, etc.).

Are there cultural differences in the ways in which these major events are reported? Are there differences between national and local newspapers in the ways in which vocabulary is used? Some examples can be accessed below.

http://www.starclassifieds.com/marketplace/category/Announcements/Births
http://www.iannounce.co.uk/Lancaster-Guardian/428/Birth/birth?_fstatus=search
http://www.canadianobituaries.com
http://www.theguardian.com/tone/obituaries
http://www.obituaries.com/ns/obituariescom/oits.aspx

Further exploration will also probably reveal how different contexts deal with these life and death issues. An alternative assignment on a similar theme would be to look at the way in which the death of a major world figure has been reported in different newspapers around the world.

23.2.2 People and places

Focus on how a particular place is represented, looking particularly at the lexical and semantic dimensions of the text but also exploring aspects of genre. Choose two different genres and compare how the representations of the place and its inhabitants vary in, for example:

- holiday brochures
- encyclopaedia entries
- tour guides
- geography books
- blogs and other online sources
- literary texts
- TV programmes
- consumer sites such as TripAdvisor

To help you better appreciate differences, do some genre swaps by re-writing a text from a holiday brochure as an encyclopaedia entry or a geography book.

23.2.3 Words and meanings and extended meanings

On p104 above, words such as *house* and *home* were explored for their different meanings and associations as well as the patterns they create inside and outside different phrases.

Compare the ways in which any two dictionaries of English provide entries on very common words. Either choose a word/words for yourself, or explore how common words such as:

book and *run*
or
head and *arm*
or
green and *blue*
or
black and *white*
or
face and *head*

are structured in the dictionaries. Words for colours and the human body are interesting, especially since they are sometimes difficult to translate because the words (and the collocations and idioms that the words form a part of) can have different cultural meanings in different parts of the world.

Alternatively, look in a dictionary to see which words have long entries because they have many different meanings and/or can: i) be different parts of speech (e.g. verbs and nouns); ii) form many different **idioms** with different meanings. A good example is the word *break* (which can have many different meanings; it can be both a verb and a noun and it forms lots of idioms in which the word *break* is central). Find three words similar to *break* either in English or in your own first language and list at least ten different meanings for each of your words, either as a single word or as it is used in an idiom. What do your explorations in the dictionary tell you about words and word meanings?

23.2.4 Metaphors and metonyms

Collect examples of metaphors in use in different texts. For example:

- News articles
- Advertisements
- Sports reports
- Recipes
- Other texts about food, for example diets
- Prayers and religious texts
- Medical discourse

Examine the ways in which the activity described is socially and culturally constructed and what it may in turn reveal about the ways in which human life is metaphorically structured. Do the same for a range of metonyms in texts. Are metonyms more or less powerful in what they reveal about underlying patterns of human behaviour? Can you find examples in your texts where metaphors and metonyms operate together? For example, parts of the body (*head, ear, mouth*) can be used both metaphorically and metonymically, especially in phrases such as *lend me your ear*. Find examples from other languages and analyse why such figures of speech are difficult to translate from one language to another.

23.2.5 Corpus word searches: talking and writing

Choose ten random words. Compare how the same words occur in corpora of spoken and written English. What does this reveal about the differences and distinctions between spoken and written language use and usage?

Now take a list of the top forty most frequent spoken words (see p140) and explore how frequent any five of these words are in a written English corpus. What does this reveal about the differences and distinctions between spoken and written language use and usage?

23.2.6 *Should* searches

Look back at the UN Women ads on pp108–9 above, where Google searches were used to reveal key underlying ideologies. In a corpus of your choice, explore the most common patterns that emerge from searches on key phrases. Start with:

> *Women should...*
> *Men should...*

Explore the contrast between men and women indicated by the searches. Are the Google results different from your own? If so, why? If not, why not?

Take your searches further and choose some more starting points, for example:

> *Children should...*
> *Students should...*

Or you could type in the name of the country in which you live followed by *should* and comment on the main patterns linked to the phrases. Try different phrases and see whether there are differences when modal verbs other than *should* (for example, *can, must, might*) are used in the search box.

For advice on access to corpora and on undertaking more detailed corpus related projects, see *Corpus Resources and Projects*, p222.

Section C

Grammatical Level

Aim: Section C will increase your awareness of how grammatical structures help to shape meanings in texts. This will enrich and deepen the level of detail you are able to offer in any text analysis.

CONTENTS: PART II, SECTION C

- 24 Introduction
- 25 Grammar and cohesion
- 26 Grammar and representation
- 27 Grammar, speech and language change
- 28 Grammar and politics
- 29 Conversational grammar
- 30 Texting grammar
- 31 Creative grammar
-     **Review your skills**
-     **Ideas for assignments**
-     **Commentaries for Part II**

CHAPTER 24

Introduction

In this section the focus will be on grammar. Grammar is a key element in the way language is organised and in the way it works. The focus will be on some key features of grammar, but the aim is not simply to identify and name these features; the aim is to explore how grammatical structures and patterns can make meaning.

Understanding better how some of the patterns of grammar work can illuminate literary texts, political rhetoric, formal writing such as academic discourse, media texts, instruction manuals and more. However, it is important not just to look at rules and patterns but also to look at texts where rules are creatively broken. The approach to grammar will be to find interesting examples of usage where you can see the relationship between the choice of particular structures, and the creative making of certain meanings or identities.

This book is not attempting to teach a comprehensive grammar course, and nor is it teaching about different grammars. Although we do assume that you know basic grammatical forms such as *noun, verb, adverb, adjective* and that we do not need to explain terms like this, remember that there is a glossary at the end of the book in which a wide range of items used in the whole book, including some basic terms that are used in the study of grammar, are defined and illustrated.

The focus in this section of the book will be on some specific aspects of grammatical structure that recur across texts that you will be able to comment on meaningfully and make work for yourselves – for example:

- pronouns
- grammatical reference and cohesion
- verb tense, **modality** and transitivity
- **nominalisation**
- aspect and voice
- pre- and post-**modification**
- articles
- conjunctions and connectives
- word order
- ellipsis
- sentence types

INTRODUCTION

Most books on grammar focus on the kinds of grammatical structures we typically find in writing and in written texts. This section will also cover some of the specific grammatical structures that are characteristic of spoken language and informal writing; this is why there are headings such as 'conversational grammar' and 'texting grammar'.

Corpus material will again be used to illustrate some of the nuances of meaning associated with particular grammatical patterns, and also to go beyond simply looking at formal writing. There are opportunities in this section to collect your own texts and to do some corpus analysis for yourself.

CHAPTER 25

Grammar and cohesion

In the previous section the focus was on vocabulary, but it should have become clear that vocabulary and grammar are very interconnected. As well as some words themselves having a grammatical function, there are word meanings that build up from the fact that those words occur frequently alongside others in particular grammatical patterns.

In the sorting exercise that you did at the end of the previous section (pp114–15), grammar also played a role in enabling you to determine not just which sentence went with which, but which order the sentences should occur in. This is an important aspect of cohesion, and the simple exercise below will illustrate this idea further.

SIMPLEHUMAN

This text is part of a warranty that came with the purchase of a kitchen wastebin. The company producing the bin is called *simplehuman*.

Reading this or any other text and making sense of it involves you in seeing how the sentences fit together. This process is not just about the grammatical aspects of language, but grammar plays an important part.

Text 25.1

a simple promise

To create smart, functional tools, we start with intuitive design and solid engineering. Then we use the best materials and subject our products to rigorous testing. That's what makes a simplehuman product and why our warranty is a real promise.

simplehuman®

a simple promise

To create smart, functional tools, we start with intuitive design and solid engineering. Then we use the best materials and subject our products to rigorous testing. That's what makes a simplehuman product and why our warranty is a real promise

Lexical and semantic aspects of cohesion include the repetition of words (*promise*), variations within a word family (*simple, simplehuman*), new words (*simplehuman*) and the use of a semantic field (manufacturing: *functional tools, design, engineering, materials, products, testing*). All these elements play a part in creating what is called 'texture': the sense that a text is a whole entity.

However, there are some important aspects of **grammatical cohesion** that not only tie the text together, but also make the order of sentences look logical and help the text to move forward. For example, the word *then* in the second sentence is a conjunction that refers to time, and this helps to place the sentence as describing a second step in a process. If you had been asked to rearrange the sentences in the text from a jumbled list, you would have known that the first sentence couldn't have started with *then*. Equally, you would have known that the third sentence couldn't have begun the text. Both *then* and *that* point backwards to something that has gone before. This is called anaphoric reference, and you were introduced to this aspect of reference in the previous section. The term *that* is demonstrative or deictic: like *this*, *these* and *those*, it points to something – in this case, the processes described in the text's previous two sentences. Language items can also point forwards, in which case they are using cataphoric reference. There are cataphoric references in this paragraph and the previous one, in the form of a colon and a dash.

Conjunctions like *then* are an important aspect of grammatical cohesion. There are many of them and they can express a range of different meanings, as illustrated in the table below. Conjunctions are sometimes called **connectives,** highlighting their connecting function.

25.1 CONJUNCTIONS

Conjunction		
	Additive (to add or to give an alternative)	Examples: *and, but, furthermore, in addition* It's raining **and** it is heavy **but** it'll soon pass.
	Temporal (time links between events)	Examples: *then, finally, up to now, the following week* **First of all**, we're going to the cinema and **then** out for a meal.
	Causal (one thing causes another)	Examples: *so, consequently, as a result, because* I've stopped eating chocolate **because** I am on a diet.
	Adversative (things contradict or require concessions)	Examples: *however, yet, although, on the contrary, nevertheless.* Gill is a good friend, **although** we don't see each other much now.
	Continuatives (things follow on in steps)	Examples: *well, now, ok, right, anyway, after all.* **Anyway**, let's not wait for the bus.

GRAMMAR AND COHESION

CONNECTIVES AND DEICTICS

Look at the following short texts and underline the connectives which create cohesion across the different sentences in the texts. See if you can classify the connectives according to some of the categories in the previous chart.

Also, underline any deictics and explore the role they may have in establishing cohesion.

> **From a website memorial to a friend:**
> My friend Jessica always wanted to be called Jessie but she introduced herself as Jessica. As a result everyone called her that.

> **From an official report on pesticide control:**
> Few countries have satisfactory legislation on pesticides or government officials who can enforce it. In contrast, use of pesticides in Europe, Japan and North America is backed by government controls which limit their use. Furthermore, where it cannot be regulated, farmers are given detailed advice to help them.

> **From a blog about environmental issues:**
> They can't just close their eyes and say that there will be no accidents on the road because the facts this year prove this. Then again, they will probably say it's too expensive to put up proper road signs. In that case, they are just saying human life is cheap. That's my opinion, anyway.

> **From the instructions on a bottle of cough medicine:**
> This cough medicine should be taken twice a day. The medicine is in liquid form and is for oral use only. If you forget to take a dose, then take the next dose when needed. No more than a single dose should therefore be taken at any one time.

Activity 25.1

There is a commentary on this activity at the end of Part II.

CHAPTER 26

Grammar and representation

This unit focuses on the role of grammar in constructing **representations,** which is all about presenting seemingly natural pictures of the world and the people and things in it. There are many aspects of grammar that contribute to ideas about how the world is, but a particular focus here is on **verbs**. The unit covers transitivity, **active** and passive voice, modal verbs, the tense of verbs, and also what the effect can be of missing verbs out altogether.

26.1 TRANSITIVITY

Both **transitive** and **intransitive** verbs are common in English. Transitive verbs are more common. A transitive verb is a verb that needs an **object** – something or someone affected by the verb – to complete its meaning. For example:

> Rabbits *love* carrots.
> Geoff *watched* three films in one evening.

The verbs here (*love* and *watched*) don't make much sense on their own and need the objects (*carrots* and *films*) to make sense.
    An intransitive verb doesn't need an object:

> She *sneezed*.
> An hour *elapsed*.

Some verbs can, however, be transitive or intransitive, depending on the meaning. In the following sentence, for example, the verb *start* is intransitive:

> An hour elapsed before the match *started*.

But below the verb *start* is used transitively:

> They *started* the engine.
> She *started* a new job last week.

Transitivity is all about agency – the extent to which people and things are seen as active in the world. This may seem an abstract idea, but grammatical choices can construct some powerful messages about what seems 'only natural'. The next activity will help you to see how grammar – particularly the nature of the verbs chosen – plays an important role in constructing and representing a sense of reality. If you are able to identify grammatical features when you are analysing a text, then you are able to show evidence for your interpretation, making your evaluation more rigorous.

TRANSITIVITY AND GENDER

Below is a piece of romantic fiction. It tells a story about how men and women behave, and it does this through making language choices, particularly grammatical choices. Start by reversing all the pronouns in the text, turning 'he' into 'she', and changing the names. Make up some names of your own, but stick to the patterns in the text: for example, if a first name and surname is given, provide both; but if only a first name is given, provide that.

When you have finished, think about how the pictures you get of the male and female characters have changed. Focus on those aspects of language that now seem odd when associated with each of the characters.

Now, from your list, identify some of the language choices associated with the characters:

- Are the verbs transitive or intransitive?
- What is the nature of the verbs involved – are they about actions, or feelings?
- Apart from verbs, are there other examples of language that represent the characters in particular ways?
- How do your findings above relate to ideas about the characters as more or less active and in control?

There is a commentary on this activity at the end of Part II.

Text 26.1

ROMANTIC FICTION

> It had been so different the evening that she had encountered Damian Flint for the second time. The first time he had flirted outrageously with her and she had dismissed him, knowing that nothing could have come of the meeting anyway. But now she couldn't quite get him out of her head and she had gone to this party, half-hoping that, as a friend of Gemma, he would be there too. He was.
>
> Claire did not feel attractive. She had come to the south coast to rest after her operation and all the problems with her boyfriend, Charles, but the weather had been too hot, freckles and little red blotches had come out on her face and she knew she looked unattractive and unexciting. Until Damian had taken her out onto the patio and kissed her.
>
> "It was better meeting you second time," he had said softly, gently holding her hand in his and only letting her go very slowly. She trembled a little and almost sighed under her breath as she looked at his lean soft brown complexion, his full but gentle lips and his dark blue eyes. "Are you angry with me?" His eyes confronted her. And she blushed violently at his words, knowing that she was rather pleased to be with him. He kissed her again and this time she clung to him, his mouth only leaving hers after what seemed a very long time. She tried to speak but only moaned listlessly as his fingers pressed her and deepened and she pressed helplessly to get closer to him.

26.2 LOOK! NO VERBS!

If verbs are so powerful, what happens when they are removed from a text – does it collapse in a heap? Actually, a sentence doesn't have to have a verb at all. Sentences without verbs are sometimes called **minor sentences** and you will see them in many places.

MENU

For example, here is part of a menu which offers rail customers some snacks on their journey:

Text 26.2

> **Traditional banoffee tray bake**
> A classic sweet cake with banana flavour, toffee fudge pieces and a vanilla frosting.
>
> **St Clements loaf cake**
> A light citrus sponge with crystallised ginger, candied orange and lemon peel.

While the menu doesn't have any verbs at all, there are some verb forms in the text below, which is an estate agent's advert describing a house for sale. However, there is a difference in the verb forms used. 'Have moved' is a **main verb,** giving a sense of completed action, but although 'featuring' and 'offered' are both verbs, in this text they appear as **non-finite** forms, which means that they suggest something ongoing and not finished.

ESTATE AGENT'S ADVERT

Text 26.3

> **FOR SALE**: Kimpton Village. Semi-detached Edwardian cottage featuring three spacious bedrooms. Open-plan kitchen. Peaceful commuter village with easy train access to Manchester city and airport. Well-maintained gardens. Owners have moved to Singapore. Offered for quick sale.

There are good reasons why both the menu and the estate agent's advert might not want to suggest finished action – after all, they are both offering descriptions of things in ongoing states – in both cases, things for sale. Menus strive for a timeless quality: no customer wants to think that the items on offer are time-limited. Similarly, no house buyer wants to think of the bedrooms suddenly shrinking in size or the gardens running to weeds. In both texts, then, the omission of verbs or the use of non-finite forms can help to suggest a permanent state of reality. In contrast, the fact that the house owners have already gone abroad – the reason for the quick sale – is described via a finite verb, 'have moved'.

132 GRAMMAR AND REPRESENTATION

Activity 26.2

VERBS

Although we tend to think of storytelling as fast-action narratives, this is not always the case. The use of non-finite verb forms can be part of a literary author's descriptive repertoire. Read the text below, where Dickens makes deliberate use of certain verb forms. His choices are explained and analysed in the notes that follow the extract.

Text 26.4

BLEAK HOUSE

Here are the opening four paragraphs from Charles Dickens' novel *Bleak House* (1852–3). Dickens is one of the major nineteenth century English novelists who saw the legal system of the country as a source of corruption and as a major obstacle to progress. Here the 'Lord Chancellor' is the head of the legal system.

One of the most striking features of Dickens' use of language is that the opening three paragraphs only rarely contain a single main verb. What effect does it have on you as you read it?

> London. Michaelmas term lately over, and the Lord Chancellor sitting in Lincoln's Inn Hall. Implacable November weather. As much mud in the streets as if the waters had but newly retired from the face of the earth, and it would not be wonderful to meet a Megalosaurus, forty feet long or so, waddling like an elephantine lizard up Holborn Hill. Smoke lowering down from chimney-pots, making a soft black drizzle, with flakes of soot in it as big as full-grown snowflakes – gone into mourning, one might imagine, for the death of the sun. Dogs, undistinguishable in mire. Horses, scarcely better; splashed to their very blinkers. Foot passengers, jostling one another's umbrellas in a general infection of ill temper, and losing their foot-hold at street-corners, where tens of thousands of other foot passengers have been slipping and sliding since the day broke (if this day ever broke), adding new deposits to the crust upon crust of mud, sticking at those points tenaciously to the pavement, and accumulating at compound interest.
>
> Fog everywhere. Fog up the river, where it flows among green aits and meadows; fog down the river, where it rolls defiled among the tiers of shipping and the waterside pollutions of a great (and dirty) city. Fog on the Essex marshes, fog on the Kentish heights. Fog creeping into the cabooses of collier-brigs; fog lying out on the yards and hovering in the rigging of great ships; fog drooping on the gunwales of barges and small boats. Fog in the eyes and throats of ancient Greenwich, pensioners wheezing by the firesides of their wards; fog in the stem

> and bowl of the afternoon pipe of the wrathful skipper, down in his close cabin; fog cruelly pinching the toes and fingers of his shivering little 'prentice boy on deck. Chance people on the bridges peeping over the parapets into a nether sky of fog, with fog all round them, as if they were up in a balloon and hanging in the misty clouds.
>
> Gas looming through the fog in divers places in the streets, much as the sun may, from the spongey fields, be seen to loom by husbandman and ploughboy. Most of the shops lighted two hours before their time – as the gas seems to know, for it has a haggard and unwilling look.
>
> The raw afternoon is rawest, and the dense fog is densest, and the muddy streets are muddiest near that leaden-headed old obstruction, appropriate ornament for the threshold of a leaden-headed old corporation, Temple Bar. And hard by Temple Bar, in Lincoln's Inn Hall, at the very heart of the fog, sits the Lord High Chancellor in his High Court of Chancery.

There are, of course, verbs in this opening to the novel. In the opening paragraph there are verbs such as 'retired', 'waddling', 'splashed', 'jostling', 'slipping', 'sliding', and so on. The verbs all serve to create an atmosphere of constant action and movement in the big city. Yet there are no **finite verbs** in main **clauses** in the text. There is thus a difference between the following two sentences, the first of which (1) contains a main finite verb, the second of which (2) does not:

(1) Foot passengers jostled one another's umbrellas and lost their foothold at street corners.
(2) Foot passengers jostling one another's umbrellas and losing their foothold at street corners.

As in the estate agent's advert, main finite verbs provide a kind of anchor for the action. You know clearly when something took place and that the action was completed. In the second sentence above you are left suspended, knowing that the action is ongoing, but awaiting a main verb to give you your bearings. If the sentence had been written in the following way, the 'anchor' for the action would have been in the verb *arrived,* which is a finite verb in this case:

Foot passengers jostling one another's umbrellas and losing their foothold at street corners *arrived* at the bank.

A finite verb is thus a verb which tells you when something happened (past or present), how many were/are involved (singular or plural) and who the participants are ('you'/'we'/'I', etc.). By contrast, when a **non-finite** -*ing* form is used the verb can be referring to any number, or tense, or first, second or third person.

Sentence (2) above is a kind of model for many of the sentences in the first three paragraphs. Sentences such as the following therefore serve to create a sense of both disorientation and dislocation. All the activity of London is confused and directionless, and it is not clear what timescale people are in. The present **participles** ('ing' forms) in particular convey a feeling of continuous action which could almost be timeless.

> London.
> Implacable November weather.
> Smoke lowering down from chimney pots...
> Dogs, undistinguishable in the mire.
> Foot passengers, jostling one another's umbrellas...
> Fog in the eyes and throats of ancient Greenwich pensioners, wheezing by the firesides...
> Gas looming through the fog in divers places...

Given the timeless character which is imparted to these descriptions, it is perhaps not surprising that Dickens can suggest that London has an almost prehistoric feel to it – 'and it would not be wonderful to meet a Megalosaurus, forty feet long or so, waddling like an elephantine lizard up Holborn Hill'.

26.3 TENSE AND WORD ORDER

In the final paragraph of this opening to *Bleak House* main finite verbs are restored to the sentences of the text. In particular the main verb 'to be' is repeated: 'The raw afternoon is rawest, and the dense fog is densest, and the muddy streets are muddiest...'. The presence of a main verb is most noticeable in the final sentence:

> And hard by Temple Bar, in Lincoln's Inn Hall, at the very heart of the fog, *sits* the Lord High Chancellor in his High Court of Chancery.

Here the main finite verb is *sits*. The action and location of the Lord High Chancellor is thus clearly situated. Indeed, the **word order** is structured so that the location of the main **subject** of the sentence ('the Lord High Chancellor') comes first in the sentence. He sits:

> hard by Temple Bar in Lincoln's Inn Hall at the very heart of the fog.

Structured differently, the sentence might have read:

> The Lord High Chancellor sits hard by Temple Bar in Lincoln's Inn Hall at the very heart of the fog.

This structure would be more normal and would follow the conventional word order for sentences in English in which the subject ('The Lord High Chancellor') occurs first and is then followed by a main finite verb ('sits').

One of Dickens' purposes may be to delay the subject so that it has more impact as a result of its occurrence in an unusual position. It also has a very particular impact as a result of being in the simple **present tense** ('sits') when readers of a novel or of any kind of narrative might expect verbs to be in the simple **past tense** ('sat').

However, 'sits' suggests that the Lord High Chancellor always sits there and is a permanent landmark in this landscape. The simple present tense in English carries this sense of a permanent, general, unchanging truth, as in scientific statements such as:

Oil floats on water.
Mice have long tails.
Two and two make four.

In this final paragraph one of the main effects which Dickens creates may be to imply that the legal system of the country is in a state of permanent confusion, or else it creates states of confusion which cannot be changed. Furthermore, both in these opening paragraphs and in the novel as a whole *fog* assumes symbolic importance, reinforcing a sense both of general confusion and of not being able to see clearly. The Lord High Chancellor as the head of the country's law-making and legal institutions is always 'at the very heart of the fog' and nothing will alter this position. For this reason, perhaps, choices of language and of the structure of the sentence position 'the Lord High Chancellor' and 'the heart of the fog' together.

26.4 ACTIVE AND PASSIVE VOICE

The order of words and phrases in the sentences of texts is important. We have seen this in the word order of the last sentence of the opening to *Bleak House*. It is also important for the analysis of texts to identify those verbs which are active and those which are **passive**. The choice of active or passive **voice** enables us to place subjects and verbs in different positions and to give different emphases to the way meanings are made.

For example, the choice of verbs in the active voice shows clearly that a subject takes an action which has an effect on an object:

They *sold* their apartment last year.
Over fifty candidates *take* the examination every summer.

These sentences can, however, also be expressed using a passive voice. For example:

> The apartment *was sold* by them last year.
> The examination *is taken* by over fifty candidates every summer.

In the passive sentences the object of the previously active sentence has changed position and is now at the beginning of the sentence. The verb has changed its form too; it is now formed from the verb 'be' together with the past participle form of the original verb (that is, *sold* → *sold*; *take* → *taken*). Also, the previous noun and pronoun subjects are now headed by a preposition (*by*), giving us *by them* or *by over fifty candidates*.

Note that the passive can be made with other forms of the verb too:

> The package *will be delivered* direct to your home.
> The door *has been locked*.
> The match *is being shown* live on three different channels.

The subject can also be left out of the sentences, as follows:

> The apartment was sold last year.
> The examination is taken every summer.

A structure in which we remove the phrases with subjects is often a way of depersonalising a text. For this reason legal documents or academic writing in some subjects such as science commonly use the passive voice in order to stress impersonal or institutional processes rather than those that highlight an individual.

However, when a subject is omitted the people, forces or agents behind an action can be downplayed or not even seen at all. Compare the following sets of sentences:

> French lorry drivers blockaded the port. (active voice)
> The port was blockaded by French lorry drivers. (standard passive voice)
> The port was blockaded. (passive voice with no agent)
> Sue told me that you are leaving the company. (agent is clear – Sue)
> I was told you were leaving the company. (agent unclear)

Of course, the choice of the passive voice is not simply an alternative structural or another stylistic option. It may seem neutral, but it can be chosen for a purpose which is not neutral; the agent can be removed from a text in order to conceal who is responsible for an action. The agent is omitted if you do not know who it is or if you don't want it to be known. Newspaper articles often use passive structures such as 'it is thought that' and 'it is said that' because they don't want to reveal individual sources – or because they are offering conjecture and speculation rather than fact.

ACTIVITY 26.3

ACTIVE AND PASSIVE VOICE

Rewrite the following short texts. Rewrite text 1 from the active to the passive voice and text 2 from the passive to the active voice. What differences do you see after your rewrites? What advantages are there in using both these voices? Are there valid reasons for using the passive, or are the reasons always to hide something? Additionally, consider the role of the **modal** verbs *may* and *must* in text 2. What is their function and purpose? How are they different?

Text 1
I sent a questionnaire to over 100 people in different age groups. I asked them how many texts they sent in a day and whether they used abbreviations. I found that over 50% of people over 50 said they used abbreviations.

Text 2
If payments are not maintained, your apartment may be repossessed. The bank must be informed if payments are made after the end of the month.

There is no commentary on this activity, as there is more than one way that the texts could be rewritten and each version will suggest a subtly different interpretation.

Activity 26.4

MANUALS AND REGULATIONS

Analyse the following texts, the first of which is an introduction to a chapter from a book on first aid and the second an extract from examination regulations for the submission of a thesis. Pay particular attention to the role of cohesion and the use of passives in the text. What particular features of the grammar in each case are appropriate to their respective purposes?

Text 26.5

ENVIRONMENTAL INJURIES

This chapter deals with the effects of injuries and illnesses that have been caused by environmental factors such as extreme heat or cold.

The body is protected by skin. It helps to maintain body temperature within a normal range. Skin can be damaged by fire, hot liquids and by caustic substances. Such injuries are often sustained in incidents such as explosions or chemical spillages.

The effects of temperature extremes can also impair skin and other bodily functions. Injuries may be localized --- as in frostbite or sunburn – or generalized, as in heat exhaustion or hyperthermia. Very young children or elderly people can be most affected by the problems that are caused by extremes of temperature.

First Aid Manual (Dorling Kindersley)

Text 26.6

UNIVERSITY EXAMINATION REGULATIONS

A candidate who has been granted leave to supplicate by a department shall be required to submit to the Examination Board a copy of his or her thesis, incorporating any amendments or corrections required by the examiners and approved by the Faculty, with a view to deposit in the appropriate university library.

[For candidates admitted on or after 1 October 2013: candidates are also required to submit an electronic copy of their thesis to the library, unless an exception to this requirement has been granted by the Examination Board.]

There is a commentary on this activity at the end of Part II.

CHAPTER 27

Grammar, speech and language change

Section B, on lexis and semantics, began with a look at some very frequent words. Drawing on language corpora, the focus there was on the words most frequently used in writing.

In this section, the focus so far has also been on writing, but there is also a lot to say about the grammar of spoken language. Research on spoken language is a relatively recent phenomenon, because it is only recently that high quality recording and the large-scale archiving of spoken language have been possible. Research has shown up the fact that speakers often use different structures from those that are used in writing, and it has also become clear that many of the labels we have traditionally used for aspects of grammar don't really fit with how things work in speech. A simple example of this mismatch is the concept of the sentence, which is often used when discussing writing. Speakers often don't speak in sentences, so the term **utterance** is often used for stretches of speech. We looked at a good example of a stretch of utterances in the activity involving two friends talking in Section B (p116).

There is no such thing as just 'writing' or 'speech', however, only individual occurrences of communication which may be particular types of speech or writing, or which may interweave aspects of both modes. Within the last twenty years the proliferation of new forms of communication has made the idea of any simple labeling problematic, so it isn't good enough to simply say something is 'like speech' or 'like writing' unless it is clear what specific aspects of speech or writing are being referred to. For example, people sometimes say that using internet chat is 'like speech'. If that means that it is composed in real time, then the comparison seems reasonable – although when online there might be none of the non-verbal communication that accompanies face-to-face interactions. If it means the language is spoken aloud, that could be true or not, depending on the tool being used. If it's being composed just at the keyboard, then it's clearly not an oral-aural communication. However, if it's keyboard-based but with access to a microphone and headphones, or all of these plus a webcam, then it is neither simply speech nor writing, but a **multimodal** interaction where each mode is being shaped by the presence of the others. In summary, it is important to avoid large-scale generalisations and to be as specific as possible about what aspects of spoken or written language are being referred to.

In this section, we will look at some aspects of speech grammar that have been revealed in corpus research, and we will also look at the idea of language change. Of all the types of communication we are involved in, formal writing tends to be the most conservative. But not all writing is conservative. Many of us engage in informal writing every day, in the form of emails, SMS, tweets and other digital texts – and some of these more interactive forms of writing can absorb features and patterns from informal speech and disseminate them very quickly. While informal styles used to be reserved for people we know well, this is no longer necessarily the case, as we can broadcast informal styles worldwide to complete strangers via social media. Changes can therefore spread rapidly, and between people who wouldn't normally be in contact with each other.

The corpus used below is based on British English, but there are corpora now available for many different varieties of English around the world. [See the section of the book on Corpus Resources and Projects, p222.]

27.1 FREQUENCY LIST

As in the case of the list of frequent written words we looked at in Section B, the list of words below is collated from the hundred-million-word British National Corpus and the two-billion-word Cambridge English Corpus. The sample is a corpus of five million of the most frequent words in spoken English.

In work on language corpora, the analysis of grammar begins with individual words and how they behave across stretches of text. The list highlights single words, but you will see how these individual words play important grammatical roles:

Text 27.1

1	THE	21	ON
2	I	22	OH
3	AND	23	WE
4	YOU	24	HAVE
5	IT	25	NO
6	TO	26	LAUGHS
7	A	27	WELL
8	YEAH	28	LIKE
9	THAT	29	WHAT
10	OF	30	DO
11	IN	31	RIGHT
12	WAS	32	JUST
13	IT'S	33	HE
14	KNOW	34	FOR
15	MM	35	ERM
16	IS	36	BE
17	ER	37	THIS
18	BUT	38	ALL
19	SO	39	THERE
20	THEY	40	GOT

SPEECH 'TOP 40'

Try to answer the following questions:

- Some words on this list don't look like words and you wouldn't be able to find them in a dictionary; for example *mm, er, erm* and *oh*. Why do you think these might feature so frequently in a spoken corpus? Are they words? Do they have a role in grammar?
- Why is *yeah* so frequent and why is *yes* not in the top forty?
- Thinking back to the coverage of the term *right* in Chapter 20 (p102), what might explain its presence in the top forty for speech?
- Compare this list with the frequency list for writing on p82 in Section B. How do the lists compare? What are the differences and similarities?

There is a commentary on this activity at the end of Part II.

Activity 27.1

27.2 SMALL WORDS, BIG CHANGES

It is noticeable that all the words on the list are small words. That is, they are monosyllables and they do not have more than four letters. 'So', 'How' and 'Like' stand out in particular, as they might not have been in the same list if it had been constructed fifty years ago. Looking at these three words in context is revealing of how the grammar of spoken English is constantly changing.

Each one of them used to be used in certain ways and each one of them has now changed. By looking at hundreds of examples of their use in a multi-million-word list, it is possible to see that younger speakers especially are using them in these new ways in the grammar of English. But interestingly, so too are older, educated speakers who might be inclined to deny that they do so.

All the examples below are taken from corpus databases in the Cambridge English Corpus and the British National Corpus.

27.2.1 SO

The word *so* is commonly used with a negative adjective in typical sentences like:

> I was **so** unhappy to have to leave my dog when I went on holiday.
> I was **so** unfit and just not up to climbing the stairs.

Speakers now seem more and more to use *so* with *not*. Here are two examples, one from the media:

> *I was so not ready to take an exam that day.*
> (Preferred formal usage: *I was so unready/unprepared to take an exam…*)
> *And I'm thinking 'I am so not fit for this expedition'.*
> (Preferred formal usage: 'I'm so unfit for this expedition.')

Younger speakers in particular have also taken to using *so* to emphasise almost anything – nouns, verbs and adverb phrases – although such usage is frowned on by many older speakers. Here are two examples:

> [Teenager commenting on a mobile phone]
> *That phone is just so last week.*
> [TV character warning her schoolmate that she'll get into trouble for wearing large earrings to school]
> *You're so going to get it from Mrs Webster.*

People are now using *so* in this way in their daily lives, although it is likely to take some time before it is used in written English or appears more widely as a standard usage in dictionaries and grammars.

Another reason why *so* is in the top forty is that it is common in spoken English as a **discourse marker**, functioning to enable a speaker to switch topics, to bring one part of a conversation or talk to an end and to start another, almost as if the speaker is beginning a new paragraph. (Of course, paragraphs do not occur in spoken language, which is why such words act as a kind of 'punctuation'.)

> *So, it's now five o'clock. Are we going out for dinner or staying in?*

It can also occur in lectures or talks:

> *So, we've covered the main history of nineteenth century physics; now we'll look at the twentieth century.*

Such usage is sometimes found in written English in informal communication, but in written formal English phrases such as *thus* or *therefore* or *in conclusion* are more likely in the case of sentences covering topics such as physics.

So is also common in sports reports and in live reports on television and radio, where it is used to highlight that what follows is immediate and in real time:

> *So I'm here in Oklahoma after the tornado…*
> *So now it's the penalty shootout and one team will be eliminated for sure.*

As well as featuring in spoken language, 'so' also has a life in multimodal contexts and can be creatively manipulated to express emotion, as in this SMS between friends:

> *I am sooooooo sorry.*

27.2.2 HOW

The next small word is *how*. The way it's used has undergone a grammatical change. It is traditionally used, among other ways, in **exclamations**. Its conventional use as an exclamation goes like this:

> *How smart **you look** today!*
> *How stupid **I am** to forget that!*
> *How absurd **it all seems**!*

How is followed by the structure used for statements, that is to say a subject then a verb (marked in bold). Here are some recent corpus examples, the first from an everyday conversation and the second from the media:

> *How confusing **is that** for Christ's sake!*
> *How rubbish **is that** as a toy!*

Note here how the subject and the verb have changed places, into the word order associated with questions, not exclamations. The speaker in the second example (How rubbish is that as a toy!) uses the question word order, but she also uses *how* with a noun (*rubbish*), whereas traditionally it was used with adjectives. Vocabulary changes quickly; even though it changes more slowly, grammar also changes.

27.2.3 LIKE

The final example is *like*. *Like* is becoming ever more widely used. One of the most frequent uses of *like* in spoken English is to focus attention, usually by giving or requesting an example.

> *A: I fancy going somewhere really hot for holiday this year.*
> *B: What, **like** the Equator or the Mediterranean or **like**…?*

A common structure in English conversation is *like what*.

> *A: What did you get up to today?*
> *B: Not a lot. There were a few computer things going on.*
> *A: **Like what**?*

Here, 'Like what?' stands for 'such as'.

Like can be placed in the final position in order to qualify a preceding statement. It also indicates that the words chosen may not be quite adequate to explain what is intended.

> *Then she got out of the car all of a sudden **like**, and this bike hit her right in the back.*
> *It was a shattering, frightening experience, **like**.*

In some cases *like* acts as a 'filler', enabling the speaker to pause to think what to say next, or to rephrase something. Pauses marked in seconds (…) can occur either side of the word.

They think that (2.0) **like** *(1.0) by now we should be married and if we were married then it's ok* **like** *(1.0) to get on with your life and do what you want.*

Like is also used in the structure *It + be + like*, a phrase which introduces an example or analogy of some kind.

It's **like** *if you go to another country you always get muddled up with the currency in the first few days.*
It's **like** *when I go to the doctors there's always loads of people in the surgery breathing germs all over you.*

One increasingly common use is illustrated by the following corpus examples:

I was **like** *'Oh, thank God for that!' you know.*
After forty minutes she says "I don't like this music." And I was **like** *"What do you want me to do?"*
And my mum's **like** *non-stop three or four times 'Come and tell your grandma about your holiday'.*

Like has recently found a new role for itself: it can now replace verbs like *say* and *tell* when we report our words or the words of others. *Like* is one of the fastest changing words in spoken English and could soon be a top twenty or even a top ten word in spoken English. At the moment, however, such uses are not at all common in formal written English.

In online contexts, *like* also has a new lease of life as an approval marker on social media sites (where its opposite is 'unlike' rather than 'dislike'). This is what is being referred to on the greetings card below:

Activity 27.2

SPEECH GRAMMAR

The following small words and phrases all appear in the top hundred in most corpora of the English language.

OK   you know   I mean   well   kind of   stuff

How are these used? What functions do they have? Can they easily be translated into other languages? Do they have the same functions in different languages?

There is no commentary on this activity.

As with the example of *like*, these forms of grammar, though common in spoken English, are not *exclusive* to spoken English. If writers want to achieve a sense of immediacy and the suggestion of an interpersonal interaction, using these forms in writing can be effective. So you may well see the words above in such contexts as email communication, advertising copy, and some notes, letters and memos – basically, anywhere that informality is the preferred style. Examples of such texts occur in some of the following units.

CHAPTER 28

Grammar and politics

This unit shifts its focus from informal spoken language towards more formal spoken language in the form of political discourse.

28.1 CRITICAL LANGUAGE AWARENESS

Politicians are skilful in their use of words and often have advisers and scriptwriters who spend a lot of time shaping their messages with them and for them. It is important for us to try to see how this is done linguistically and rhetorically, and to see through the shaping to the underlying political messages that are conveyed. In fact, we began to do this earlier when we looked at the way transitive and intransitive verbs could be used to indicate particular gender roles and thus reveal particular ways of seeing the world, particular (sometimes stereotypical) belief systems and particular political ideologies. This type of work is sometimes referred to as **critical discourse analysis (CDA)** or critical language awareness.

We will look below at a longer text and at the role played by a range of grammatical and lexical features, including small words of the kind found in the top forty list on page 82 and 140. However, there is one feature of language – **nominalisation** – that it is important to be attentive to at the interface between grammar and **ideology**.

28.2 NOMINALISATION

We can form nouns in English from different parts of speech. So, the adjective *bright* can form the noun *brightness*, and the verb *fly* can form the noun *flight*. Nominalisation refers to this process of noun formation. Nominalisation is common in formal academic and technical writing as it can contribute to a more impersonal style.

For example, the first sentence (1) below uses pronouns *we* to put human subjects in the picture. This is transformed in sentence (2) into a nominalised style in which the description of processes reduces and diminishes the personal involvement. Here the verb *advance* becomes the noun *advance*, the verb *discover* becomes the noun *discovery* and even the adverbial phrase *significantly more* is transformed into the noun *increases*.

1. In the 1960s we *advanced* our study of microbiology to the point where we *discovered significantly more* about the structure of food bacteria.
2. In the 1960s *advances* in microbiology led to *increases* in *discoveries* of the structure of food bacteria.

In the unit on *Active and passive voice* (p135) we saw how the passive voice can be used without reference to agents. Nominalised forms can also be used without reference to agency. In certain contexts this can mean that the cause of something or a responsible individual agent can be concealed or at least made less significant.

For example, look at the first sentence below, which is written in an active voice with agency clear to see.

1. The Fixel company *closed* two factories in Korea today and over 300 workers *lost* their jobs.

Now look at the new version below, which uses nominalisations (*closure/ losses*):

2. The *closure* of two factories in Korea today resulted in over 300 job *losses*.

Quite often these switches in focus are subtle and (often deliberately) difficult to detect when reading or hearing a text quickly. Sometimes, too, the words that are significant are very small and even more difficult to detect.

28.3 SMALL WORDS, BIG ROLE

In the frequency list at the beginning of this section the personal pronouns *I* and *you* are very frequent, demonstrating that they form a frequent part of communication of all kinds. These very ordinary-seeming words and the patterns produced by them can have powerful and not always noticed effects, especially when used by politicians in political speeches.

28.4 THE LANGUAGE OF POLITICS

The extract below is from a speech given by Barack Obama in Chicago in November 2008, when he was President Elect of the USA. The grammatical patterns are varied, but pronouns figure prominently. The pronouns used here are significant, but they form a part of a set of persuasive techniques that include other aspects of grammar. Read the notes that follow and look at how the different features that are described contribute to the overall impact of the speech.

POLITICAL SPEECH: OBAMA AND 'YES, WE CAN'

Text 28.1

This election had many firsts and many stories that will be told for generations. But one that's on my mind tonight is about a woman who cast her ballot in Atlanta. She's a lot like the millions of others who stood in line to make their voice heard in this election except for one thing – Ann Nixon Cooper is 106 years old.

She was born just a generation past slavery; a time when there were no cars on the road or planes in the sky; when someone like her couldn't vote for two reasons – because she was a woman and because of the colour of her skin.

And tonight, I think about all that she's seen throughout her century in America – the heartache and the hope; the struggle and the progress; the times we were told that we can't, and the people who pressed on with that American creed: Yes, we can.

At a time when women's voices were silenced and their hopes dismissed, she lived to see them stand up and speak out and reach for the ballot. Yes, we can.

When there was despair in the dust bowl and depression across the land, she saw a nation conquer fear itself with a New Deal, new jobs and a new sense of common purpose. Yes, we can.

When the bombs fell on our harbour and tyranny threatened the world, she was there to witness a generation rise to greatness and a democracy was saved. Yes, we can.

She was there for the buses in Montgomery, the hoses in Birmingham, a bridge in Selma, and a preacher from Atlanta who told a people that "we shall overcome". Yes, we can.

A man touched down on the Moon, a wall came down in Berlin, a world was connected by our own science and imagination. And this year, in this election, she touched her finger to a screen, and cast her vote, because after 106 years in America, through the best of times and the darkest of hours, she knows how America can change. Yes, we can.

The president's message is clear and positive and forward-looking, and the message is made more powerful by linking past and present: a past when people, especially African Americans, were disempowered and disenfranchised and a future in which democracy and a collective will can prevail.

Some of the main features of the grammar of the speech are:

1. Abstract nouns and nominalisation.
Words here such as *hope*, *struggle* and *progress* are nouns that have equivalent verbs. The use of nominalised forms here means that Obama does not need to clarify who or what was struggled against, what was hoped for, and how progress was measured. The nouns are abstract, but are also sometimes used as if they were animate. It gives a dynamism to the speech in which big ideas sit alongside personal individual voices.

> *the heartache* and *the hope*, *the struggle* and *the progress*
> *America* can change
> She saw *a nation* conquer fear itself

2. Voice.
The passive voice is sometimes used without agents being mentioned.

> *we were told* that we can't.
> *women's voices were silenced* and *their hopes dismissed.*
> *a democracy was saved.*

'We were told' by whom? Who silenced women's voices? When referring to the unnamed powerful forces in society the passive voice is used; but when referring to liberation from these forces the active voice is used:

> she *touched her finger* to the screen and *cast her vote*.

3. Nouns plus postmodifying structure.
(the postmodifying structure (underlined) adds extra information to the noun.)

> despair *in the dustbowl*
> depression *across the land*
> a new sense *of common purpose*

These patterns provide a more formal and detached overview, but the speech is counterbalanced and made more informal and interactive by a direct address to the audience with a use of **singular** and plural personal pronouns.

4. Personal pronouns.

> *I* think about all that *she's* seen
> Yes, *we* can
> …that's on *my* mind tonight

The rhetoric of this speech suggests a common purpose. The refrain of the plural personal pronoun *yes, we can* includes everyone in the vision of change to a better future.

Obama's main strategy of making things personal is perhaps not to draw attention to or otherwise make salient the content of his message, but rather to focus on the creation of an interpersonal rapport and relationship with his audience, assuming that they know what he is referring to when nominalisation is used. In this context the president is a politician for whom communicating with an audience, identifying with them and involving them in the presentation is paramount. It's an interactive and informal style, although in keeping with a public address to thousands of people it contains more formal structures too. The way he presents what he says is, it seems, almost as important as what he says. The use of pronouns in particular is central to this strategy.

CHAPTER 29

Conversational grammar

We noted in the introduction to this unit that we would be looking at patterns of grammar that are more common in spoken than in written texts. A start was made earlier by looking at how some of the most important and frequently spoken words in the language can be subject to change over time, but are also central to everyday interactions. There are also features of grammar that give a text a more informal or 'spoken' character. One of the most common features is **ellipsis**, an aspect where grammar can connect strongly with pragmatics.

Ellipsis is a grammatical structure in which subjects and verbs are omitted because speakers can assume that their listeners (or their readers) know what is meant (the words and phrases in brackets below are the ellipted elements):

Didn't know that film was on tonight.	*(I)*
Sounds good to me.	*(It, That)*
Lots of things to tell you about the trip to Barcelona.	*(There are)*
A: Are you going to Leeds this weekend?	
B: Yes, I must.	*(go to Leeds this weekend)*

Ellipsis is common in spoken English, but it is one of the clearest indications of an interactive, interpersonal, dialogic style when used in writing.

INFORMAL GRAMMAR

The following text is from a review in a national newspaper of the previous night's television programmes. It is written in an informal, chatty style. Look for examples of ellipsis. What other features of the language make it informal?

There is a commentary on this activity at the end of Part II.

Activity 29.1

Text 29.1

TV REVIEW

Good. Thank God that's over. The Olympics. All that warmth, good will and tears. Even at the bloody taekwando. It was getting tiring. Now we can get back to more familiar territory. Like murder. Which you don't have to wait long for in Ruth Rendell's *Thirteen Steps Down* (ITV).

I wonder how Rendell came up with the profession for Mix, her protagonist. Hmmm, shall I make him an accountant, or a carpenter... no. Got it. He will be a gym-equipment repair man, specialising in cross-trainers. Anyway, it's an excellent job for him – ideal for a stalker. And the actor, Luke Treadaway, is brilliant in the part, a thoroughly convincing weirdo psychotic obsessive.

The murder – the first, I fear there may be more to come in part 2 – is horrid (yeah, as opposed to those really nice ones). ... Rarely can a dead person have looked so utterly dead. Then under the floorboards she goes. Big mistake, Mix: schoolboy error. Never put the body under the floorboards. Just you wait. It'll come back to haunt you. And what about the face in the attic that keeps appearing in the window?

There are subplots and loads of loose ends to tie up. Whatever happens I don't think it's all suddenly going to be fine – oh, it's just another lodger up there in the attic. No, there's a gnawing sense of foreboding and dread, bad shit ahead.

***

Wow! *Escape from Colditz* (Channel 4). What an AMAZING story. In the Second World War, it was considered a moral duty for captured British officers to try to escape, and they came up with the most ingenious and insane schemes to try to achieve it. This has to be the craziest of all.

A group of army officers built a glider out of floorboards, bedsheets and porridge. A system of pulleys and a falling bathtub was to catapault them from the prison roof to freedom.

They never got to try it out, though. The war spoiled everything by ending.

But now a team has rebuilt it. And it works. Kinda. I wouldn't have enjoyed that landing – quite bumpy. But then I would almost certainly have just stayed in my cell, sitting out the war, amorally.

Sam Wollaston, The Guardian

CHAPTER 30

Texting grammar

SMS CONVERSATION

Here is an extract from an exchange of text messages:

A: gotta go
B: ttyl
A: talk to you soon
B: which means tomorrow right?
A: I'd forgot that
B: cos we're seeing David.
A: must go. alright. see you later alligator.

Text 30.1

This was called a 'conversation' above, but how far does it fit that description? There are some distinctive grammatical features to think about in answering that question.

Right is, as we have seen, commonly used in spoken English as a kind of tag question, as well as acting as a pre-closing item in phone calls ('alright' above seems to have a pre-closing function). Ellipsis is also common in speech. Examples of ellipsis here include *gotta go/talk to you soon/must go*. Even the abbreviation *ttyl* (talk to you later) is based on a grammatical ellipsis. All these examples involve subject deletion, where the subject of the sentence has been ellipted (often the first person pronoun, 'I'). The non-standard form *forgot* (standard form *forgotten*) is an interesting use of idiolect by writer A. Thurlow (2003) suggests that we sometimes deliberately represent our own idiolect in SMS communication, for example changing our writing to imitate features of accent, such as 'wivout' instead of 'without'.

Also interesting are a relative clause and a **subordinate clause** that do not seem to 'belong' to a main clause:

which means tomorrow right?
cos we're seeing David.

These structures are frequent in conversational exchanges and maintain an interactive conversational feel as the content of the main clauses (while absent) is understood by the speakers and it is therefore almost redundant for them to be 'spoken'. Texter A also signs off with a common and playful idiom *see you later alligator*.

> **Activity 30.1**
>
> **SMS VARIATIONS**
>
> Here are two SMS texts taken from a million-word corpus of e-communication in the Cambridge English Corpus. What patterns of grammar do you notice in the two texts? How similar are they and why? How dissimilar are they and why?
>
> There is a commentary on this activity at the end of Part II.

Text 30.2

TWO SMS EXAMPLES

Message sent between two friends: male aged 24 (sender) and female aged 22

> Hi, did two shifts tonite and am off to bed. But still fancy the film tomoz. Ur still ok for this right? How about meet up at I dunno 6 or something outside the Chinese take away. Thatll mean we can still have a bite to eat and stuff? Whatyoufink?

Message sent from mother (aged 52) to son (aged 19).

> What are the plans for this weekend? Are you, as you suggested, meeting us at Auntie June's for the birthday tea? Would you like to be picked up by us and, if so, at what time? Or are you, after all, driving to Matt's first and then meeting us there? Let us know whatever is most convenient? X

CHAPTER 31

Creative grammar

As we have seen, grammar is a key element in how meanings are made in and through formal and informal spoken and written language, including in texts which are written but have some conversational features. The fact that there are rules of grammar also means that effects can be created when the rules are broken. When rules are broken, mistakes and misunderstandings can occur. But when we break or bend rules it can also be an opportunity for playing creatively with language. For example, here are a couple of examples of how an estate agent can draw attention to their business by bending grammatical rules in a striking way. Note here how adjectives (*happy, smart*) are used as if they were nouns:

> *Find your happy at Rightmove* (Rightmove Estates Agents, UK)
> *Selling your home? Smart knows where to be seen* (Zoopla Estate Agents UK)

> **GRAMMATICAL CREATIVITY IN POETRY**
>
> Read the poem overleaf, which was written by the American poet Lorine Niedecker (1903–1970). The word *cover* here is a noun and refers to the plastic foil lid which covers a tin or packet of popcorn. There is a word missing from the final line – try to guess what this is. The word shows creative rule breaking.

Activity 31.1

Text 31.1

POPCORN-CAN COVER

> Popcorn-can cover
> screwed to the wall
> over a hole
> so the cold
> can't ....in
>
>   Lorine Niedecker

The complete text of the poem is printed on p182. There is also a brief commentary on some suggested effects produced by the rule breaking.

Grammatical creativity is by no means restricted to poets or writers of fiction. Here are the names of two hotels using grammar in creative and playful ways:

The Tuck Me Inn (USA)
The Nobody Inn (Exeter, UK)

The names involve a creative play on the preposition *in* in the phrasal verb (*tuck me in*) and on the adverb *in* the phrase *Nobody is in*. They also rely on the fact that *in* and *inn* are homophones – that is, they are pronounced in the same way, even if they are written differently and have different grammatical functions.

Activity 31.2

TITLES AND NAMES

What is creative about the following? What part do grammatical, lexical and phonological patterns play in the creative effects?

Sofa So Good	(furniture store)
Making Waves	(hairdressing salon)
There's No Present like the Time	(jewellery store)
Prime Minister flies back to front	(newspaper headline)
Toasting Brad Pitt in Cannes	(film report)
Feta Compli	(Greek salad in a box)
Lighten up your garden. Plant bulbs.	(A garden centre shop)
Travel yourself interesting	(online travel company)

There is a commentary on this activity at the end of Part II.

GRAMMATICAL CREATIVITY IN CONTEXT

Grammatical effects do not exist in isolation. Grammatical choices work alongside the other language levels you have been studying in Part II to create meaning – and, of course, interpretation also involves you in bringing your own experiences to bear in making sense of any text.

Look at the text below, which is part of a booklet called *For Goodness Sake*, from a well-known sandwich shop with outlets in several different countries including Hong Kong, France, the USA and the UK. The booklet covers different aspects of fresh food, including its sourcing and preparation.

How do you view the phrase *eating fresh* in this advertisement? Is it ungrammatical? How might different speakers of English view this phrase?

What features of language use are also striking in this advertisement? What part is played by aspects of textual design and the other levels of language you have studied so far? To what extent are these features creative?

There is no commentary on this activity.

FOR *GOODNESS* SAKE

We asked some of our food team...

'What's goodness to you?'

They chatted about the
many ingredients in our shop kitchens and
the benefits of eating fresh.

They also shared their thoughts and ideas
on being bright, healthy and well.
We think they're rather fun
so have written some of them down
in the back of this little book... A sort of
glossary of good to do things.

(for *Goodness* sake)

158 CREATIVE GRAMMAR

Activity 31.4

CREATIVE GRAMMAR OR 'WRONG' GRAMMAR?

The following texts show that rule-breaking can occur with the use of English in many different contexts and circumstances. Which texts here contain real mistakes and which are intentional acts of rule-breaking for creative or other purposes?

There is a commentary on this activity at the end of Part II.

Text 31.3 **EXETER CRUISES**

Text 31.4 **BURGER ME**

ORANGE MY DAY

November 2014
Orange the World in 16 days
From 25 November, the International Day for the Elimination of Violence against Women, to 10 December, Human Rights Day, the 16 Days of Activism against Gender-Based Violence Campaign is a time to galvanize action to end violence against women and girls around the world.

A JOB ADVERTISEMENT FOR A PROOFREADER

There are ten grammatical mistakes in this ad for a job.

 Top edit Associates. Hong Kong and Singapore.

Is this the job for you?

If your able to spot ten mistakes here, then there likely be good opportunity for you as a copy editor with our company. We need graduates which have eye for details and interested for informations relevant to computing technology. If you're used to read documents careful and have good word processing skills, let us know by sending your cv and portfolio by post or email too →

Top edit Associates. Hong Kong, Singapore and Cape Town
Head office: Braodway Towers
Overway,
Singapore 0561
email: Jefferson@editass.com

31.1 REVIEW YOUR SKILLS

Now that you have considered grammar in more detail, go back to the texts that have appeared throughout this book so far, and pay particular attention to their grammatical features. Choose a specific text and see how far you can apply the grammatical tools you have just learned about. Write up your analysis in a formal way.

31.2 IDEAS FOR ASSIGNMENTS

31.2.1 Romantic fiction

Find examples of romantic fiction either in international novels and magazines (usually magazines for women) in English or in novels, short stories or magazines in your own first language. Are the patterns of transitivity that are described here the same or are they different? Try changing the pronouns and names in the text to start with, in order to identify some patterns.

31.2.2 SMS texts

Collect examples of your own SMS texts that have been sent to you, either in English or in your own first language, especially those from people of different ages. Are the same features present? If so, why? If not, why not?

31.2.3 Multilingual SMS

The following exchange of texts involves two female university students. They are from Hong Kong. They use English to communicate but also interweave text chat and transliterated Cantonese (the language most commonly used in Hong Kong – the translations are given in brackets below).

Viki: it's snowing quite strong outside.....be careful
Sue: I will, thx
Viki: wei wei...lei dim ar?
Sue: ok, la, juz got bk from Amsterdam loh, how r u?
Viki: ok la.. I have 9 tmrw
Sue: HAHA, I have 2–4 ....soooooooooooo happy
Viki: che...anyway...have your rash gone?
Sue: yes, but I have scar oh...ho ugly ar!
Viki: icic...ng gan yiu la...still a pretty girl, haha!!

[Cantonese translations: *wei wei...lei dim ar* – hi, how are you?; *ng gan yiu la* – it doesn't matter; *ar, loh* and *la* are discourse markers in Cantonese]

Why have the girls created this hybrid form of language, mixing styles and languages in this way? Would standard English grammar and vocabulary be appropriate here? What is the function and purpose for the girls of communicating in this way? How does the language (and grammar) reflect the context of communication? Are there mistakes in the texts or is the use of language fundamentally inventive and creative? What does it tell us about English as a language in the world today? Can you find other examples in your own language where English is used alongside other languages? Are the functions and purposes the same as in this exchange?

31.2.4 Small words

So and *like* and *just*

a) Collect more examples <u>in written English</u> of *so* as a discourse marker and *like* when used to give examples. Where do you find them? In tabloid newspapers? In legal documents? In weather forecasts? In advertisements? What do your examples tell you about formality and informality in writing?

b) Given the frequency of our use of small words, they are well worth investigating in everyday spoken English. To do this, you need to think about these issues: how can they be recorded and analysed? How important is it to obtain examples in a wide range of settings? How different would the examples be if one list was recorded from a nightclub and the other from the BBC World Service? How have internet conventions changed our use of some words? For example, we now use *like* and *unlike* in new ways on some social media sites, to signal approval or disapproval. Are there other terms that would appear on frequency lists derived from corpora that are only included on social media sites?

c) There are many interesting words on the list, but the word *just* could be investigated as a first step. There are many different meanings to the word, but in spoken discourse it is commonly used to soften utterances such as requests. *Could you just open the window?* is much softer as a request than *Could you open the window?* and indicates that the speaker does not want to make the request seem like an imposition on the listener.

Explore the extent to which the word is used in this way in written texts. Is it as common? If so, why? If not, why not? What might this tell us about differences between speech and writing?

31.2.5 Grammar and politics

Record some speeches or collect some recordings that have already been made. Analyse the material in stages, focusing on pronouns but also on any other structures that you see as significant. You might also want to compare the use of pronouns in political speeches and in advertisements. For example, advertisements use pronouns to involve us, to encourage us and to mislead us:

> *It could be you!* (UK National Lottery)
> *I can't believe it's not butter* (ad for a margarine spread)
> *Be good to yourself* (ad for slimming foods)

There are some excellent resources online for studying political speeches, for example the archive www.americanrhetoric.com

162 COMMENTARIES FOR PART II

31.2.6 Grammar and news discourse

Many newspapers have their own online sites, and as a result you can view the way that the same story is treated in different sources. Choose two sources and analyse the way the same story is presented, paying particular attention to the way grammatical features contribute to meanings.

31.2.7 Grammar and creativity

Advertisements use grammatical features for a number of reasons, including getting our attention and involving us, as suggested above. They can sometimes do this by creative rule-breaking, as you have seen in this section. Collect a range of texts that demonstrate creativity in grammar – as well as advertising you could think about jokes and riddles that rely on grammatical ambiguity, literary texts, greetings cards, and online sources such as Twitter.

31.3 COMMENTARIES FOR PART II

SECTION A

Activity 11.1

SIGNS AND MEANING

Text: CCTV

The text works by blending the image of a guard dog with that of a camera, suggesting that the camera acts as a guard dog in its prevention of crime.

The words are intertextual because they echo a notice that is commonly displayed in the UK by homeowners where they want to warn the public that they have a dog – 'Beware of the Dog'. 'Beware of the CCTV' uses this same idea, but is sited here on commercial premises that are under construction.

The name of the company – Triton – involves a classical reference to Greek mythology, in the form of a god. This suggests both seriousness and strength, as does the chain symbol. The company also has endorsements by several organisations, reinforcing the idea that they mean business.

The text is culturally specific in a number of ways. The type of dog pictured would be recognisable to UK viewers of the notice as often in a guard dog role. The whole idea of using dogs to guard premises could be culturally specific, as well as the idea of CCTV itself. Some estimates of CCTV usage suggest that the UK has 20% of the world's CCTV cameras.

ACTIVITY: LITERARY TECHNIQUES

Text: Ladder of Years

David Crystal's *The Cambridge Encyclopedia of the English Language* (1995) lists four main functions for punctuation: grammar, where features such as full stops and commas mark out grammatical units; prosody, where such symbols as speech marks, question marks and exclamation marks indicate that someone is speaking; rhetoric, where some forms of punctuation – most notably colons and semicolons – map out aspects of argument or explanation (as in this paragraph); and semantic nuance, where features of emphasis such as quotation marks suggest a particular attitude to a word or phrase being 'marked out'.

Anne Tyler uses punctuation to mark out grammatical units in the same way as writers of many other types of text.

However, what is most noticeable is Tyler's extensive use of the prosodic and the semantic nuance functions. This is hardly surprising, given that these are concerned with constructing a sense of voice, and with establishing attitudes.

- *Examples of the prosodic function*: within the language of the characters themselves – speech marks, lines of dots suggesting a voice trailing off, question marks, exclamation marks, italics to suggest emphasis; within the language used by the narrator – brackets and dashes in lines 22 and 58 to suggest a change in pace as a result of adding extra information.
- *Examples of the semantic nuance function*: quotation marks in the narrator's report of Delia's thoughts in lines 6 and 7; the same in the narrator's commentary in lines 37 and 54.

Despite these extensive markers, there is still much about the way the characters speak that has to be described by the narrator. Here are some examples: 'she called over her shoulder'; 'he lowered his voice'; 'she murmured through ventriloquist lips'; 'he whispered'; 'he startled her with a sudden burst of laughter'; 'he told her too loudly'. These examples illustrate that, in the end, written language cannot do justice to the subtleties of speech. All it can do is to give us some signposts as readers, via devices such as punctuation marks, to help us create the idea of speech in our heads.

Activity 11.3

BREAKING THE RULES

Text: art'otel

The letter follows the conventional rules of letter writing in having some contact details in the top right corner, indicating where the letter is from. It opens the letter by addressing the recipient and it closes with a conventional form of wording – 'with warm regards' – followed by the manager's signature on behalf of the hotel. The letter is separated into paragraphs, each of which deals with a particular aspect of information that the hotel wishes the guest to be aware of. Bold type emphasises these key points.

In some other respects, the letter is unusual and unconventional. Where letters would normally be uppercase, for example at the beginnings of sentences and on proper nouns, lower case is used. This suggests a level of informality – this hotel wants to present itself as a bit different from an ordinary hotel, as a place that has a personal touch; its own name is in lower case too. We might use lower case letters in messages to people we know, where we don't feel that we have to use formal standard English. Indeed, the fact that the arriving guest is presented with a personalised letter rather than just pointing them to a hotel information book tells us that the hotel sees its identity as different from others.

The letter also has interesting graphics, in the top right-hand corner and at the bottom of the page. The creativity in the verbal language accompanies other forms of creativity in the letter's artwork, which in turn reflects the art that the hotel is displaying inside its building. The letter tells us something about the featured artist and his connection with the history of the city of Berlin. The theme and presence of art fits with the name and identity of the art'otel group, and the text's conscious adoption of creative rule-breaking language is underlined in wishing the guest an 'artrageous' stay.

Activity 12.1

USING THE PHONEMIC ALPHABET

'ough' words

rough	/rʌf/
dough	/dəʊ/
thoughtful	/θɔːtfʊl/
ploughman	/plaʊmən/
through	/θruː/
Scarborough	/skɑːbərə/
coughed	/kɒft/
hiccoughed	/hɪkʌpt/

EXPLORING THE REPRESENTATION OF SOUNDS

Poetry extracts (Item 2).

Examples a) and b) are plosives, b) uses more voiced sounds.

Example a) suggests the explosive force of bullets (compare this with the sounds in 'rat-a-tat').

b) tries to evoke the duller thud of drops on a hard surface.

Examples c) and d) use voiceless fricatives, suggesting the light friction of wind and breath.

Example e) suggests the repeated and overlapping calls of doves and continuous hum of bees.

Example f) uses the repetition of voiceless plosives /t/ and /k/ to suggest a lighter sound alongside the heavier voiced plosive /b/ in 'bells', onomatopoeia in words such as 'tinkle' and 'jingle', and some complex internal rhythm and rhyme patterns to create a kind of musical soundscape.

Summary of broad categorisations:

- Voiced/voiceless: louder, heavier, a fuller sound/softer, lighter, a thinner sound
- Plosives: percussive sounds – banging, striking, tapping
- Fricatives and affricates: friction – hissing, scratching
- Nasals and approximants: continuous sound or motion – flowing, rippling, humming

Some of the effects are cumulative: particular sounds are repeated within a short space (termed 'alliteration' when the sounds are at the beginnings of words). Individual words occurring on their own may or may not have in-built sound effects: for example, while 'murmur' may suggest the hum of mumbled talk – as 'mumble' itself may – the word 'immemorial' has no particular sound profile.

Activity 12.2

VOWEL PATTERNS

Repetitions
/e/ helter skelter   jet set   harum scarum   airy fairy
/ɪ/ willy nilly   big wig   nitty gritty
/æ/ hanky panky   fat cat   namby pamby
/ɑː/ arty farty
/ɒ/ hotch potch   collywobbles
/ʌ/ lovey dovey   hugger mugger
/iː/ eebie jeebies
/ɔɪ/ hoity toity   hoi polloi
/əʊ/ roly poly

Contrasts
/ɪ/ and /ɒ/ flip flop   hip hop   sing song   ping pong   ding dong   tick tock   wishy washy
/ɪ/ and /æ/ shilly shally   pitter patter   mishmash   spick and span   knick knack   jim jams   tit for tat
/iː/ and /ɔː/ see saw
/ɒ/ and /ɜː/ topsy turvey

These terms belong to informal contexts of language use. Some are so unfamiliar on the page that their spelling is uncertain: for example, is it 'colliewobbles' or 'collywobbles'? 'hoy polloy' or 'hoi polloi'? This is the language of personal anecdote rather than public lecture, although many a public lecture would benefit from the liveliness and energy contributed by these vigorous little items. Many express motion, emotion, muddle and incoherence – 'helter skelter', 'eebie jeebies', 'mishmash', 'hotch potch'; others strike arch attitudes about certain types of people – 'fat cat', 'hoi polloi'; some are straightforwardly onomatopoeic – 'tick tock'.

EXPLORING HOMOPHONES

Activity 12.4

a kneads, needs
b arms, alms
c bruise, brews
d course, coarse
e sole, soul
f caught, court
g lesson, lessen
h quarts, quartz
i cause, cores, caws
j rose, rows, roes
k sent, scent

a heir male = airmail
b flay quay = flaky
c conned oar = condor
d pyre nears = pioneers
e infer know = inferno
f mill inner = milliner
g bling curd = blinkered
h clap tout = clapped out (slang for 'worn out')
i anna kissed = anarchist
j bone apart = Bonaparte (Napoleon).

Commentary on Text 13.2: Hedy's speech

If you look for the words that the adult pronounces beginning with a /s/, like 'sun' and 'circle', you can see that Hedy pronounces these with a [d]. However, it seems that she can pronounce [s] at the end of a word. In these cases, though, [s] is not the target pronunciation. She pronounces 'fish' with the [s] at the end rather than /ʃ/. If we rely on the data provided here as a representative sample of Hedy's speech, she only pronounces /s/ one way – as [d]. Why does Hedy choose [d] as her pronunciation of /s/? If we compare the features of the two sounds we can see that although [d] is a plosive and the target pronunciation [s] is a fricative, they are both made at the same place of articulation, the alveolar ridge. Perhaps then, the child is nearly getting the target pronunciation right. The choice of [d] seems not to be random.

If we compare how Hedy pronounces consonant clusters in comparison to the adult speech, we find that she pronounces only one of the two sounds. In most cases it is the first consonant that is retained, and the second one is elided (missed out). So, in 'drums', the /r/ is not pronounced and it becomes [dʌms]. 'Green' is the same. However, in 'sky', neither of the target consonants is pronounced as in the adult speech. Instead, Hedy produces [gaɪ].

We could analyse this as the /s/ being elided, and the target /k/ being pronounced as the voiced equivalent [g]. The same thing seems to be occurring in 'stripy'. Children are known to often produce voiced consonants in place of voiceless ones before a vowel, but it is possible that something more complex is happening in this case. Consider the pronunciation of the word 'sky': if you pronounce it normally as [skaɪ] and then try to pronounce it as Hedy does, but with the /s/ – [sgaɪ], you should notice that the two pronunciations sound the same. This is because in English, the difference between voiced and voiceless plosives is neutralised when they follow /s/. So the /p/ in 'spot' sounds a bit like a [b] and so on. Is it possible that Hedy hears this slight pronunciation quirk and follows it even though she cannot yet produce /s/ in that environment?

Commentary on Text 13.3: Omar's writing
Omar (aged 5) enhances his story with a picture where a ghostly figure makes 'ooooo' sounds, in an attempt to provide something of an atmospheric soundtrack. This also occurs within the text itself: the reader knows that the words 'The Spirit, The Spirit' need to be pronounced in a 'spooky' way, as a result of their having wobbly lines round them. It's difficult to say exactly where this convention is from, but likely contenders could be comics and those science-fiction films where the screen 'dissolves' as the narrator goes back in time to remember 'when it all began'. Note the very logical sound-based spelling, 'ones a pone tieem' for 'once upon a time'.

SECTION B

MORPHEMES

Text: Matalan
The use of words beginning with *re* makes a pattern that draws the attention of the reader. The pattern is subtle though. In the case of 'reuse' and 'recycle' *re* is a bound morpheme (a prefix) that emphasises that something is being done again. By the time we read 'reduce' and 'rewards' (where *re* is not a prefix and where the words *reduce* and *reward* are self-standing free morphemes), a connection between all the words is created. The connection suggests that the company Matalan repeatedly offers rewards and reduces prices again and again. There is also the suggestion that it is able to give customers financial rewards and to reduce prices because it protects the environment as a result of recycling, making the reduction in prices and its rewards to customers an ethical act.

Activity 17.1

MORPHEMES *(continued)*

Text: Andrex: eco roll

The Andrex ad illustrates structural semantic patterning (*soft/rough*) and the way in which new words can be creatively developed by extension from old words (*recycle* → *upcycle* – the word also echoes the word 'upgrade' to something superior). Visually there are also circular patterns everywhere, a clever use of the shape *e/*eco where the dog is sleeping in an 'e' (eco – ecological) shape to suggest the environment (it's green material in the original text and 'green' is the word most associated with the environment and, politically, with environmental matters). The text also sets up a relaxed dialogic exchange with the reader with some marked informal chatty features in the way words and phrases are used (*at last, actually*). The use of the word *loo* (which is an informal word for toilet) and the contraction *it's* reinforces the informality. This is also an advertisement for a company that has used the Labrador dog so many times intertextually in its advertisements that the breed is sometimes referred to as the Andrex dog.

Activity 17.1

WORD FORMATION

Text: Comfort on sale

The sale is a furniture sale and involves a feeling of comfort associated with soft armchairs that you float down onto like a feather, or which have seats that are as soft as feathers. The text assumes a cultural connection between ideas of comfort and feathers (feather mattresses, feather duvets). *Comfort* is an abstract word and does not fit as commonly with the word *sale* as do more material, less abstract things such as armchairs or sofas. However, the new word sit*isfaction* (which does not exist in a dictionary), which only involves the change of one letter from the word 'satisfaction', cleverly and creatively joins together sitting and satisfaction to suggest a new form of comfort. The creative strategy is foregrounded in the text via the graphological device of separating the word 'sit' by using upright letters and bold type to divide it from the italicised, non-bold remainder of the word. This shows readers that the creation is deliberate and not a spelling error. The expression 'satisfaction guaranteed' is something of a cliché so this creative strategy refreshes what would otherwise be a rather tired and predictable piece of text. The offer of 0% interest is constructed on the poster at an angle to catch your attention, almost as if it were a kind of afterthought.

Activity 17.3

Activity 18.3

COMPLEXITY

Text: Techno and Metal

The text draws on two semantic fields – music, and the mechanics of car engineering. Both these fields are invoked by the terms 'techno' and 'metal'. 'Techno' in musical terms can refer to the high tech music associated with the German band Kraftwerk; it can also refer to German car companies' use of technology, exemplified by Audi's advertising slogan 'Vorsprung durch Technik' (advancement through technology). In contrast, the Swedish profile of music and cars is associated with 'heavy metal' music and strong car bodies. The overall idea is that German techno is outdated in both music and cars – it's time for some Swedish strength and power instead. The shooting of the picture of the car from behind reinforces the idea of raw speed with the car disappearing fast from view round a tight bend. The references to the different traditions in music and engineering suggest that the target audience is mature (and perhaps male). 'Bored of' is now frequently heard instead of the previous 'bored with', at least in speech, giving the text a contemporary, colloquial feel.

Activity 20.1

MULTIPLE MEANINGS

Text: Rodney's Oyster House

The word 'bed' here can refer both to an oyster bed and to the bed in which the consumer of the oysters (and the wearer of the napkin) habitually sleeps. 'Just out of bed' therefore refers both to the freshness of the oysters and, cheekily, to the idea that the customer might be lazy and might only recently have got out of bed. The fact that oysters are often associated with extreme luxury and pampering, as well as with romance, strengthens the ambiguity of the phrase further.

Activity 21.1

PAIRS AND CONNOTATIONS

childless   childfree

'Childless' suggests that a couple are biologically unable to have children; 'childfree' suggests that it is a positive decision not to have children as part of a family or in a specific place such as a restaurant or holiday resort.

to father a child   to mother a child

PAIRS AND CONNOTATIONS (continued)

'Fathering' a child has connotations of a physical biological act; 'mothering' a child suggests a long-term commitment closely associated with emotional involvement.

regime   government

'Regime' suggests that a country is controlled by an unelected group; 'government' is more strongly associated with democratic election.

terrorist   freedom fighter

'Terrorist' suggests a view of an individual fighter who is hostile to a group (usually a national group) and has pejorative associations; 'freedom fighter' may be used to describe the same individual but from a positive position. Much depends on the viewpoint or ideology of the individual selecting the word. Similar opposing meanings are created when it is said that a country has been *liberated*, when others would declare that it has been *invaded*.

unemployment benefit   jobseeker's allowance

'Unemployment benefit' suggests that unemployment is out of the control of the individual and that benefits are therefore a social entitlement; 'jobseeker's allowance' restricts the money paid only to those willing to actively seek work and suggests more directly that unemployment is the responsibility of the individual.

firing people; rightsizing; making economies

'Firing people' involves a transitive verb with an actor or agent responsible for individuals who lose their jobs; 'rightsizing' and 'making economies' omit any reference to people. 'Rightsizing' is commonly used intransitively, thus removing responsibility for job losses; 'making economies' works again to remove reference to the actual act of firing people and also underlines that employing people is solely an economic process where only money matters.

increased job insecurity   increased flexibility

These phrases echo the way words are used in the previous example. Changing contracts leads to 'increased job insecurity' for the employee, but increased flexibility allows greater power to be maintained for the employer and is only rarely in the interests of the employee.

slim; slender; thin; skinny; scrawny; emaciated

All these words have different connotations. The words on the left are positive (especially 'slim' and 'slender') and are often used as compliments, but as we move along the line the words become increasingly negative and pejorative, underlining the many different ways in which the human physical shape can be viewed, at least in most Western or Western-oriented societies.

Activity 21.1

Activity 21.4

CONNOTATION AND COLLOCATION

Text: Muscat

The *Muscat* text is interesting both for what is says and for what it doesn't say. Much depends on how readers are positioned or allow themselves to be positioned when reading the text.

The text works very hard to reassure visitors that images of the Arab and Muslim world that may be created outside the region are not always accurate. It precisely and deliberately combines different lexical sets and lexical contrasts (sophisticated, tolerant, embracing, warm, welcoming, no excessive consumerism and shimmering turquoise seas). We should also note here the way in which biblical gold and frankincense (and dates!!) are combined as part of the country's history and tradition.

It is also interesting to note the ways in which the text presents a world that is actually not very local, but is rather more a globalised world of tourism where everything is presented through Western (?) eyes and to meet expectations of safety, order, harmony and uniformity – and with no rough edges. Local differences and local cultural distinctions are re-registered and re-accented to mediate a lifestyle modelled for a globalised consumer. It is the kind of text that works hard to reveal as well as conceal. What does the text not say about Muscat as a destination for holidaying travellers?

Activity 22.2

METAPHOR AT WORK

Text: Encounters Dating

The *Dating* ad is deliberately playful and over-sentimental, but the text knows that it is working in this way and the ad works well in this tongue-in-cheek manner. The main metaphors of *bucket* and *spade* suggest two things (and two words) that naturally go together and are associated with holidays, even childhood holidays on a beach by the sea, where times are innocent and adult daters can remember them as being uncomplicated. They may be led to expect that Encounters dating is similarly uncomplicated.

The text is very densely patterned with lots of repetition, lexical echoing and cohesive repetition and variation; in other words, there is a textual patterning that reinforces the multiple choices open to dating couples that are offered by the agency.

This is a good text with which to begin some research and to explore how online dating companies advertise and present themselves verbally in different cultures. This is likely to be very variable internationally. How do such agencies work in your country and/or culture?

COHESION

Text: Jumbled sentences

The correct sequence of sentences is:

1. Add the butter and onions to the saucepan. Allow them to cook gently on a medium heat for about 15 minutes, or until they are soft and lightly browned.
2. The playwright Harold Pinter was born in 1930. The author of over 25 plays and several books of poetry, he won the Nobel Prize for Literature in 2005.
3. *Man critically ill after overnight mountain rescue.* A man is seriously ill in hospital today after exposure to extreme cold during a mountaineering expedition with friends in the Swiss Alps.
4. You are entering a holy site. All shoes and socks must be removed before entering.
5. Take two tablets every four hours. Do not exceed the stated dose without consulting your doctor.
6. Sow between April and May in a prepared seed bed. Cover lightly with soil and keep moist.

The sentences at 1 have a lexicon of cookery and recipes (*cook, saucepan, butter, onions*) with an imperative sequence (*allow, add*) suggesting a sequence of instructions. The sentences at 2 link *playwright* and *plays* across sentences and the words are also lexically cohesive with *literature* and *poetry*. The sentences at 3 have a context of a newspaper report with a headline followed by more detail. There are lexical repetitions and morphological patterns in words such as *ill* and *mountain/mountaineering*. Our cultural knowledge also connects the Swiss Alps with mountains. The sentences at 4 depend much more on the cultural knowledge that it is common to remove footwear to enter holy sites. The sentences at 5 indicate a lexicon of medicine with the words *tablets, dose, consulting* and *doctor* linking across sentence boundaries. The sentences at 6 are connected by a lexicon associated with gardening (*sow, seed, soil*). The imperatives given here in the sequence suggest either a gardening book or instructions on a seed packet.

Activity 23.2

COHESION AND SPEECH

Text: Two friends

As is the case with the written sentences above, there are a number of cohesive lexical links across speaking turns as the topic of the workplace and its physical environment is discussed and developed (e.g. *desks, office, canteen, reception area*). Also interesting here is the way in which the conversation is maintained by means of responses and questions that invite responses. These include non-verbal and verbal responses such as *mmm* and *erm* and *yeah*, but also responses that link very clearly with what has just been said and comment on it (e.g. *I suppose so, I think so, I do*). Questions, including tag questions that invite these responses include *isn't it? Would you?* Both speakers also make connective links between and across their own utterances (*all the same, what's more*). Discourse markers that both link and signpost that the speaker is changing the topic include words such as *anyway*.

Activity 23.3

COHESION AND POETRY

Text: *Offerings*

The poem *Offerings* is by the Malaysian poet Hilary Tham. It is a poem containing lexical patterns and associations that are rich and varied. The poem attempts to capture feelings of disappointment and rejection, maybe even of a love that is not returned, and the main actions of the speaker are conveyed by means of tightly cohesive sets of words that grow incrementally in intensity and in contrast.

The first line of each stanza describes physical actions that vary as the speaker becomes ever more uncertain of the right approach. The progression is from the more neutral verb *came*, moving to the delight of *danced*, to the more furtive *crept*, and then to the more potentially angry or desperate movement associated with the verb *strode*. The cohesive links across the four stanzas between the verbs

came, danced, crept, strode

are matched by a parallel movement as the object of the 'offerings' acts with a similar increasing intensity of action, indicating a growing decision not to accept the offerings of the flowers and to openly display a rejection of them. The verbs

put, dropped, shredded

start with a more neutral *put* and progress to the destructive act of *shredded*. They words collocate in that they are all physical actions and

COHESION AND POETRY *(continued)*

to this extent they are related, but they are distinguished by a growing strength and intensity in the actions they depict.

'Hybrid orchids' (which may suggest flowers – and feelings – that are not pure or natural but are grown by a more artificial or manufactured process) are *offered* in return, but this action has its basis in the original lack of certainty that feelings would be reciprocated and offerings matched. The flowers – *lotus, raintree blooms*, and *lilac orchids* – are not matched with similarly genuine offerings and the final stanza turns on a series of lexical contrasts that reflect a complex mix of feelings of rejection, anger, 'despair' and frustration. It leads to the sudden deepening of the sequence of action verbs of movement relating to the hands that now result in the verb *crushed*.

The lexical patterning of the poem works to reflect this growing realisation that the offerings will be rejected. The actions of the hands are paralleled by the verbs showing a combined radiance of the flowers and the excitement of the speaker

sparkling, flaming, trembling

that subsequently grow into the destructive action of *clenched* as the hybrid orchids are offered and it is seen that genuine feelings are not returned.

There is also a further cohesive patterning created by the natural environment of the setting in which the connections between the words lead from the natural and elemental (*sun, sunset, midnight*) to the cold, hard, manmade *gravel* of the patch between them.

Connections between the words in the poem are established in which ever more powerful and intense verbs are displayed, only to be then reversed by lexical contrasts that reveal the realisation that the offerings have come to nothing.

Activity 31.3

SECTION C

CONNECTIVES AND DEICTICS

> **From a website memorial to a friend:**
> My friend Jessica always wanted to be called Jessie but she introduced herself as Jessica. As a result everyone called her that.

Here, *but* is an additive conjunction. The deictic *that* is anaphoric and refers back to the name Jessica.

> **From an official report on pesticide control:**
> Few countries have satisfactory legislation on pesticides or government officials who can enforce it. In contrast, use of pesticides in Europe, Japan and North America is backed by government controls which limit their use. Furthermore, where it cannot be regulated, farmers are given detailed advice to help them.

In contrast is an adversative conjunction. *Furthermore* is a continuative conjunction. *It* is an anaphoric pronoun which refers to the noun 'legislation'.

> **From a blog about environmental issues:**
> They can't just close their eyes and say that there will be no accidents on the road, because the facts this year prove this. Then again, they will probably say it's too expensive to put up proper road signs. In that case, they are just saying human life is cheap. That's my opinion, anyway.

Because is a causal conjunction. *Then again* is an adversative conjunction (it has the meaning of 'on the other hand'). *In that case* is an additive conjunction; *anyway* is a continuative conjunction. *This* at the end of the first sentence is a deictic referring to the whole previous clause about ignoring the number of accidents. *That* (in the phrase *that's my opinion…*) is a deictic pointing cataphorically.

> **From the instructions on a bottle of cough medicine:**
> This cough medicine should be taken twice a day. The medicine is in liquid form and is for oral use only. If you forget to take a dose, then take the next dose when needed. No more than a single dose should therefore be taken at any one time.

This in the first sentence is a deictic pointing to the medicine. *And* is an additive conjunction. *Then* is a temporal conjunction. *Therefore* is a causal conjunction.

TRANSITIVITY AND GENDER

Text: Romantic fiction

General points about agency:

- Claire seems very passive and does not have any agency. She reacts to actions taken by Damien. He kisses her. She certainly kisses him but is not shown to be the agent; rather, she is the object. In other words, it is she who is kissed.
- Damien's feelings are not really described and they have to be inferred from his words and actions.
- Claire's actions are almost all to do with her feelings.
- Claire is the subject of some of the sentences (*she trembled, she sighed*) but they are all actions that do not have any outcomes. She can act, but not on anything or anyone else. The only exception is the sentence *she dismissed him.*
- When she acts she does so in spite of herself or she is shown to fail; for example: *She tried to speak.*
- Damien acts on her but Claire is passive and only acted upon by her own emotions and physiological reactions.

Further details about the grammar of the text:

One way in which an imbalance in agency between the man and woman is reflected in the text is by the manner in which transitive and intransitive verbs are used.

The verbs associated with Damien's actions (*kissed, took her [onto the patio], confronted*) are mainly conveyed by transitive verbs, whereas Claire's actions are mainly conveyed by intransitive verbs. For example:

Transitive: *kissed, hold* (her hand), *took her* [onto the patio], *confronted*
Intransitive: *trembled, sighed, moaned, hoping*

There are also patterns that show that even parts of his body also control her actions and make her passive in his presence.

His mouth leaving hers... His fingers pressed her...

The impression created by this text and by much romantic fiction written in this style is that women are helpless in the presence of attractive men and have no choice but to submit helplessly. Note too how in some similar examples of romantic fiction **prepositions** such as *up* or *above* and *over* are used to describe the physical position of the man, suggesting that the female is nearly always in a lower, inferior and less powerful position.

Activity 26.1

Activity 26.4

MANUALS AND REGULATIONS

Both these texts are highly impersonal. The text from the first aid manual is broadly scientific and focuses on detached information, containing a number of passive forms (*can be damaged by fire; illnesses that have been caused by; can be most affected by*). Nouns and noun phrases (*extremes of temperature/heat exhaustion*) are used rather than pronouns which would make the text too personal. For example, 'the heat can exhaust you' would not normally be appropriate in a text giving guidance and instructions. The use of the modal verb 'can' suggests possibilities rather than restrictions or certainties.

The 'regulations' text is similar. Passives are common (for example, *candidates are required…*) because the focus here is on institutional rules and regulations. Modal verbs which limit and control are used (*shall be required*). The regulations cannot be personal or centred on individuals because they apply and have to apply to everyone in exactly the same way. The phrase *A candidate who has been granted leave* would sound therefore very inappropriate in this context if it were written *If we have granted you leave*. As in the case of the first aid manual, nouns and noun phrases underline the focus on processes. Nouns such as *amendments* and *corrections* are used rather than modal expressions with a pronoun subject ('you may correct' or 'you may amend'). See also the discussion of nominalisation on p146.

Activity 27.1

SPEECH 'TOP 40'

Some words on the list do not look like words because they do not seem to refer to anything in the way that words in a dictionary have reference to ideas or things or entities and can therefore be defined. Words such as *mm* and *er* are best described as 'vocalisations', but they still have a very important function and purpose as they allow speakers to agree, to deliberate, to hesitate, to express some surprise, and so on. The vocalisations depend quite a bit on intonation (depending on intonation, *mm* can signal that you agree or disagree), but without these vocalised forms a lot of meaning would be lost in face-to-face conversations where speakers have to deal with talk with an immediacy that is not necessary when composing or responding to written communications. In the written list too (see p82) many of the most frequent words are key grammatical words (articles, prepositions, pronouns, **determiners**, core verbs such as 'is' and 'was') that provide the glue enabling messages to hang together. Of course, this is also true of spoken communication, but it is more the case here that the most frequent words are essential to interaction and to negotiating face-to-face exchanges in real time. The word *yeah* is

SPEECH 'TOP 40' (continued)

significant here because it commonly signals 'feedback' from a listener to the speaker (also called *backchannels*) that is mainly supportive to the speaker. It shows that channels of communication are open, that the speaker may continue, and sometimes that the listener agrees with what is being said. Words such as *so* and *right* on the list also enable speakers to signal and signpost what they are saying almost in the manner of punctuation. Although there is, of course, no such thing as punctuation in spoken language, these words function in ways similar to the spaces which mark new 'paragraphs'. For example, *right* and *so* both enable speakers to signal that the next step in the conversation should be taken (see p102 for further discussions of the word *right*).

Activity 27.1

INFORMAL GRAMMAR

Text: TV review

The style is clearly cultivated to engage the reader in a dialogue or, more accurately, a chat about the previous night's television programmes. It's as if the writer is talking to us the following day over a cup of coffee at work, or while we are walking from one class to another at college. It is an intimate, involving style. It's also creative in that it breaks some of the rules of formal written English that are not normally expected in a film or TV programme review in a national newspaper (although if you read this column regularly it is not surprising). Of course, some readers may be irritated by what may appear to be an attempt to be cool or hip by writing chatty prose that is too self-consciously democratic (*we*, the writer and the reader, are all one, *we* experience all this together). Some may feel it is the language of the texting and Facebook generation where spoken styles predominate, even though the language is inscribed in written texts. Others may like it and feel that the review is highly creative in both style and effect.

Whatever judgements are made, this is a very distinctive way of writing along a continuum from formal to informal, and is characterised by a very marked use of particular grammatical patterns, woven into the text in a highly skilful way.

Further details about language features of the text
Vocalisations and responses

There are even some words which are written exactly as they are spoken in casual speech. For example, *hmmm* is not really a word; it is more a vocalisation in everyday speech that commonly expresses hesitation. *No* is, of course, a more conventional word and is distinctly dialogic, with the speaker/writer talking aloud with himself or with a supposed listener/reader:

Activity 29.1

INFORMAL GRAMMAR *(continued)*

I wonder how Rendell came up with the profession for Mix, her protagonist. **Hmmm**, shall I make him an accountant, or a carpenter… **no**. Got it. (l.6)

Yeah (l.9) operates in a very similar way, and the use of *oh* (l.15) likewise.

Even the very first word of the review, *Good*, captures a sense of an ongoing conversation with the speaker/writer that is moving on to another topic:

Good. Thank God that's over. The Olympics. All that warmth, good will and tears. Even at the bloody taekwando. It was getting tiring. Now we can get back to more familiar territory. Like murder.

Exclamations

Wow (l.17) is an exclamation (called *exclamatives* in some grammars) that is used in emails and texting, but is normally more common in writing when used in dialogue – that is, between quotation marks.

Wow! *Escape from Colditz* (Channel 4). What an AMAZING story. (l.24)

Its spoken character here is further reinforced by the capitalised AMAZING, almost as if the writer wants to highlight the word as spoken in a much louder volume.

Vague language

Another example is the use of the phrase *kinda* (l.34):

Kinda = kind of

The full informal sentence here would normally be *It kind of works*, but the use of *kind of* here – with this very spoken inflection (*kinda*) – is delayed until after the main clause. *It works. Kind of.* In spoken grammar *kind of* and *sort of* are commonly used by speakers to express a deliberate vagueness. Speakers don't want to sound too definite, too assured or too certain of their facts. It is a common characteristic of spoken grammar.

Ellipsis

There are numerous examples of ellipsis across this review.

Big mistake	(l.14)	*(it was a)*
Schoolboy error	(l.14)	*(it/that was)*
Got it	(l.7)	*(I've)*
Quite bumpy	(l.35)	*(it was)*
Like murder	(1.3)	*(we can get back to territory like murder)*

SMS VARIATIONS

Message sent between two friends male aged 24 (sender) and female aged 22.

> Hi, did two shifts tonite and am off to bed. But still fancy the film tonite. Ur still ok for this right? How about meet up at I dunno 6 or something outside the Chinese take away. Thatll mean we can still have a bite to eat and stuff? Whatyoufink?

Message sent from mother (aged 52) to son (aged 19).

> What are the plans for this weekend? Are you, as you suggested, meeting us at Auntie June's for the birthday tea? Would you like to be picked up by us and, if so, at what time? Or are you, after all, driving to Matt's first and then meeting us there. Let us know whatever is most convenient? X

There are big differences in grammar in these two texts which in part reflect the ages of the two texters. Text 2 is much more formal. The clauses are, as is often the case in formal writing, interrupted by finite and non-finite subordinate clauses:

> Are you, <u>as you suggested</u>, meeting us at Auntie
> June's…   (as you suggested)
> Would you like to be picked up by us and, <u>if so</u>, at what time? (if so)

The grammar also contains no use of ellipsis.
   By contrast, text 1 contains several uses of ellipsis, creating a highly informal, interactive, matey and chatty character as a result.

> Did two shifts tonite   (I did two shifts tonight)
> Ur still ok for this right?   (You are still ok for this, right?)

Notice how the ellipsis is layered alongside other more informal, 'spoken' forms such as vague language (*6 or something*; have a bite to eat *and stuff*). Notice too how dialectal or idiolectal forms are used (probably playfully): for example, *Whatyoufink*? (What do you think?). Furthermore, punctuation is very correct in the second SMS text, indicating the clause structure and clause boundaries very deliberately and precisely. In the first text punctuation is more optional; for example *thatll* (that'll) *ur* (you are), etc.

Activity 31.1

GRAMMATICAL CREATIVITY IN POETRY

Full text of Popcorn-can cover:

> Popcorn-can cover
> screwed to the wall
> over a hole
> so the cold
> can't mouse in
>
>   Lorine Niedecker

The use of the word *mouse* here might be guessed from the small hole in the wall, but it is unexpected. *Mouse* is most used commonly as a noun and is not normally used, as in the final line here, as a verb. The effect of this creative use of grammar and the creative breaking of grammatical rules is to suggest the cold creeping unnoticed into the room rather like a mouse might. If you are frightened of mice, there might be an analogy with the fear someone might have of the cold sneaking into their home in the depths of winter. Note too how the sound of the word *mouse* also breaks the previous sequence of similar vowels and letters – *over, hole, cold* – which adds a further unsettling and unexpected effect to the use of the word *mouse*.

Activity 31.2

TITLES AND NAMES

Sofa So Good echoes the phrase *so far so good*.

Making Waves is an idiom that refers to causing a stir or to drawing attention to something (the hairstyle perhaps). The word *waves* is part of the lexicon of hair and hairstyles.

There's no present like the time refers to buying a watch as a present (expensive, perhaps, since it is from a jewellery store). The slogan also echoes the proverbial phrase 'There's no time like the present', which refers to the advantage of doing something quickly, maybe without too much thought.

Prime Minister flies back to front: *Front* is a noun which means the territorial position of an army. The prime minister returns to make a further visit to troops at the front. But *back to front* is an adverbial phrase which means doing something in the wrong order, such as putting a shirt on that faces the wrong way.

TITLES AND NAMES *(continued)*

Toasting Brad Pitt in Cannes: Brad Pitt is an American film star and director. Toast can mean to celebrate someone with a drink such as champagne, but the verb can also mean subjecting something to heat, as in making toast from bread. The headline is ambiguous; it may suggest the review is critical or complimentary.

Feta Compli: Feta is the name of a Greek cheese. The phrase is an intertextual echo of the French phrase *fait accompli* used in English to mean something that has already been done and cannot be changed. The perfect salad?

Lighten up your garden. Plant bulbs: Bulbs are the seeds for plants such as daffodils and tulips. The word *bulb* is also used to refer to electric light bulbs.

Travel yourself interesting: There is an intertextual echo here of a common English phrase *make yourself interesting*. The structure involves a **reflexive verb** *make yourself* followed by an adjective or noun/noun phrase. (Other examples are *make yourself strong*, *make yourself a cup of tea*.) *Travel* is not used in this structure, so the slogan (from the company Expedia) is striking and memorable as a result and suggests that you have to make an effort by yourself if travel is to be interesting (in this case, perhaps by doing all your own travel research and arrangements online).

CREATIVE GRAMMAR OR 'WRONG' GRAMMAR?

Text 1 Exeter Cruises involves a spelling mistake (it should be *inconvenience*) and a possible grammatical mistake involving **subject verb concord**. The texts says *Exeter Cruises is* when in most grammars of English it is more common to say *cruises are*, so that the plural verb *are* goes with (that is, is in concord with) the plural noun *cruises*.

Of course, this may not be a mistake, since it depends on whether we see *Exeter Cruises* as a singular or plural entity. If the phrase is being used to refer to the name of the company it would normally be singular. If it refers to the cruises themselves, it should be plural. The writers of temporary notices tend not to worry too much about grammatical niceties.

Text 2: Burger me involves a noun *burger*, which we might interpret as being used as a verb. It may have the meaning of 'give me a burger', or, if it is a noun, then the phrase uses a strong ellipsis and means 'what is the right or best burger for me?'. The phrase draws attention to itself

CREATIVE GRAMMAR OR 'WRONG' GRAMMAR?
(continued)

because of the unusual grammar, creating a striking headline for the article on burgers which follows in the magazine.

The text is taken from the front page of a weekend magazine published in Hong Kong, and the associations of the phrase within Hong Kong English-speaking cultures may be different (or it may be a deliberate attempt to be even more striking and attention-attracting). In some parts of the world and in some social contexts the phrase may break taboos, as it echoes the phrase 'bugger me' which is often said as an expression of surprise and annoyance and may be considered by some to be vulgar and offensive. For this reason the word 'bugger' may not always be in all English language dictionaries.

In **Text 3 Orange my Day**, *orange* – which is normally either an adjective or a noun – is employed strikingly as a verb to raise awareness of the need for action on domestic violence against women. The use of a deliberate 'creative' error together with the striking colour orange achieves a clear and memorable effect, breaking rules for a definite purpose.

However, the word orange has different cultural resonances in different parts of the world. For example, the colour orange is closely associated with the Protestant religious movement and there are 'Orange Day' marches in support of religious groups. In the past these have led to violent clashes with 'green' Catholic groups, especially in Northern Ireland. Therefore, being told to 'orange your neighbourhood' would have a very different meaning within Irish cultures. Some years ago the telephone company Orange had to change the use of its slogan '*The future's bright, the future's Orange*' in Northern Ireland for the same reason.

Text 4: Here is a correct version of the job ad.

Is this the job for you?

If you are able to spot over ten mistakes here, then there is likely to be a good opportunity for you as a copy editor with our company. We need graduates who have an eye for detail and are interested in information relevant to computing technology. If you're used to reading documents carefully and have good word processing skills, let us know by sending your cv and portfolio by post or email to →

The **Job Ad** breaks rules in a number of ways. Grammatical mistakes are not normally expected in advertisements, particularly in job ads for editors. However, the mistakes are deliberate in order for potential applicants to measure how well they can recognise mistakes. There are more than ten

CREATIVE GRAMMAR OR 'WRONG' GRAMMAR?
(continued)

grammatical mistakes, although strictly speaking some could be said to be spelling mistakes. Here grammar rules are used for real purposes; the mistakes are not creative in themselves in the same way as the texts above – *orange your neighbourhood* or *burger me*, or the last line of 'Popcorn-can cover'.

However, the overall effect of the complete text is strikingly unusual, original and creative. Creative language nearly always involves a break with expectations. The expectations can be at the level of vocabulary, grammar or phonology, and can also, as here, involve our genre-based expectations of what a text should normally look like and how a text should normally be.

Part III

Building up

Texts and contexts

Aim: Part III will help you to keep in mind the larger questions about how texts represent the world around us. The ideas in this part of the book complement the more text-internal work of Part II, as well as the research skills of Part I. Taken together, they ensure that any text analysis you do is well planned, rigorous and well balanced.

CONTENTS: PART III

32 The dimensions of texts: place and time

33 Textual perspectives and point of view

34 Texts as discourses: culture and gender

35 Dialogues: genre and intertextuality

   Review your skills

   Ideas for assignments

   Commentaries for Part III

CHAPTER 32

The dimensions of texts

Place and time

Two important dimensions of context are the physical setting for any piece of communication, and the time frame within which it takes place. These dimensions were introduced in Part I as important aspects of analysis (see pp15–18). This section of the book will take both of those dimensions in turn, and consider them in some detail across a range of text types.

32.1 THE 'HERE' OF FACE TO FACE TALK

In face to face encounters, a shared physical presence means that not everything needs to be spelled out: significant items and events in the environment can be indicated non-verbally or via 'pointing' (deictic) words such as 'this', 'that', 'here', 'over there'. Deixis, which is Greek for 'demonstrate', is all about points of reference: deictic terms tell us to pay attention to certain aspects of the environment. This can include references to people as well as things: pronouns such as 'he' and 'she' can be effective short-cuts between those with shared knowledge.

> **TEST YOURSELF**
>
> In Part I you were introduced to the idea of recording spoken language as a method of collecting data (see p24). You also transcribed part of a speech given by Michelle Obama, in order to think about the role of transcription conventions in marking features of speech and of context. The following activities will help you to understand more fully what context means, in terms of spoken language. It is not simply something that is external to language, but is often strongly connected with the language choices that speakers make at any particular moment.
>
> In the work done at the lexical and semantic level (Part II, Section B), the importance of deixis was discussed when considering why certain terms such as 'here' and 'there' featured frequently in word lists from corpus searches.
>
> In the transcript below, an instructor is demonstrating something to an apprentice. Can you guess what the activity is? See if you can pick out all the deictic terms. (The answer is at the end of Part III.)

Activity 32.1

Text 32.1

INSTRUCTION

I = Instructor
A = Apprentice
(.) = Normal pause
[ ] simultaneous speech

> I: if you start here (.) um (.) what you can do (.) is take this up gradually (.) stopping to just check (.) this is even (.) [then]
>
> A: [what] about this side (.) how do you keep it out of the way
>
> I: well (.) just get one of these (.) and clip it up (.) and forget about it
>
> A: right (.) so take that up [gradually]
>
> I: [yeah] make sure it's level (.) don't get carried away (.) you can always come back to it later
>
> A: so then which way do you go
>
> I: up here (.) then the same the other side (.) the top and front last (.) then you can see for yourself (.) how the shape's coming on (.) and the top and front (.) should take their shape (.) from the rest (.) that's the skill really (.) judging as you go (.) even though you have the main idea (.) in your head

Activity 32.2

RECORD AND TRANSCRIBE SOME TALK

In order to gain more understanding of the role of deixis in speech, record and transcribe an informal conversation, preferably one involving some kind of practical activity such as cooking, making something or playing a game. You should be present at the recording. You can be an observer or a participant – either is fine. If it's not possible to record an interaction in a 'live' way, then record a practically-based programme from the TV or internet and transcribe a small extract from it. Then make two different kinds of transcription:

1. Just transcribe the talk itself – don't add in any explanations of non-verbal behaviour or any details about the physical setting of the talk. Give the transcript to someone who was not present at the original recording, and ask them to interpret the interaction. Get them to focus on what was happening and how the participants were behaving.

> 2. Now add in the extra elements that you feel need to be included in order for readers to understand how the interaction worked: for example, participants' movements and positions, gestures and actions, or other aspects of the physical environment. Test out this transcript, focusing on the extent to which the interpretation you get is different from your previous one. Draw some conclusions about the role of deixis in talk, and the difference between having a conversation and transcribing it.

Activity 32.2

> **WRITING UP**
>
> When you have finished recording, transcribing and testing yourself and your material, write up your conclusions in the form of an essay entitled 'The role of context in spoken language'.

Activity 32.3

32.2 THE 'THERE' OF DIGITAL COMMUNICATION

Of course, not all our interactions are face to face. Nowadays we spend large amounts of time in digital interactions of various kinds, all of which present us with contextual challenges. When phones changed their fixed landline connections and went mobile, a frequent part of opening exchanges involved location details – perhaps they still do. In early chatroom dialogues between strangers, location (along with age and sex) were the most frequently requested items of information. The chatroom data below, taken from a study of students working online for the first time during 2000, shows how participants created the idea of three-dimensional space by their choice of certain deictics – 'here', 'there' 'in here', 'out there'. The lines are not part of a continuous dialogue, but are opening lines from different participants as they started the chat tool. The examples are reproduced here with their original spellings and punctuation:

STUDENT CHAT

Text 32.2

> HELLO! ANYONE THERE!!
> Is there anybody here apart from me
> Is anyone in group 1 and in the chat room at this precise moment
> Is anybody from our course in here today?
> Helo is anyone there
> no one here so what can i do
> Sorry I'm late...anyone there?
> Is there anybody there?
> is anybody coming in?
> nobody here either
> is anyone there?
> is there anyone there yet?
> look, here i am
> anyone there?
> Hello spirits is their any one out there?
>
> (Goddard 2005)

In a medium where one's interlocutor is invisible, checking that there is someone 'there', wherever that location is, becomes a key communication skill. This is especially the case when a 'chat' tool is part of a company's sales pitch. For example, below is an extract from a 'chat' session between a customer (called 'you' in the data) and a telecommunications salesperson (Dave). The customer is enquiring about buying an iPhone:

SALES CHAT

Text 32.3

> **Dave:** let me help you with link to check iPhone deals
> **You:** ok, thanks
> **Dave:** Please Click here for the iPhone deals
> **You:** thanks for your help Dave
> **Dave:** Please click on above link and have a look at all 3 iPhone
> **Dave:** iPhone 5, iPhone4s and iPhone4
> **Dave:** Did the link work for you?
> **You:** Not been yet, I'll go now (I'm making the dinner while also doing this!)
> **Dave:** Multi-tasking!!!
> **Dave:** let me know once you select price plan
> **Dave:** Hope we are still connected
> **You:** yep still here
> **Dave:** Great!!

COLLECT SOME DIGITAL DATA

In Part I, digital data was discussed as an interesting source of material for analysis (see pp27–29), and a practical activity illustrated the challenge of disentangling the disrupted turntaking that can often occur in real-time writing.

However, there are many different kinds of digital communication, so which types you collect, and how many, is up to you. Think about SMS messages, social media posts, specialist forums, emails, online games, as well as 'chat' (i.e. real-time writing) in its various forms, such as the 'help' tools offered by some commercial websites. Each of these sources will involve users in employing different language strategies, but any of the sources could be useful for exploring deictic aspects of language.

Explore the role of deixis in your data, focusing particularly on ideas about space and location. Do the physical aspects of where people are, or where the interaction is happening, feature in the data in a significant way? To take an example from research on mobile phone use, Thurlow (2003) showed that SMS messages were often used for social planning and organising. If his study continues to reflect current practice, does location form an important part of such messages? Location details could be simply factual in messages about meeting up (for example, 'just coming into the station now'; but they could also signify what another person is experiencing, helping to construct a picture of events (for example, 'at doctor's with dad, he's had a fall, am worried'). Or have images and video overtaken words in depicting scenes?

Draw some conclusions about how important the contextual aspect of space/location is within digital communication, and about how details are communicated.

Activity 32.4

32.3 THE 'EVERYWHERE' OF ADVERTISING

It might seem that because advertising is all around us, it would be pointless to explore the idea of space. This is far from the case – advertising is all about placement, and placement is about the strategic use of space. In other words, some spaces are more fruitful than others.

If we take the idea of advertising in its broadest sense, as promotional texts in general and not simply as texts that sell products (Goddard 1998), then artefacts such as carrier bags, coffee mugs and t-shirts provide mobile spaces for advertisers to colonise: our bodies carry their messages everywhere. At the same time, our phones and computers host advertising that is increasingly targeted to our own personal spaces.

Text 32.4

COFFEE CUP

The advertiser has placed the voice of a notional coffee drinker on the side of the cup, dramatising the experience of enjoying the drink. The message faces out towards potential further customers, and is constructed as a personal endorsement by the coffee purchaser, regardless of what they actually thought of the drink they'd bought. In a way, the advertising is ventriloquising the consumer, putting words in his or her mouth.

Activity 32.5

INVESTIGATE ADVERTISING

Avoiding the more familiar forms of product advertising, explore some of the promotional messages that are in your environment. You might think about institutional texts (for example, church hoardings, school or college logos) or the possessions we carry around with us, wear, or use (for example t-shirts, sportswear, shopping bags, food packaging, napkins, coffee cups). You could also focus on the idea of unusual placements – for example on trains, alongside roads, on the sides or backs of trucks, or the moving ads that are displayed around pitches at sports fixtures. You saw in Part I of the book that there is material to be collected everywhere we look, and if you have been collecting material as you go, you may well already have some advertising you could take from your own collection.

32.4 LITERARY SPACES

In literary texts, the idea of space is most familiar in terms of setting, or place. Because literary texts create fictional worlds, the deictics involved are termed 'displaced'. The aspect of place, along with the time frame used for the action in the story, features within the broader concept of **point of view** – the overall perspective from which the narrative unfolds. Studying point of view would also normally include looking at whose voice appears to be addressing us: this area will be considered in detail in the next unit.

The idea of physical space goes beyond the scenery of any imagined place, and takes in all the visual aspects of the story's presentation, including how the characters look, their actions, and what is reported to us indirectly as well as what we are directly shown.

THE DIMENSIONS OF TEXTS

NOVEL OPENINGS I

The opening of any novel offers a unique opportunity to set up a strong sense of place, and populate it with the people who are going to feature in the story. Below are two novel openings. Identify all the details of language that help you to visualise the scene, including aspects of the characters involved. There is a commentary on this activity at the end of Part III.

Activity 32.6

ORDINARY THUNDERSTORMS

Text 32.5

Let us start with the river – all things begin with the river and we shall probably end there, no doubt – but let's wait and see how we go. Soon, in a minute or two, a young man will come and stand by the river's edge, here at Chelsea Bridge, in London.

There he is – look – stepping hesitantly down from a taxi, paying the driver, gazing around him, unthinkingly, glancing over at the bright water (it's a flood tide and the river is unusually high). He's a tall, pale-faced young man, early thirties, even-featured with tired eyes, his short dark hair neatly cut and edged as if fresh from the barber. He is new to the city, a stranger, and his name is Adam Kindred. He has just been interviewed for a job and feels like seeing the river (the interview having been the usual tense encounter, with a lot at stake), answering a vague desire to 'get some air'. The recent interview explains why, beneath his expensive trenchcoat, he is wearing a charcoal-grey suit, a maroon tie with a new white shirt and why he's carrying a glossy solid-looking black briefcase with heavy brass locks and corner trim. He crosses the road, having no idea how his life is about to change in the next few hours – massively, irrevocably – no idea at all.

William Boyd

Text 32.6

61 HOURS

Five minutes to three in the afternoon. Exactly sixty-one hours before it happened. The lawyer drove in and parked in the empty lot. There was an inch of new snow on the ground, so he spent a minute fumbling in the foot well until his overshoes were secure. Then he got out and turned his collar up and walked to the visitors' entrance. There was a bitter wind out of the north. It was thick with fat lazy flakes. There was a storm sixty miles away. The radio had been full of it.

The lawyer got in through the door and stamped the snow off his feet. There was no line. It was not a regular visiting day. There was nothing ahead of him except an empty room and an empty X-ray belt and a metal detector hoop and three prison guards standing around doing nothing. He nodded to them, even though he didn't know them. But he considered himself on their side, and they on his. Prison was a binary world. Either you were locked up, or you weren't. They weren't. He wasn't.

Yet.

Lee Child

As well as representing aspects of space, the literary texts also set up particular time frames. The first text in particular has some very complex shifts of time: the text starts by pointing to future time, moves to the present, then to the recent past, goes back to the present, then points forward to the future. In fact, it is very difficult to separate the two dimensions of space and time, as each shift in time frames a new picture. The second text – which has a time reference in its title – is written in the past tense but points forward to the future. Both texts point to future time with an ominous sense of foreboding – a good narrative technique for texts in the thriller genre, as these are.

Activity 32.7

NOVEL OPENINGS II

Collect some opening paragraphs from different novels, and analyse how the contextual factors of space and time are constructed.

32.5 TEXTS AND TIME(S)

The discussion of the literary texts above has focused on time as it is used internally, to structure the opening of narratives. However, there is also time in the plural – the times, or different eras, that writers work in.

The same two aspects of time – internal and external – can be considered with reference to any text, not just to literature. With reference to external time, texts date; social values and practices can change, objects become obsolete, language use can become archaic and different languages can come to prominence or fade away.

Looking back at the non-literary texts already considered in Part III can illustrate both these aspects of time. In the real-time texts (*Text: Instruction*, *Text: Student chat*, *Text: Sales chat*) time has significance internally because of the conventions established in any community around appropriate timings – for example, the length of time that is seen to be acceptable when waiting for others' responses. The importance of timing is less obvious in *Text: Instruction* because we do not have access to the very many signals that would have occurred between participants in the original face to face interaction, registering how the various actions were being understood. However, in the online texts, participants have no knowledge of the physical circumstances of their interlocutors. The students feel the need to check out whether other people are logged on, but also sometimes to indicate their own time frames; this may have been because any piece of writing could be read by others after the authors had left the room. The terms in bold refer to temporal factors:

> Is anyone in group 1 and in the chat room *at this precise moment*
> Is anybody from our course in here *today*?
> Sorry "m *late*...anyone there?
> is anybody *coming in*?

In the sales chat, the salesperson has the additional pressure of trying to get as many sales as possible, so speed in dealing with customers and in closing deals is of the utmost importance. His prompts force the customer to justify why she has not responded:

> Dave: Did the link work for you?
> You: Not been yet, I'll go now (I'm making the dinner while also doing this!)
> Dave: Multi-tasking!!!
> Dave: let me know once you select price plan
> Dave: Hope we are still connected
> You: yep still here

There are also external aspects of time that are relevant. Mediated contexts (communication involving technologies of various kinds) such as *Text: Student chat* and *Text: Sales chat* are highly shaped by the affordances and limitations of the technologies at any one time. The participants behave as they do because of what the system allows them to do: in those examples, participants could not see each other, and there were no icons indicating keyboard activity. Language choices also change as a result of familiarity and experience. The students in the chat text were not familiar with online contexts, so it was all very otherworldly to them; it would be very different now that digital communication has become an unremarkable part of many people's lives. In terms of the content, too, time is a factor: currently new technologies such as the iPhone 5 will soon become 'old', dating the text (see Goddard & Geesin 2011).

The era in which any text is produced is also subject to some large-scale factors where space and time are inextricably linked. The coffee cup was photographed on a public street in a Swedish town in 2011, existing alongside many other texts in the environment that were written in English. In Scandinavia at this point in time English language texts are a very common sight, with many, especially younger, citizens able to use English quite fluently. The growth of English as an additional language in areas such as Scandinavia is relatively recent compared with those countries that have had English in use for many years, often as a result of former colonialism – for example, in India, across the Caribbean, in some African countries, and in some areas of south east Asia, local varieties of English are well established and are considered academically as part of a network of **World Englishes**. However, the growth of global corporations using English everywhere they operate, the increased mobility of populations, and above all the expanded scope for communication facilitated by new technologies have accelerated the use of English in many further parts of the world, where English has gone from being a foreign language to being a kind of lingua franca – used as a common language between speakers who have different first languages (Jenkins 2009; Saraceni 2010).

The existence of local varieties of English has implications for all speakers of English, particularly where interpreting language choices is concerned. For example, the phrase 'Oh Thank Heaven!' seen on the coffee cup (p194) might suggest different kinds of speakers when read either by a native speaker of English or by a speaker of English as an additional language.

JUMP

Similarly, the English used in this ad, for a German radio show from Dresden, might suggest different meanings to English users of different kinds. Presumably for the show's producers, however, having an English name suggests a level of global reach and therefore sophistication.

Text 32.7

Ideas about how texts might be read and interpreted form a particular focus in the next unit.

Sometimes, however, texts rely so much on specific contexts of appearance that it is hard to achieve any kind of interpretation without some quite detailed knowledge of what was going on at the time the text was produced. An example of this was a car advertisement that appeared in the UK in 2013 promoting a new edition of the Mini Cooper. The ad used the hook 'Beef. With a lot of horses hidden in it'. You can see the advert at this web address: http://www.campaignlive.co.uk/news/1171261/

This appeared at a time when it had been discovered that many food products supposedly containing beef were, in fact, horsemeat. There was a public outcry not just at the fraud involved, but also at the whole idea of eating horse, which was – and still is – generally viewed as culturally unacceptable in the UK. This ad cleverly turns the idea of the fraud on its head, seeing it as a positive quality to have 'beef' on the outside and 'horse' hidden within. However, 'beef' and 'horse' are not simply labels for animal meat, but work as metaphors for strength and power – with horse referring to horsepower, a term that traditionally describes the output power of engines. The ad maintains a reference to the food crisis in its description of 'an unexpectedly generous helping' of 211 horsepower. The advertising copywriter rode the wave of topicality and immediacy, exploiting the current events of the time. You could say that this text sacrificed longevity for the power of tapping into the moment. This idea of powerful but momentary currency is illustrated by the fact that permission was refused to reproduce the advert in this book. Clearly, it is now seen by the company and/or the advertising agency as an out-of-date campaign that would no longer connect with readers.

32.6 IDEAS FOR ASSIGNMENTS: TEXTS AND TIME(S)

Choose a specific aspect of time as it has been covered in this unit, and collect some data from a context of your choice in order to explore it. Here is a summary of what has been covered:

- The importance of timing in real-time communication. You could concentrate on face to face speech, real-time writing, or multimodal tools which involve a variety of channels.
- The idea of changes in how different communication tools work. You might think back to the different technologies you have had to learn, as new gadgets have been produced.
- The way in which texts become dated in their references to things, people and events. You could find some much older historical texts and explore potential changes. Texts that explicitly address aspects of social behaviour – such as etiquette manuals – are interesting for their coverage of public attitudes and values. Other texts could include newspapers, comics and magazines.
- The use of English in new contexts, as a lingua franca. You could explore whether, or to what extent, English is in evidence in your environment, focusing on the type of English used and on its purposes.
- How some texts might deliberately key in to current debates and require inside cultural knowledge for their interpretation. You are most likely to find this strategy in advertisements and promotional texts, because they want to show contemporary relevance.

CHAPTER 33

Textual perspectives and point of view

Reading and interpreting any text is a dynamic process. It is not simply a question of decoding what has been put there, as if it were a formula. People bring their own experiences to bear in interpreting a text, and this means that no two individuals will have exactly the same response. At the same time, there are aspects of texts that can be identified as part of a set of communicative strategies. In the end, interpretation is a process of negotiation between what is in the text and what people bring to it. This chapter focuses on this idea of negotiation, paying particular attention to the relationships between the negotiators.

You may have come across different terms for these negotiators, for example:

producer – consumer
sender – receiver
addresser – addressee
speaker – listener
writer – reader

These terms come from different subject areas and each pair reflects the emphasis of their particular area. 'Producer' and 'consumer' come from sociology and media studies, reflecting the idea of texts as artefacts that are bought and sold in marketplaces. Literary texts and advertisements are examples of this idea. 'Sender' and 'receiver' come from communication studies, suggesting the electronic basis of early communication systems. 'Addresser' and 'addressee' and 'speaker' and 'listener' emphasise spoken language and have origins in rhetoric and linguistics, while 'writer' and 'reader' suggest a focus on writing and literature.

There are no hard and fast rules about which terms are most appropriate, but it is important to realise that the choice of terms suggests a particular focus. For the purposes of this chapter, the terms 'writer' and 'reader' will be used. This does not mean that only written words will be considered, however. 'Writing' will need to encompass different aspects of communication, including that of spoken language when represented on the page or digitally, plus all the visual aspects of texts we encounter both on paper and in electronic contexts.

33.1 NARRATORS

writer
narrator
text
narratee
reader

The term **narrator** describes the constructed persona that appears to be addressing us from the text. For example, in *Text: Coffee cup* (p194), there was a representation of spoken language, in the form of *Oh Thank Heaven!* This is made to seem like speech because of its apparent spontaneity, expressing the relief and pleasure of having a good cup of coffee. 'Oh' is classified as a 'response cry', a spilling over of emotion in response to a stimulus. You looked at response cries in Part II, (see p65 & pp72–3). 'Thank Heaven' is a mild imprecation, again expressing a release of emotion. No strong swearing here – our narrator is a very polite figure.

Although this writing has been devised by a copywriter and is therefore the product of a writer, the voice produced is that of a narrator – a fictionalised figure, in this case enjoying coffee. A different narrator was seen in *Text: Ordinary Thunderstorms* (see p195) where William Boyd, the writer, creates the persona of a kind of tour guide with a difference – one who can anticipate future events:

> Let us start with the river – all things begin with the river and we shall probably end there, no doubt – but let's wait and see how we go.
> Soon, in a minute or two, a young man will come and stand by the river's edge, here at Chelsea Bridge, in London.
>   There he is – look – stepping hesitantly down from a taxi, paying the driver, gazing around him, unthinkingly, glancing over at the bright water (it's a flood tide and the river is unusually high).

The narrator's use of 'we' suggests an inclusiveness – he or she is standing with us, pointing out those things we need to pay attention to. S/he is constructed as a helpful figure, ready with an explanation of why the young man should look at the river.

FIND THE NARRATOR

Collect a range of texts and describe the nature of the narrators in them. You could start with the novel openings you collected previously. Then add some non-literary examples — for example, advertising, personal ads, social media posts, comics, notices, textbooks. If you already have a collection of texts from your work in Part I, review your texts and make a selection. Regardless of whether writers are consciously creating a narrative voice, explore the persona they have constructed by focusing on their language choices. If you want to explore spoken language, collect (or select) some speech data such as voice mails, podcasts, speeches, lectures, or sports commentaries, and explore the nature of the figure that is being projected.

Activity 33.1

33.2 NARRATEES

If a narrator is a constructed figure who appears to be addressing us from the text, a constructed figure who appears to be being addressed is termed a **narratee**. While you might be a reader of a text in the flesh-and-blood sense, a narratee is a fictionalised reader, constructed from all the assumptions that are made about who is being addressed — both explicit and implicit — by the text. A quick way to understand the nature of this constructed figure is to recall an experience where you felt that a text was being addressed to someone else — someone who wasn't you or anyone like you. At that point, you are perceiving the difference between a real reader and a fictional narratee.

If the aim of the text in question is persuasive, then the narratee figure needs to represent something that the real reader can connect with. This may not be a realistic picture of themselves at all. In fact, many advertisements work by creating fantasy figures that are aspirational rather than achievable.

The idea of an idealised narratee figure can be seen below, in the bathroom notice. The text is from an international chain hotel in the UK. The message is written in both English and Danish.

Notice how the narrator uses the plural pronoun 'we', referring to the company as a caring organisation that is already engaged in ecologically sound practices. Readers are invited to 'join us in our conservation efforts' and help preserve precious resources by 'working together'. There is no sense of 'us and them' here: hotel proprietors and guests are constructed as one big happy family.

204   **TEXTUAL PERSPECTIVES AND POINT OF VIEW**

Text 33.1

BATHROOM NOTICE

The narratee as constructed by this text is someone who has a strong desire to protect the environment, and who would therefore naturally support the hotel's initiative. In other words, the narratee is assumed to need no persuasion to do the right thing – a persuasive message in itself.

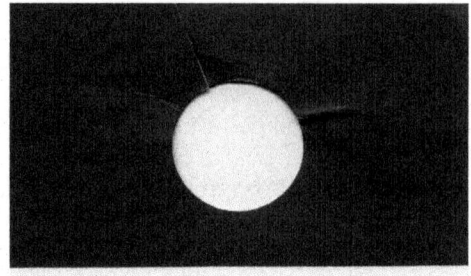

WE CARE ABOUT THE ENVIRONMENT
We are committed to undertaking practices
that preserve our natural resources.

While it is our practice to change towels every day, we are supportive of our guest's desire to help protect the environment. If you prefer, here is what you can do to join us in our conservation efforts.
LEAVING A TOWEL ON THE RACK MEANS:
"I will use it again."
LEAVING A TOWEL IN THE BATHTUB MEANS:
"Please exchange."
Working together, we can conserve millions of liters of water, save energy and minimize the release of detergents into the environment.
Thank you and enjoy your stay!

VI TAGER HENSYN TIL MILJØET
Det er vigtigt for os, at benytte metoder,
der bevarer naturlige ressourcer.

Det er vor praksis at skifte håndklæder hver dag,
men samtidig vil vi gerne efterkomme vore gæsters ønske
om at beskytte miljøet. Hvis De ønsker det,
kan De gøre følgende for at hjælpe os med at
gøre en indsats for miljøet.
HÆNGES HÅNDKLÆDET OP BETYDER DET:
„Jeg bruger håndklædet igen."
LÆGGES HÅNDKLÆDET I BADEKARET BETYDER DET:
„Skift venligst håndklædet."
Sammen kan vi spare millioner af liter vand og energi samt
minimere udslip af skadelige stoffer i miljøet.
Idet vi takker for Deres hjælp,
ønsker vi Dem et behageligt ophold!

Activity 33.2

FIND THE NARRATEE

Go back to the texts you assembled in order to explore the idea of a narrator. Think about the texts again, but this time explore the way narratees are constructed – what attitudes, values and shared knowledge are being assumed? Identify the language features in the text that contribute to the construction of the narratee figures.

CHAPTER 34

Texts as discourses

Culture and gender

Individual texts create discourses through repeatedly representing people, things, areas of experience, ideas and events in particular ways. The previous discussion of narratee figures suggested that these fictional constructions were based on assumptions. Assumptions are the building blocks of discourses, creating stories about 'what things are like'.

34.1 CULTURAL STEREOTYPES: WHAT ARE 'WE' LIKE?

In *Text: Bathroom notice*, the plural pronoun 'we' was used by the narrator to denote a corporate identity. However, pronoun use is not necessary to suggest that a particular group is being referenced.

Social group identities can be suggested in a number of different ways. Sometimes, a set of practices or characteristics associated with a group can be used as part of a text's message.

BEER MAT

For example, a Swedish bar that called itself an 'English pub' used beer mats to explain how to get a drink by referring to a British tradition where customers go to the bar to get their drinks — an alien tradition in Sweden as well as many other countries across the world, where service is at customers' tables.

Text 34.1

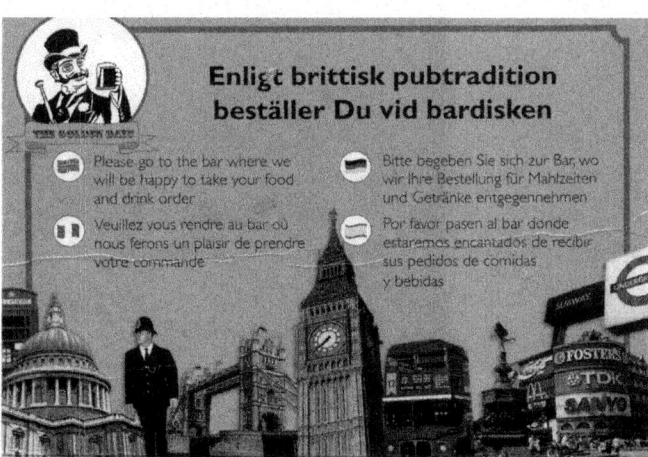

The Swedish text at the top reads 'According to British pub tradition, you order at the bar'.

The text below also represents a notion of British cultural traditions, this time in the form of afternoon tea. This is an older tradition associated with wealthier social groups with the leisure time to take a meal at about 3pm, consisting of sandwiches and cakes (including scones, a type of cake) accompanied by tea to drink.

Both texts present British culture in a deeply traditional way, the first involving images of London from a former time and the second a playful description of ritualised behaviour: 'raising one's pinkie' refers to extending the little finger when holding a teacup, a supposed mark of refinement. 'La-di-da-ness' suggests people putting on a performance of being from a higher social class. The texts are about a notion of Britishness – valuing tradition, being overly concerned with social class – rather than particularly addressing British readers, or coming from British sources (Radisson Blu was formerly owned by Scandinavian Airlines). Discourses about different cultural groups don't necessarily involve the respective groups at all; they can be stories told about them and exchanged by others.

Text 34.2

AFTERNOON TEA

The text reads

'"PARTICIPANTS MUST MAINTAIN THEIR LA-DI-DA-NESS WHILE SCOFFING SCONES AND GOBBLING TURKEY SANDWICHES, EXTENDING ONE'S PINKIE AS ONE SIPS ONE'S TEA IS COMPULSORY.'

ANALYSING CULTURAL REPRESENTATIONS

Below are two further texts where a particular cultural group is being represented by others. Both are from UK publications, and both play with language use and images that are associated with the group in question.

Text: Times Higher is the front page of a monthly magazine aimed at university staff. The article being referred to inside the magazine concerns the plan by Dutch universities to produce more specialist students.

Text: clas ohlson is an advert from a free UK newspaper called *Metro*. A version of this newspaper is published in many different European countries, each edition being tailored every day to the particular country in question. The text is advertising a new Swedish shop (similar to IKEA) that is opening in Leeds, UK.

How do the writers of the texts use language and images to represent the different cultural groups?

TIMES HIGHER

Text 34.4

CLAS OHLSON

There is a commentary on this activity at the end of Part III.

34.2 GENDERED DISCOURSES: WHAT ARE 'HE' AND 'SHE' LIKE?

Throughout this book, discourses – repeatedly talking and writing about people and things in particular ways – have been seen as powerful in constructing our notions of reality, of 'how things are'.

In the Grammar section in Part II, you saw how choices of particular verb structure – specifically transitive and intransitive constructions – can paint very different pictures of how men and women are supposed to be. In considering the difference between a text and a discourse, we need to show that a pattern of depiction extends beyond a single text or genre, recurring in different contexts and adding to an overall representation.

Language and gender isn't just about women, or about how men and women interact on the pages of romantic fiction aimed at female readers. Even in such fiction, although the stereotyping of women is more obvious, there are powerful constructions of masculinity too – men are seen as powerful, assertive, sexually expert and dominant. Just because these qualities might be seen as more positive doesn't make them any less stereotypical. Also, the fact that men might not read romantic stories doesn't change things: we saw in the previous unit that ideas about groups can be exchanged without the involvement of the group being depicted. So you could see romantic fiction as a discourse exchanged between women about stereotypical masculinity, as well as femininity.

Of course, men also receive projections of ideal masculine identities from sources of material that are aimed at them, and in recent years, depictions of masculinity have become more mainstream as they have been seen as an untapped market in consumer cultures. Regardless of the genre being analysed, discourses of gender are also intertwined with those of sexuality; idealised depictions of both men and women are often 'heteronormative', where the figures involved are assumed to be heterosexual.

ANALYSING A GENDERED DISCOURSE

In the romantic fiction text you studied earlier, the male figure was constructed as active, affecting the (female) object of his romantic interest both physically and psychologically. But what if there is no obvious person in the frame, for a male figure to act upon? Can a depiction of active, powerful masculinity still be produced via the language choices in evidence in the text?

Look at the text overleaf, which is the front cover of an edition of *Men's Health*, a popular magazine in the UK aimed at male readers and with a mid-range price tag.

- Is there evidence of the same verb structures you studied in the Grammar section of Part II? Try to identify any transitive verbs and think about how they work.
- The front cover includes many imperative structures (expressions that give orders). To what extent is this a characteristic of magazines in general, or do you see this as part of a gendered discourse?
- The title of the magazine suggests a semantic field of health. How is health defined by the lexis used in the text?
- How do the graphological aspects of this text, including the image, contribute to its overall message?
- How would you describe both the nature of the text's narrator (the voice addressing you) and that of the narratee (the person supposedly being addressed)?
- There are many examples of the use of numbers in this text. Why do you think that is? Are there other discourses being referenced here, and if so, what are they?
- Are there presumptions of sexuality as well as messages about gender in how this text might be understood?

Activity 34.2

 Text 34.5

MEN'S HEALTH

There is a commentary on this activity at the end of Part III.

CHAPTER 35

Dialogues

Genre and intertextuality

35.1 WHAT IS A GENRE?

In the previous unit you were starting to think about the relationship between single texts and the larger system of discourse that each single text helps to construct. The term 'genre', like 'discourse', also refers to a system. However, in the case of genre, the system is based on types of text and not necessarily on the topic or ideas contained within it. For example, magazines constitute a genre, or text type (see McLaughlin 2001), as do birthday cards, junk mail, and social media sites.

Genres are different from discourses because a discourse can be composed of many genres. For example, in thinking about gendered discourses, you might cross many genres – and you did so, in going beyond romantic fiction to think about magazines and other types of text.

Genre names describe the different types of communication that are in circulation at any one time within a society, and these labels tend to be associated with a particular function or goal. For example, some texts are directly selling goods, as is the case with many pieces of advertising. However, there are many other functions too: birthday cards reflect a particular custom in some cultures of marking the day an individual came into the world; gravestones can be seen as marking departures. Genres can be spoken as well as written, or a mixture of forms. A political speech and an exchange at the supermarket checkout are both genres, as is a digital post containing writing, images, and speech.

Different cultures vary in the socially significant texts they have as part of their communicative repertoires. Also, genres change through time, they are not fixed or unalterable: the term 'social media site' had to be invented to describe a new form of communication; the term 'email' used the idea of the postal service to describe a new kind of electronic posting; the term 'junk mail' created a new sub-genre, of mass circulation paper-based mail that was of little value. The latter reminds us that genres clearly vary in how they are valued across any culture.

> **Activity 35.1**
>
> **GENRES**
>
> Make a list of all the different genres you can think of, then discuss the following:
>
> - Which genres do you habitually use in your everyday life?
> - Which genres are most and least valued in your culture?
> - Which genres are promoted and assessed in the education system?
> - Which genres will be the most important in the years ahead, and what skills will they require in their communicators?

35.2 INTERTEXTUALITY

Texts and genres do not exist in watertight categories. It is important to remember that genre labels are socially produced, which means that people can have different opinions about how to define them. A text can be seen as part of a particular genre by one person, but not by another. For example, one person might regard an image on their t-shirt as a piece of art, or a church billboard as an informative poster, while another person might see both these texts primarily as a form of advertising.

Texts themselves are also not necessarily 'pure' in the sense that they belong just to one category. In terms of purposes, a text can be both informative and persuasive: think of a university prospectus, or a clothes catalogue. It can also contain many references to other texts, a phenomenon identified earlier as 'intertextuality'.

Intertextuality can be a useful strategy to harness the power of other texts and achieve a connection with particular target groups. We saw in the previous activity that there were some connections between a textual representation of masculinity and an idea of scientific knowledge. Intertextuality can act like a badge of group membership. It can also be used to invoke genres that are seen as powerful in society as a whole because they are associated with influential individuals or groups such as (in Western cultures) scientists or lawyers.

Intertextuality can operate in complex and different ways, sometimes even within a single communication context. For example, the billboard below, displayed in an airport, was advertising the shopping facilities by imitating the style of flight departure screens. Another text in the same series announced FINAL CALL: FOR CHRISTMAS SHOPPING:

GO TO: GREAT CHRISTMAS DEALS

Text 35.1

In contemporary times where traditional paper-based texts or those such as the billboard above exists alongside electronic resources, analysing how the different modes operate is an intertextual activity in its own right.

This complexity is illustrated by the digital material available at the web address below. The material is a tourist guide compiled by Wrexham Council, in Wales, a part of the UK that still has significant numbers of Welsh language users as well as bilingual speakers of Welsh and English.

The site creators have taken what was a paper-based text and turned it into a digital version. You can see the whole guide by clicking on the 'Hello World' Visitor's Guide, or if you prefer, just read it online.

https://www.wrexham.gov.uk/english/leisure_tourism/publications/real_wrexham.htm

Activity 35.3

HELLO WORLD

Answer the questions below by writing some notes on each, then turn your notes into an analytical essay. The title of the essay should be 'Hello World: A text analysis of a digital tourist guide'. If you work your way through the questions one by one, you will find that a possible structure for your essay will emerge. Of course, you are also free to cover the points in a different order and make your own essay plan:

- How would you describe the language of the narrator on the opening page? (Hello World – Visitor's Guide). What kind of narratee is constructed by the language choices in the text?
- Focusing on both the opening page and on the Guide itself, identify all the digital features that have been incorporated into the pages and explain how those features shape the way you read the text. Has the fact that the guide was originally a paper booklet limited or distorted the electronic version?
- What semiotic aspects of the material are significant?
- Summarise the overall purpose of the guide – what (and who) is it for? What different areas of Wrexham life are covered? How are each of the sections introduced, and what images sit alongside the language used?
- Focus on a particular aspect or section, and analyse the language in detail. Concentrate on the lexical and semantic features of the text and explain the choice of any significant words and phrases. What grammatical features would you highlight as contributing to the way the text works? What pragmatic assumptions are at work in the text? Are there any aspects of sound symbolism in evidence and, if so, why are they there?
- What advantages and disadvantages are there for Wrexham Council in placing the guide online? Think about ideas of physical placement and about any temporal factors involved.

35.3 REVIEW YOUR SKILLS

Write a response, in a formal essay style, to each of the following:

1. Discuss the importance of space and time in analysing the context of texts.
2. Define the concepts of 'narrator' and 'narratee'. Why are these concepts important in analysing texts?
3. Explain the difference between a 'text' and a 'discourse'. Choose a particular discourse and explore how it is constructed, how it works and how it is maintained.

4. 'Genres are not easy to define and they are also not fixed.' Discuss this statement.
5. Assess the importance of intertextuality in text analysis work.

35.4 IDEAS FOR ASSIGNMENTS

35.4.1 Gender

In the Grammar section of Part II you were asked to research romantic stories in order to consider how men and women are portrayed. Now look further than this one type of writing and collect and analyse other types of material. Your analysis should explore the idea of gendered/sexualised discourses, and how language choices in texts construct particular identities. Choose a specific focus, for example:

- Texts that are often read by men, or which appear to be aimed at them.
- Texts that are seen as general readership (such as some newspapers), but focusing just on how male figures are portrayed. For example, here is an image from a Scandinavian edition of the *Metro* newspaper (referred to earlier) which offers a very different image of masculinity from the Men's Health picture:

SCANDINAVIAN METRO

Text 35.2

- Texts that come into our homes, texts that are seen in local shops or texts that we often interact with: for example, catalogues, junk mail, cards of various kinds, social media sites and other forms of digital communication. How are men and women constructed in these texts, and how do they construct themselves?

35.4.2 Cultural representations

Pick a cultural group or place with which you are familiar, and collect and analyse some representations from sources such as travel literature, textbooks, prose fiction, news reports, magazines and websites.

Think about whose perspective the texts are written from, where the texts were placed, and when they were written.

Think about the narrative figures involved – who is narrating the texts, and what assumptions are made about the narratee(s)?

To what extent do the texts contribute to particular discourses about people and places?

35.4.3 Intertextuality

Find some texts that use genres in interesting ways, or that include aspects of intertextuality as part of their message. Explore how different groups interpret the texts you have collected. Write up your results in the form of an analytical essay.

35.5 COMMENTARIES FOR PART III

Activity 32.1

INSTRUCTION

The activity is hairdressing. The instructor is teaching the apprentice the skills of cutting hair. Deictics include 'this', 'that', 'here', 'these', 'it', 'you', 'top', 'front'.

Activity 32.6

NOVEL OPENINGS

Ordinary Thunderstorms
The deictic term 'there' positions the narrator as a spectator of the scene, which is specified as a river, then as the Thames at Chelsea Bridge. The narrator talks to a fictional addressee as if he or she were standing nearby, saying 'let us start', 'let's wait' and 'look', as if the addressee was physically present and sharing the perspective.

The spatial movement of the opening starts at the macro-level perspective of the river, then zooms in to focus on the man, naming him and giving extensive details about his attire as well as explanations of his situation, and ends with a micro-level focus on the corner trim of his briefcase.

NOVEL OPENINGS *(continued)*

61 Hours

A character identified as 'the lawyer' is introduced early on but it is quite a while before the idea of a prison is referenced. There is a sense of the lawyer visiting an organisation of some kind because of the reference to the 'empty lot', but it is not until the prison guards are mentioned that it is clear what kind of institution it is. Details of the weather suggest a bleakness that is strengthened by the repetition of 'empty', and 'nothing'. The fact that the lawyer puts overshoes on indicates a carefulness, and the narrator's representation of the character's binary view of the world suggests a sense of order and boundaries. There are 'sides' created by the characters' respective occupations as well as the sides demarcated by the X-ray machine and the metal detector. However, this order is clearly about to be challenged.

Times Higher

The image and the language work together to represent the Dutch as cultivating 'prize specimens'. This phrase is ambiguous and the ambiguity is reflected in the image. It refers to tulips, which the Dutch are famous for growing. These are not just any old tulips, though – they are rare specimens, the kinds of flowers that were bought and sold for high prices during Holland's 'tulipmania' in the seventeenth century. Many of these flowers were painted at the time by Dutch artists, and the image suggests an oil painting, with figures depicted in rich clothes (but with tulips instead of heads). The costumes could also be referring intertextually to academic dress, in its often overblown and antique decoration.

The phrase 'blooming marvellous' is also deliberately ambiguous and polysemantic. Flowers 'bloom', so 'blooming' could refer to the tulips – but 'blooming' is also used in the UK as a mild swear word, to replace 'bloody', so the phrase could be acting as a form of praise for what Dutch universities are planning to do – that is, grow students who are 'prize specimens', specialists in their field of study.

clas ohlson

The whole text is written in lower case, with no punctuation, suggesting an unconventional approach, a creative overturning of old ways. The use of lower case could be connected with the store's own name – clas ohlson – which is itself written in lower case. Even the proper nouns Swedes and Leeds are not exempted from the text's rule-breaking. The idea of treating everyone the same, of making no concessions to wealth and status, is something that people in the UK associate with Swedish culture. The Swedish store IKEA has a reputation for producing affordable furniture for mass consumption.

clas ohlson *(continued)*

Activity 34.1

The language constructs a very plain-speaking, straightforward message, but uses English that has been given a Swedish 'makeover' in its use of a diacritic mark, double letters and a compound word – 'usefulshöpp'. This remains understandable to readers of English while also suggesting Swedishness. Because UK residents have been exposed to some Swedish via their experience of IKEA, clas ohlson is able to take a chance on using this artificial form. However, it does resemble real aspects of Swedish language, which sometimes uses this mark on the vowel 'o' and which also uses double letters where English would have a single one – for example, in the Swedish word 'hotell'.

Activity 34.2

Men's Health

There are many uses of transitive verbs denoting physical action – 'lose 9kg', 'detox', 'burn' calories, 'make' 2013, 'build' arms, 'press' here, 'shift' fat – suggesting that masculinity is all about doing things rather than being in certain states of mind or feeling things. Imperative structures tend to feature strongly in magazines for both sexes because these publications are often about self-improvement, but they are particularly noticeable here, perhaps because of the active nature of the verbs. They produce a dominant-sounding narrator who doesn't tolerate failure, and a narratee who is clearly in need of direction.

Health is represented as strength and physical power, as being athletic – 'strong, lean & fast'. It is also associated with looking good, which means having muscular arms, no fat, six-pack abs and looking like famous figures from action movies. The magazine's version of health is represented as easily achievable: one hundred reps can build 20% more muscle; fifteen minutes a day will achieve six-pack abs; nineteen pills can get rid of fat; even mind-blowing sex is achievable by pressing a 'button'.

The very specific nature of the numbers and various quantifications add to the assured nature of the narrative – it suggests knowledge and scientific expertise, proven results. Target sights and tick boxes suggest aims and achievements, the kinds of self-assessment sheets that are used in gyms during workouts. The magazine rates itself as '100% useful'.

Although the definition of masculinity in both the language and the images is very narrow here, it cannot be directly associated with either heterosexual or gay identities, although the idea of sexual orientation in terms of desired other would be clarified on page 61 of the magazine.

A checklist for text analysis

> *This is a basic starter kit which is designed only in order to enable first steps and first observations to be made. Many features, including some covered in the book, are not included here.*

FIRST QUESTIONS ABOUT A TEXT

- What do you notice?
- How does the text affect you?
- Where did the text come from?
- What type of text is it? What is the text for?
- How do you initially interpret the text? What is your first response to it?

TEXT, TEXTURE AND IMAGE

- What is the initial impact made by the shape and texture of text on the page: print size? pictures and images? drawings? type of font? signs and symbols? camera angles? colour? movement (in the case of video or digital texts)?
- What is in the background/foreground? What is the balance of print to pictures or images? Are there parallels and patterns in the text? Are patterns broken with and deviated from?
- What is not in the text that might be expected?

VOCABULARY, GRAMMAR AND DISCOURSE

Vocabulary

- What is the balance of lexical and grammatical words? Are there word families in the text?
- Are the words and phrases specialised or general? If specialised, what semantic field is being used and why?

- What connotations are suggested by the words? Are the meanings more literal or more indirect and pragmatic in meaning?
- What kinds of patterns are created by the words? Are there parallels and repetitions? Are there synonyms and antonyms, metaphors and metonymies? Are any patterns broken?
- What level of formality is suggested by the lexical choices made?
- What is the nature of the cohesion (lexical and grammatical) made in the text? What is the role of conjunctions and discourse markers? Are they more formal or more 'spoken' and conversational?
- Are there any expected features of vocabulary that are not in the text?

Grammar

- What is the effect of grammatical words? Look first for smaller grammatical words – for example, definite/indefinite articles? Pronouns/personal and possessive pronouns/plural and singular?
- What kind of deictic expressions are there? Are they temporal, spatial, social?
- How many adjectives are used and what point of view do they convey?
- What kinds of nouns are used? Are they mainly abstract or concrete? How complex are the noun phrases?
- What tenses are used? Is the text mainly in the active or the passive voice?
- What kinds of verbs are used – action verbs? verbs of perception and cognition? Are the verbs mainly transitive or intransitive? Are modal verbs and modal expressions used? Are the modal verbs used for control and regulation, for permission, for possibility, for obligation?
- What kinds of sentences are there in the text? Short or long sentences? Finite or non-finite?
- Are there mostly statements? Are there any imperatives? How many questions are there?
- Does the text mainly consist of main clauses? Are there many subordinate clauses? Is the clause structure more complex or more simple in structure? Is ellipsis common?
- What level of formality is suggested by the grammatical structures used?
- Are there any expected features of grammar that are not in the text?

Discourse(s)

- To what extent are words, phrases and grammatical structures used to reveal and conceal ideologies?
- What is the point of view of the text? What beliefs and values are revealed? Do you accept or resist the point of view?
- Are there any intertextual references? Does the text remind you of other texts that express similar views about the topic?

Sound, speech and dialogue

- How many speakers are there? What are the speakers using language for? What kind of genre or speech event are the speakers engaged in?
- Is the talk spontaneous or planned? Is it part of a routine or freely composed? Are the speakers using one language or are they code-mixing and switching?
- Who initiates speaking turns, who holds the floor and for how long? Is the speaker male or female? Who controls the topic?
- Are there interruptions, overlaps or pauses in the exchanges? Who interrupts? What terms of address are used?
- Are there (in video texts) any obvious paralinguistic features and is there any evidence of facial or bodily gestures?
- What are the most noticeable sound patterns? What are the similar and dissimilar sounds? Is there rhyme and are there patterns such as alliteration and assonance? Do vowel and consonant sounds cluster in particular ways?
- How is sound represented on the written page? Are accents and dialects represented?
- Is there anything which is missing or unexpected?

Digital text

- What are the affordances and limitations of the communication tool?
- Is the text interactive and interpersonal, or more of an individual or corporate one-way product? If it is interactive, do both participants have the same tools or different ones?
- How do the different possible modes of communication relate to each other? Do some characteristics of the text resemble conventional writing and, if so, which?
- Are there any aspects of the environment that resemble the spoken context and, if so, which?
- Are there aspects of the text that are nothing like former modes of communication?

NEXT STEPS

> Continue by reading (looking, listening) several more times, increasing observations of the forms, functions and meanings of language and image and developing interpretations of them.

Corpus resources and projects

This section includes some guidance on available corpora that you might want to use in your assignments or as a part of further studies in corpus-based language exploration. There are many different corpora available around the world, and although the most common language is British and American English, there are corpora in different Englishes and several in many other world languages too. Most corpora are up-to-date and are drawn from contemporary language sources, others have been compiled in the past twenty to thirty years, and some are more historically based and give information about language change over time.

Some of these corpora are owned by publishers for their own research and access is not normally allowed, but other corpora allow free downloads. Some corpora may need to be bought by individuals or by a school or library, and some allow all their material or at least selected samples to be used online for student research projects. Not all corpora web addresses remain constant, but general Google searches will usually reveal relevant details and information about access.

EXAMPLES OF CORPORA

Corpus of Contemporary American English (COCA) - 450 million words of American English. - The Corpus of Contemporary American English (COCA) is the largest freely-available corpus of English, and the only large and balanced corpus of American English. The corpus is equally divided among spoken discourse, fiction, popular magazines, newspapers, and academic texts. It includes twenty million words for each year from 1990 to 2012, and the corpus is also updated regularly.	http://corpus.byu.edu/coca/

The Corpus of **Glo**bal **W**eb-**B**ased **E**nglish **(GloWbE)** ■ This is composed of almost two billion words from 1.8 million web pages in twenty different English-speaking countries around the world. GloWbE is pronounced like "globe" and is linked to the 450-million-word Corpus of Contemporary American English (COCA) (see above) and the 400-million-word Corpus of Historical American English (COHA). All three corpora are housed at Brigham Young University in the USA and sections of them are available for free download and/or more general access.	http://corpus.byu.edu/glowbe/
British National Corpus (BNC) 100 million words of English consisting of: ■ A written part (90%) including newspapers, periodicals and journals, books, letters and memoranda, essays etc. ■ A spoken part (10%) includes conversation, recorded in a demographically balanced way, as well as a range of spoken language from business or government meetings to radio shows and phone-ins etc.	http://www.natcorp.ox.ac.uk/what/index.html
Hong Kong PolyU Language Bank ■ The PolyU Language Bank, developed in the Department of English at Hong Kong PolyU, is a large archive of language corpora made up of a wide range of written and spoken texts totalling over 12 million words. Corpus searches can be performed using the Bank's built-in web-based concordancer, enabling the easy use of corpus resources for language learning and research.	http://langbank.engl.polyu.edu.hk/indexl.html

Wellington Corpus of Spoken New Zealand English (WSC) ■ 1 million words of spoken New Zealand English collected in the years 1988 to 1994. ■ The corpus consists of 2,000 word extracts and comprises different proportions of formal, semi-formal and informal speech. Both monologue and dialogue categories are included, and there is broadcast as well as private material collected in a range of settings. ■ 75% percent of the corpus is informal dialogue.	http://www.victoria.ac.nz/lals/resources/corpora-default/corpora-wsc
Vienna-Oxford International Corpus of English (VOICE) ■ VOICE is a one-million-word corpus of English as it is spoken by non-native-speaking users in different contexts. These speakers use English successfully on a daily basis all over the world, in their personal, professional or academic lives. The VOICE team sees these users not as language learners but as language users in their own right. The VOICE project has run from 2005 to 2013 and may be extended. ■ The speakers recorded in VOICE are experienced **ELF (English as a lingua franca)** speakers from a wide range of first language backgrounds. VOICE includes approximately 1250 ELF speakers with approximately fifty different first languages (disregarding varieties of the respective languages). In the initial phase VOICE focuses mainly, though not exclusively, on European ELF speakers. ■ Interactions are recorded in a variety of settings including professional, educational, informal, functions (exchanging information, enacting social relationships), and with different participants' roles and relationships (acquainted vs. unacquainted, more socially powerful vs. less socially powerful).	http://www.univie.ac.at/voice/

International Corpus of English (ICE)	http://ice-corpora.net/ICE/INDEX.HTM
<ul><li>The International Corpus of English (ICE) began in 1990 with the primary aim of collecting material for comparative studies of English worldwide.</li><li>Each ICE corpus consists of one million words of spoken and written English produced after 1989.</li><li>To ensure compatibility among the component corpora, each team is following a common corpus design, as well as a common scheme for grammatical annotation.</li></ul>	ICE Great Britain http://www.ucl.ac.uk/english-usage/ice/icegb.htm ICE East Africa http://www.ucl.ac.uk/english-usage/ice/iceea.htm ICE India http://www.ucl.ac.uk/english-usage/ice/iceind.htm ICE New Zealand http://www.ucl.ac.uk/english-usage/ice/icenz.htm ICE Philippines http://www.ucl.ac.uk/english-usage/ice/icephil.htm ICE Singapore http://www.ucl.ac.uk/english-usage/ice/icesin.htm ICE Ireland http://www.qub.ac.uk/ice-ireland

A FIRST STEP TOWARDS CORPUS-BASED LANGUAGE PROJECTS

A corpus-based language project can involve you in more extended research into words, phrases and larger stretches of language. Here are some first steps that can help you to start such projects.

- Begin by selecting a word or linguistic feature that you find either interesting or problematic. It may also be a feature that is striking in a text because of its typography, layout or use of colour.
- Conduct a literature review on the selected linguistic feature by reading, for example, books, book chapters or online articles that report on some corpus linguistics research studies. The bibliography and references at the end of this book can help, but see in particular Cheng (2011) which offers a very practical guide. Then write a summary of the reading, discussing how useful it is for your own project.

- Develop a research question or questions, giving a clear and logical rationale for the choice of linguistic feature, supported by what the literature says or doesn't say about it.
- Either compile your own corpus of 20,000 to 40,000 words, or use a ready-made corpus. In addition, you might want to use a large multi-million-word reference corpus, for example, the British National Corpus or the Corpus of Contemporary American English (see previous pages), to make sure that your corpus is benchmarked against a larger, more comprehensive and balanced corpus – depending, of course, on the purpose and research question(s) of your own project.
- The project can be done in a group or individually. You might like to share the compilation of the corpus but do your own individual study.
- When you report on the study that you have conducted, for example in the form of an oral presentation and a written report, make sure that your description, interpretation and explanation of the findings have clear reference to the research question(s) of your study and that your conclusions take full account of how language works across whole texts, including such features of texts as image, page design and layout, colour, typography and the many other textual features covered in this book.

EXAMPLE: CONCORDANCE SEARCH

You will find another example of the kind of research you can do using a corpus in Part 1 pp22–3. In that example we looked at the differences between the uses of the words *chat* and *discussion* and we used the Collins COBUILD sample corpus.

Here is an example of the kind of search that is possible using a concordance of a very common word, in this case the word *eye*. Here we can begin to see differences between singular and plural forms of a word (here, eye vs. eyes). This case is illustrated below with a random sample of concordance lines taken from the COBUILD Concordance and Collocation Sampler (http://www.collins.co.uk/Corpus/CorpusSearch.aspx).

CONCORDANCE 1

Sample concordance lines for *eye* from the online Cobuild Concordance and Collocation Sampler

1. the Field Director keeps an **eye** on its progress, and when our
2. been adopted in several **eye** hospitals. [p] [p] Other studies have
3. was a gleam in his visceral **eye**. Christian Slater plays Clarence
4. focusing, individual right- **eye** focusing to adjust to the user's

5.   fat on thighs and buttocks is **eye** -watering even to contemplate.
6.   Under the benevolent **eye** of this Celtic talisman, Nicholas has
7.   to ridicule them in the public **eye** AND win a G SHIRT in the process.
8.   admitted that he had his **eye** on Cromack's figure, but it was not
9.   chosen by the discerning **eye** of leading art critics, including the
10.   writing. [p] The trained **eye** may find some comparison
11.   Union does not see quite **eye** to eye with Jordan on this. Recent
12.   and doesn't get his batting **eye** back before August. Both the
13.   so he naturally kept his **eye** on you. When you hadn't come out
14.   There are three types of **eye** , the first being the [f] stream [f]
15. of her created by the Private **Eye** satirists in general, and 'Mrs
16.   John Chapman-Smith, an **eye** surgeon from New Zealand, and
17. I was pleased to discover an **eye** -witness account of them written
18.   she and her father still see **eye** to eye on immigration. [p] Providing
19.   two don't exactly see eye to **eye**. I'm putting them together. They'll
20.   has not sampled a newt's **eye**, but she has found prescriptions
21.   a camel to pass through the **eye** of a needle to enter the kingdom of
22.   were glued under my left **eye** and jaw to exaggerate my bags
23. re-introduce free dental and **eye** checks. [p] Opt-out hospitals and
24.   seat. [p] The 48-year-old **eye** patient parked the ageing Morris
25.   6-3, 6-3, 6-2. [p] [h] Dallas **eye** up double; American Football [/h]
26.   Missed [/sh] [p] Nick's shut- **eye** sit-in meant he missed his shift as a
27.   pink bow that caught his **eye**. [p] He chased the kidnapper 100
28.   no longer much in the public **eye**. Although [f] Three Years in Tibet [f]
29.   as Ar-Ex or vaseline in the **eye** area. When You Wake Up Repeat
30.   ceiling. It looked like a blind **eye**. Lainey stepped over to it and swung

CONCORDANCE 2

Sample concordance lines for *eyes* from the online Cobuild Concordance and Collocation Sampler

1.   Innocent people having their **eyes** gouged out. Children tortured in
2.   Miller viewed through the **eyes** of the two women who knew him
3.   Of Love or Love In Your **Eyes** he reaches ever lower plateaux
4.   it destroyed in front of your **eyes**. You haven't got nothing, you
5.   -pale lips with deep, dark **eyes**. Try Givenchy's new Onyx Prism
6.   the tropics as well. Well, our **eyes** for this view of Brazil – because
7.   it, Fritz?" [p] The man's cool **eyes** betrayed nothing, no remorse for
8.   aping from her nurse's cap, **eyes** shining: she really was delicious.
9.   the top of his bald head. His **eyes** were bright, though, and swept

10.	ound his muffler slowly, his	**eyes**	fixed on the menu which had be
11.	[p] Ah, Christ, Stein thought,	**eyes**	hurting from too much reading st
12.	ached to their mothers. Right	**eyes**	denote characteristics inherited f
13.	this picture out through her	**eyes**	until she saw it perching on the
14.	awake, and there were two	**eyes**	in there, staring at me. Well, we'll
15.	She searched his watery	**eyes**,	attempting to find the truth; they
16.	ice, panting and crossing his	**eyes**	to make himself look like an imb
17.	ore pinched faces, sightless	**eyes**,	stumps of limbs and ragged clot
18.	son hissed without taking his	**eyes**	off Marlette. Dennison hurried do
19.	I can steer this thing with my	**eyes**	closed [p] But Baz chose Charlie,
20.	well tie a towel around your	**eyes**	and set off. [p] [p] Does that mea
21.	autumn, Rousseau has his	**eyes**	on breaking it, though he is not s
22.	by his fabulous bright blue	**eyes**.	They looked at each other and it
23.	ard Steve Hyett opened his	**eyes**.	In a hazy blur he could see his wi
24.	to wear a wig. [p] Ol' Blue	**Eyes**	sneaked in at the side door on th
25.	about its business. Such new	**"eyes"**	exist, fortunately, and they are w
26.	secretary. Frannie hadn't laid	**eyes**	on her for at least four years. Sin
27.	He sighed and closed his	**eyes**.	Wonder what Gladys engraved o
28.	stumbling against a wall, her	**eyes**	transfixed with terror. [p] Eva, let
29.	skein of wrinkles around his	**eyes**.	He was perhaps only seven or ei
30.	But she couldn't take her	**eyes**	away from Joe. "Now," he told he

From a basic first step examination of these concordance lines (just thirty random lines in each case) we can see that there are two main meanings associated with the words *eye* (singular) and *eyes* (plural). One (concordance 2) is to do with the "organ of sight" (e.g. *his fabulous bright blue eyes*) and the other (concordance 1), which has less to do with the eye as a visual organ, is more directly metaphorical and involves checking and monitoring things (e.g. *Under the benevolent eye of this Celtic talisman*), with "critical examination" (*Tibet was no longer much in the public eye*) and with considering different "various points of view" (*The Soviet Union does not quite see eye to eye with Jordan*).

This kind of investigation of metaphorical and figurative extensions to the meanings of parts of the body is also suggested as a possible assignment (see Part II p120). For further reading and discussion of lines such as these see Sinclair (2003, especially pp. 167–172).

Another interesting assignment using concordance lines in a corpus is to investigate the semantic profile of words and phrases (see Part II p107). For example, the following words are said to have a negative ('unpleasant' or 'unfavourable') semantic prosody. For each case, investigate whether this is true:

be bent on   commit   dealings   make off with   peddle symptomatic

> The above guidance relates to more formal classroom or course-based projects. Don't forget that you can also do any number of informal searches using corpora – many of these searches will help you learn a lot about how language works in texts.

KEY READING

Biber, D., Conrad, S and Reppen, R. (1998). *Corpus Linguistics: Investigating language structure and use.* Cambridge: CUP.

Cheng, W. (2011). *Exploring Corpus Linguistics: Language in Action.* London: Routledge.

McEnery, T. and Hardie, A. (2011). *Corpus Linguistics: Method, Theory and Practice.* Cambridge: CUP.

Sinclair, J. (2003). *Reading Concordances.* Harlow: Pearson.

References

PART II

Section A

Bourdieu, P. (1991). *Language and Symbolic Power.* Cambridge, Mass.: Harvard University Press.
Boyd, W. (2009). *Ordinary Thundersorms.* Bloomsbury.
Chandler, D. (1998). 'Personal Home Pages and the Construction of Identities on the Web.' Available at: http://www.aber.ac.uk/media/Documents/short/webident.html [Accessed 10 June 2015].
Chandler, D. (2004). *Semiotics: The Basics.* London: Routledge.
Fox, K. (2005). *Watching the English: The Hidden Rules of English Behaviour.* London: Hodder & Stoughton.
Goddard, A. (2005). *Being Online.* University of Nottingham PhD thesis.
Goffman, E. (1981). *Forms of Talk.* Oxford: Blackwell.

Section B

Baker, P. (2008). "Eligible' bachelors and 'frustrated' spinsters': Corpus linguistics, gender and language", in J. Sunderland, K. Harrington and H. Sauntson (Eds.). *Gender and Language Research Methodologies.* Basingstoke: Palgrave Macmillan.
Firth, J. R. (1957). 'Modes of meaning'. *Papers in Linguistics 1934–1951.* London: Oxford University Press, pp. 190–215.
Goddard, A. and Mean, L. (2009). (2nd edn.). *Language and Gender.* London: Routledge.
Herriman, J. (1998). 'Descriptions of *woman* and *man* in present-day English, *Moderna Sprak* XCII (2): 136–42.

Section C

Thurlow, C. (2003). 'Generation Txt? The sociolinguistics of young people's text-messaging'. *Discourse Analysis Online.* Available at: http://extra.shu.ac.uk/daol/articles/v1/n1/a3/thurlow2002003.html [Accessed 10 June 2015].

PART III

Child, L. (2010) *61 Hours*. Bantam.
Goddard, A. (1998). *The Language of Advertising: Written Texts*. London: Routledge.
Goddard, A. and Geesin, B. (2011). *Language and Technology*. London: Routledge.
Jenkins, J. (2009). *World Englishes: A resource book for students*. London: Routledge.
McLaughlin, L. (2001). *The Language of Magazines*. London: Routledge.
Saraceni, M. (2010). *The Relocation of English*. London: Palgrave.

Links to online references

See *Corpus resources and projects* for further links to language corpora.

Please also see the Routledge companion website for this book, at www.routledge.com/cw/goddard, where these links and any updates also feature.

PART I

Men's clothes shops:
The Throttleman
www.throttleman.es

Pull & Bear
www.pullandbear.com

Paul and Shark
www.paulandshark.it

British Library archive of historical recipe books. This page will take you to Richard II's recipe for a 'tostee' (toasted sandwich), but there are many more texts you can explore:
http://www.bl.uk/learning/langlit/booksforcooks/med/tosteehome/curytostee.html

The British National Corpus (BNC):
http://www.natcorp.ox.ac.uk

Michelle Obama's speech at the Democratic Convention, 2012:
http://www.npr.org/2012/09/04/160578836/transcript-michelle-obamas-convention-speech

Links to transcription notations:
University of Loughborough
http://homepages.lboro.ac.uk/~ssca1/notation.htm

Sean Rintel's page
http://seanrintel.com/key1/

Harvard referencing guide (Cite It Right):
http://www.otago.ac.nz/library/pdf/harvard_citeitright.pdf

PART II

Section A

Independent newspaper article about the use of mobile phones in shops:
http://www.independent.co.uk/news/uk/home-news/is-it-rude-to-pay-up-while-talking-on-your-phone-dont-all-call-at-once-8683927.html

Fred Benenson's 'translation' of *Moby Dick* into the language of graphic symbols called 'emoji':
http://www.smithsonianmag.com/arts-culture/text-me-ishmael-reading-moby-dick-emoji-180949825/?no-ist

Phonemic chart with clickable symbols and a transcription tool:
http://www.phonemicchart.com

Collection of animal noises in different languages:
http://www.eleceng.adelaide.edu.au/personal/dabbott/animal.html

Section B

British Library 'Texts in Contexts' archive:
http://www.bl.uk/learning/langlit/texts/context.html

United Nations Women (UN Women) website: article about corpus searches and sexism on the web:
http://www.unwomen.org/en/news/stories/2013/10/women-should-ads#sthash.25Smj67N.dpuf

Examples of newspaper obituaries:
http://www.starclassifieds.com/marketplace/category/Announcements/Births
http://www.iannounce.co.uk/Lancaster-Guardian/428/Birth/birth?_fstatus=search
http://www.canadianobituaries.com
http://www.theguardian.com/tone/obituaries
http://www.obituaries.com/ns/obituariescom/oits.aspx

Section C

Archive of political speeches
www.americanrhetoric.com

PART III

Mini Cooper car advertisement
http://www.campaignlive.co.uk/news/1171261/

Visitor Guide to Wrexham
https://www.wrexham.gov.uk/english/leisure_tourism/publications/real_wrexham.htm

Further reading

PART I

The *Intertext* series of books published by Routledge offers many ideas for starting research of your own. Finding a library with a full set of these books and then browsing through them (or looking at them online) will offer you a very wide range of possibilities.

Some examples of *Intertext* books

The Language of Advertising: Written texts
(second edition, 2002) Angela Goddard

Language Change
Adrian Beard

The Language of Children
Julia Gillen

The Language of Comics
Mario Saraceni

Language and Gender
Angela Goddard and Lindsey Meân

The Language of Magazines
Linda McLoughlin

The Language of Newspapers
(second edition, 2002) Danuta Reah

The Language of Politics
Adrian Beard

Language and Region
Joan C. Beal

The Language of Science
Carol Reeves

The Language of Speech and Writing
Sandra Cornbleet and Ronald Carter

The Language of Sport
Adrian Beard

Language and Technology
Angela Goddard and Beverly Geesin

The Language of Television
Jill Marshall and Angela Werndly

The Language of War
Steve Thorne

The Language of Work
Almut Koester

PART II
Graphology and phonology

Chandler, D. (2004). *Semiotics: The Basics*. London: Routledge.
Cobley, P. (2010). *Introducing Semiotics: A graphic guide*. London: Icon Books.
Hughes, A., Trudgill, P. and Watt, D. (2005). *English Accents and Dialects*, 4th edn. London: Hodder Education.
Jaworski, A. and Thurlow, C. (Eds.) (2010). *Semiotic Landscapes: Language, Image, Space*. London and New York: Continuum.
Scollon, R. and Scollon, S. (2003). *Discourses in Place: Language in the Material World*. London: Routledge.
Wells, J. C. (1982). *Accents of English*, volumes 1–3. Cambridge: Cambridge University Press.

Lexis and semantics

Carter, R. (2012). *Vocabulary: Applied Linguistic Perspectives* (3rd ed). London: Routledge.
Cruse, D. (2010). *Meaning in Language: An introduction to semantics and pragmatics*. Oxford: OUP.
Crystal, D. (2012). *The Story of English in 100 Words*. London: Profile Books.
Gardner, D. (2013). *Exploring Vocabulary: Language in Action*. London: Routledge.
Lakoff, G. and Johnson, M. (1980). *Metaphors We Live By*. Chicago, USA: University of Chicago Press.

Grammar and discourse

Carter, R., McCarthy, M., Mark, G. and O'Keeffe, A. (2011). *English Grammar Today: An A-Z of spoken and written grammar*. Cambridge: CUP.

Carter, R. and McCarthy, M. (2006). *Cambridge Grammar of English: A comprehensive guide to spoken and written grammar and usage.* Cambridge: CUP.
Cutting, J. (2014). *Pragmatics: A resource book for students.* London: Routledge.
Halliday, M. A. K. and Hasan, R. (1976). *Cohesion in English.* Harlow: Pearson.
Hewings, A. and Hewings, M. (2005). *Grammar and Context.* London: Routledge.
Jackson, H. (2002). *Grammar and Vocabulary.* London: Routledge.
Swan, M. (2005). *Grammar.* Oxford: OUP.

PART III

Baker, P. (2008). *Sexed Texts: Language, Gender and Sexuality.* London: Equinox.
Carter, R. and McCarthy, M. (1997). *Exploring Spoken English.* Cambridge: CUP.
Cameron, D. (2001). *Working with Spoken Discourse.* London: Sage.
Tagg, C. (2015). *Exploring Digital Communication: Language in Action.* London: Routledge.
Thurlow, C., Tomic, A. and Lengel, L. (2004). *Computer Mediated Communication.* London: Sage.
Thurlow, C. and Jaworski, A. (2010). *Tourism Discourse: Language and Global Mobility.* Basingstoke & New York: Palgrave MacMillan.

FURTHER READING FOR ALL PARTS

Cameron, D. (1995). *Verbal Hygiene.* London: Routledge.
Cameron, D. (2000). *Good to Talk? Living and Working in a Communication Culture.* London: Sage.
Crystal, D. (2003). *The Cambridge Encyclopaedia of the English Language.* Cambridge: CUP.
Gavins, J. (2007) *Text World Theory: An Introduction.* Edinburgh: EUP.
Goddard, A. (2012). *Doing English Language: A guide for students.* London: Routledge.
Jenkins, J. (2014). *Global Englishes: A resource book for students.* London: Routledge.
Llamas, C. and Watt, D. (2010). *Language and Identities.* Edinburgh: Edinburgh University Press.
Saraceni, M. (2010). *The Relocation of English.* London: Palgrave.
Seargeant, P. (2012). *Exploring World Englishes: Language in a global context.* London: Routledge.
Short, M. (1996). *Exploring the Language of Poems, Plays and Prose.* Harlow: Pearson.
Simpson, P. (2014). *Stylistics: A resource book for students.* London: Routledge.
Simpson, P. and Mayr, A. (2009). *Language and Power: A resource book for students.* London: Routledge.
Tannen, D. (1992). *You Just Don't Understand: Men and women in conversation.* London: Virago.
Zhu Hua (2013). *Exploring Intercultural Communication: Language in Action.* London: Routledge.

Glossary/Index

> The text below forms a combined glossary and index. Listed are some of the key terms used in the book, together with brief definitions. They are shown in bold. Not all terms used in the book are glossed here as some of the terms receive extensive explanation in the main book. This is not a complete index of descriptive linguistic and cultural terms, and therefore it should be used in conjunction with other reference books.

accent (p9): accent refers to the sounds people make when they speak. (see also → dialect)

active (p128): (see → voice)

adjective (p89): adjectives describe the qualities of people and things. Words like *rich*, *green*, *old*, *hopeless* are adjectives. An attributive adjective occurs before a noun: *the black box*; a predicative adjective occurs after a verb: *the student is intelligent* (see also → modification)

adverb (p89): an adverb indicates the place, manner, degree or frequency of an event or action. Adverbs have many different functions and can have different positions in a clause. For example: *Unfortunately, we were late for the meeting. The team reacted to the decision angrily*

affixation (p89): the process of adding an affix or morpheme to a word to create a different form of that word (for example: *cat* → *cats*), or to create a new word with a different meaning (*tank* → *tanker*) (see → prefix; suffix)

affordances (p72): things that are made possible. For example, a website can be read by many people simultaneously

anaphoric (p85): (see → reference)

arbitrary (p64): having no real connection beyond that of social convention

article (p83): the definite article is *the* and it commonly refers to things which are known or can be identified. For example: *I'll meet you at the cinema*. The indefinite article is *a/an* and is commonly used to refer to things which are not definite or specific. For example: *Can you lend me a pen?*

association (p21): (see → connotation)

assonance (p68): assonance is created when vowel sounds are repeated to produce internal rhyming within phrases or sentences. For example, *the carts rolled down the old road*.

blend (p92): a blend occurs when shortened forms of words are combined to form a single new word. For example: *smog* (a blend of **sm**oke and f**og**); *blog* (a blend of we**b** and **log**)

bound morpheme (p88): (see → morpheme)

cataphoric (p85): (see → reference)

clause (p133): a clause is part of a sentence. A clause normally consists of a subject and a verb, and a main clause must contain a verb indicating tense (also called a finite clause; see → finite). For example: *I went to Vietnam on holiday* is a main clause. Main clauses can be joined by a co-ordinating conjunction such as *and* or *but*. For example: *We decided not to have a holiday abroad this year and to stay at home.* A subordinate clause cannot normally form a sentence on its own. Subordinate clauses are dependent on main clauses. A main clause and a subordinate clause are commonly joined together with a subordinating conjunction such as *although, because* or *when*. For example: *We decided to take the dog for a walk, although it was raining.* Subordinate clauses can also be non-finite (see → finite). For example: *Entering the hall in a large black hat, she was obviously trying to be the centre of attention.* (see also → sentence)

cohesion (p114): cohesion is a term which describes the patterns of language created within a text, mainly within and across sentence boundaries or speaking turns. Cohesion can be both lexical and grammatical. Lexical cohesion is established by means of chains of words with related meanings linking across utterances and sentences; grammatical cohesion is established mainly by grammatical words such as the, this, it linking across utterances and sentences. It can also be established by ellipsis (see → ellipsis) and substitution. Substitution means that words, phrases and clauses do not need to be repeated. For example, the word *do* can be used to substitute for a verb or verb phrase: A: *Are you going to the match?* B: *I might do.* The word *so* can be used to substitute for a clause: A: *Will Jenn be at the meeting?* B: *I think so* (so here substitutes for 'that Jenn will be at the meeting'). A cohesive text is one in which the smaller lexical and grammatical parts of the text collectively organise the larger units of the text such as paragraphs or conversational turns between speakers.

collocation (p21): a collocation is two or more words that often go together. For example: *lean* and *meat* or *fat* and *cheque* occur together more frequently than by chance and more frequently than other possible patterns and combinations such as 'skinny' and 'meat' or 'heavy' and 'cheque'. Certain words keep closer company with some words than with others

concord/subject verb concord (p183): (see → subject)

concordance line (p21): line of text from a corpus, showing where the searched item occurred within a sentence or utterance

conjunction (p85): a conjunction links words, phrases, clauses and sentences. The two main types of conjunction are coordinating conjunctions and subordinating conjunctions. Coordinating conjunctions are words such as *and* and *but* and they link main clauses. Subordinating conjunctions such as *because, if, when, in order to* link a subordinate clause to a main clause. Some subordinating conjunctions such as *when, while, before, after, until, once, as soon as* are words which link a main clause and a subordinate clause by a time sequence (see also → clause)

connotation (p21): the connotations of a word are the associations it creates. For example, the connotations of *December*, mainly within British and North American culture, would be of 'cold', 'dark nights' and 'Christmas'

corpus (p2): a corpus (plural 'corpora') is a collection of texts, often consisting of millions of digitally stored words, utterances and sentences – tagged in order for them to be electronically searchable – that are judged to be representative of the ways in which people write and speak. Corpus linguistics is a significant and rapidly growing approach to the study of language

critical discourse analysis (CDA) (p146): a sub-discipline of discourse analysis aimed at uncovering belief systems and ideologies as they are conveyed through language and texts

definite article (p83): (see → article)

deixis (p84): deictics are words which point backwards, forwards and extra-textually and which serve to situate a speaker or writer in relation to what is said. For example, in the sentence 'I'm going to get some wine from that shop over there', the main deictic words are 'that' and 'there'

derivational morpheme (p88): (see → morpheme)

determiner (p178): a determiner specifies the kind of reference a noun has. Determiners include: *the, those, my, her, both, all, several, no*. The term 'zero determiner' is used to refer to phrases where no determiner is used (for example: *eat fruit*)

dialect (p44): dialect refers to the grammar and vocabulary used when people speak a language (see also → accent). A dialect is normally characteristic of a particular geographical region or social group

discourse (p2): a term used to describe the rules and conventions underlying the use of language in extended stretches of text, spoken and written. The academic study of discourse is commonly referred to as 'discourse analysis'. The term is also used to refer to the patterns which characterise particular types of language or – in its plural form, 'discourses' – to refer to habitual ways of talking and thinking about a topic, for example, discourses about food or discourses about travel

discourse marker (p102): a discourse marker is a word, phrase or clause which organises or comments on what we are saying. Discourse markers include *right, well, so, I mean, at the end of the day*. For example: *So, let's decide where we are going at the weekend* (marking a conclusion to previous discussion)

English as a lingua franca (ELF) (p224): the use of the English language for purposes of communication by speakers of different first languages

ellipsis (p38): ellipsis is used when we omit words or phrases which can be understood from the context. For example: *She went to the office and worked until it was very late in the evening* (the pronoun *she* is ellipted in the second clause). Ellipsis is also used in informal contexts of speaking when speakers share knowledge of what is referred to or when it is obvious in the situation (commonly called 'situational ellipsis'). For example: *Want some tea?* (*Do you* is understood)

etymology (p58): the study of word origins

exclamation (p143): an exclamation (or *exclamative*) is a sentence or utterance in which we express strong emotion or feelings. They are commonly accompanied by punctuation marks which highlight the expression, for example *Ouch!! Wow! That's SHOCKING…*

expressive (p64): language that connects with our emotions and sensations

eye dialect (p64): using the regular alphabet to represent sounds, rather than a phonetic or phonemic alphabet

finite verb/finite clause (p133): a finite clause is a clause that has a modal verb or a main verb marked for tense. A non-finite clause contains a verb that is not marked for tense and does not include a modal verb. Examples: *I waited for them* (finite clause); *Born in Beijing* (non-finite clause), *she was educated in Melbourne*

foregrounding (p16): the capacity of a piece of discourse to make something (words, sentences, or even an entire text) stand out and be noticeable to the reader

free morpheme (p88): (see → morpheme)

genre (p79): in language study, a type of text in any mode which is defined by its purpose, its features, or both. In literary fields, genre tends to refer primarily to the literary genres of prose, poetry and drama, but it can also refer to types of content (for example, crime or romance)

globalisation (p13): refers to a process whereby business and commerce see increased trade in more countries worldwide. It can have the effect that goods, business, services and culture appear very similar. English is a globalised language with different varieties in different parts of the world and contributes to communication worldwide (see → English as a lingua franca; see also → World Englishes)

graphology (p44): graphology refers to the physical characteristics and patterns of written text such as typeface and layout. See Part II, Section A for detailed exploration. **Grapho-phonemics** refers to the relationship between symbols and sounds

grammatical cohesion (p126): (see → cohesion)

grammatical words (p86): refers to words which have a primarily grammatical function. Words such as *the*, *an*, *you*, *on*, *which* are grammatical words. Grammatical words are the glue which hold texts together structurally. They contrast with *lexical words* such as *house*, *bottle*, *wrong*, *happiness*, *riskily*, *sport* which have a primary function of referring to content (objects, ideas, entities). Grammatical words are finite (there is only a limited number), whereas lexical words are an open class; that is, the class is potentially infinite and new lexical words can be added to a language all the time

half-rhyme (p70): (see → rhyme)

headword (p99): the headword is the key word in a word family, usually the root word (or lexeme) that will form the key point of entry in a dictionary. For example: the word *break* is a headword in a family of words consisting of related words *broken*, *breakable*, *unbroken* as well as related phrases such as *break* (a promise), *break* (a record). Headword is also sometimes used in grammar to refer to the most important word in a phrase. For example: the noun phrase *the old man in the park* consists of the headword (a noun *man*), the pre-head (*old*) and the post-head (*in the park*)

hedge(s): hedges are words and phrases which regularly soften or weaken the force with which something is said. Examples of hedges are: 'kind of', 'sort of', 'by any chance', 'as it were' and 'admittedly' (see also → vague language)

hybrid (p77): a blend of two or more elements. For example, new forms of communication are often seen as having some of the characteristics of both spoken and written language

iconic (p49): in semiotics, the term iconic refers to an image that is a picture of its referent, as in a photograph, for example

indefinite article (p83): (see → article)

ideograph (p52): a graphic symbol that represents an idea

ideology (p146): refers to a set of conscious and/or unconscious opinions or belief systems held by a group or an individual and sometimes by a whole society or political culture. It is the aim of critical discourse analysis (CDA) to uncover ideologies (see → critical discourse analysis (CDA))

idiom (p119): an idiom is a phrase that has a meaning that is independent of the meaning of the words that it consists of. For example: *over the moon* = delighted, thrilled (see also → lexis)

inflectional morpheme (p88): (see → morpheme)

intertextuality: (p12): intertextuality refers to the ways in which the meaning of a text can be shaped by its relationship to another text

intransitive (p128): (see → transitive)

lexis/lexeme (p99): lexis is another term for vocabulary, and the terms lexeme or 'lexical item' are sometimes used in order to avoid difficulties of defining what a word is. For example, the abstract lexeme 'walk' underlies all the separate instances 'walks', 'walked', 'walking'; the idiom 'smell a rat' is also a lexeme in so far as it functions in the manner of a single word (*I smelled a rat* = I suspected something). An idiom is a phrase that has a meaning that is independent of the meaning of the words that it consists of (see also → idiom)

lexical cohesion (p114): (see → cohesion)

lexical word (p86): (see → grammatical word)

metaphor/metaphorical (p675): a word or phrase which establishes a comparison or analogy between one object or idea and another. For example, 'I *demolished* his argument' suggests that arguments are like buildings that can be destroyed

metonym/metonymic (p51): a metonym entails the association of two things (such as objects and ideas) with one thing referred to as though it were the other. For example, *The White House* is the official home of the President of the USA. By metonymic association, a reference to *The White House* can stand for a reference to the president and his government – e.g. 'The White House announced new plans for health care'

minor sentence (p130): (see → sentence)

modality (p123): modal verbs have only one form and do not indicate person, number, voice or aspect. They are placed first in the verb phrase and are followed by a verb (either an auxiliary verb or a main verb) in the base form. Modal verbs such as *can, could, may, might, must, shall, should, will, would* express two main kinds of modal meaning: degrees of certainty and degrees of desirability or obligation. For example: *I might decide not to vote* (the speaker says something is possible, but is not certain); *I must text her to find out how long she's away from the office* (the speaker says that she is obliged to do something and that it is necessary). Adjectives (*possible*) and adverbs (*probably, definitely*) are also modal in meaning

modification (p123): a modifier is a word or phrase that indicates further meaning about a head word (commonly a noun) either before the head word (pre-modification) or after the head word (post-modification). The head word here is the noun hotel:

pre-modifier   post-modifier
It's the large hotel at the end of the village.

morpheme/morphology (p87): a morpheme is a basic unit of grammar in that it can function to mark a grammatical feature or structure. For example, 'walks' contains two morphemes: 'walk' and 's', the latter morpheme marking the tense and person of the basic or root morpheme 'walk'. Morphemes are normally divided into free morphemes and bound morphemes: bound morphemes occur as single words and normally only acquire meaning when joined to the free morpheme. For example: *unfriendly* is a word made up from three morphemes

– a free morpheme 'friend' and two bound morphemes 'un' and 'ly'. Morphemes are often studied as 'inflectional' or 'derivational' forms: inflectional morphemes are morphemes such as 's' and 'ed' (bound morphemes) which indicate grammatical meanings; derivational morphemes are morphemes such as 'ship' and 'dom' which can form specific grammatical categories (here *friendship*; *kingdom*). The general term for the study of morphemes is morphology

multimodal (p3): multimodal is a term which describes communication systems which use more than one mode. For example, Skype is a multimodal communication system in that a written text can be accompanied by visual signs, by pictures and by sound

narratee (p203): a fictional receiver; the person that the text appears to be aimed at

narrative (p15): a story-like construction that involves characters operating in a sequence of events

narrator (p15): the fictional teller of a story

nasal (p61): nasal sounds are produced by sending a stream of air through the nose. Sounds such as /m/ and /n/ and /→/ (for example, in the words *swim, born, sing*) are classified as nasal sounds

nominalisation (p123): refers to a process by which a word is converted from one class to another – for example, *decide* → *decision, close* → *closure*. The nominalised form is usually more formal and can be used to conceal a subject and to make a process more impersonal. Compare, for example: (1) *We closed the factory and had to sack fifty people.* (2) *The closure of the factory led to the loss of fifty jobs*

non-finite (p131): (see → finite verb/clause)

Object (p128): the person or thing affected by the verb (see also → intransitive; verb)

observer's paradox (p10): The paradox that the only way to collect natural speech is to observe it, but the very act of observation is likely to destroy its naturalness

onomatopoeia (p64): onomatopoeia refers to the use of words whose sound suggests the sense of the words. For example, *the wind murmuring softly in the valleys* imitates the sound of the movement of the wind

participle (p134): a participle is the *-ing* and *-ed* forms of the verb. *Singing* is the present participle form of *sing*; *walked* is the past participle form of *walk*

passive (p135): (see → voice)

phonology/phonetics (p44): phonetics and phonology are branches of linguistics. Phonetics deals with the production and articulation of speech sounds by humans, whereas phonology deals with underlying structures and patterns of sounds such as, for example, different patterns of sounds in different positions in words. Some of these sounds are covered in this glossary (see → plosive, voiced, nasal) but more related terms such *approximant, affricate, lateral, glottal stop* are explored in Part II, Section A. An individual sound is called a phoneme and the range of sounds in an accent or possessed by a speaker is termed a **phoneme inventory**

plosive (p60): a plosive is a sound made by a consonant when air is stopped from flowing out of the mouth and is then suddenly released. The /p/ in the word *stop* or the /d/ in the word *bad* are examples of plosives

plural (p86): a coding in grammar that indicates more than one person or entity is being referred to – for example, singular *ship, woman*; plural *ships, women*

point of view (p16): the position of the narrator of a text in relation to the text's ideas or storyline

postvocalic r (p63): pronouncing an /r/ after a vowel where there is an r in the spelling. For example, 'farm', 'sir', 'horse'

pragmatics (p38): assumptions made about what is meant, or the inferences drawn from what is said or written. Pragmatics is most easily revealed in the unspoken cultural rules that underlie our everyday routines, from our greetings and farewells in face to face interactions to rules about food, hygiene and public behaviour

prefix (p89): a prefix is a series of letters added to the beginning of a word which alters the meaning in some way, e.g. *im*possible, *re*write

preposition (p92): a preposition is a word or phrase such as *after, to, on, next to, with, in front of*. Prepositions are usually used before nouns or pronouns and they show the relationship between the noun or pronoun and other words in a sentence. They can mark the position of something, the time it took place, or how something was done. For example, *we went to London by car. Shall we meet after work?*

pronoun (p84): pronouns are words like *he, she, yourself, mine, who, this, these*. Pronouns commonly refer to or fill the position of a noun or noun phrase. Personal pronouns are *I, you, he, him, her* etc. Relative pronouns are: *which, who, whom, whose, that.* Demonstrative pronouns are: *this, these, that* and *those.* Reflexive pronouns are: *yourself, myself, themselves.* Indefinite pronouns are words such as *someone, anyone, no-one*

qualitative research method (p20): a method concerned with understanding the nature of a phenomenon. Often applied in the areas of arts and humanities to studies of human behaviour and typically drawing insights from closely focused, limited but rich data

quantitative research method (p20): a method concerned with collecting numerical data and drawing insights from large-scale studies. Often used in the fields of social science and science

rebus (p53): a system whereby a word or part of a word is represented by a picture. Commonly used for fun in modern-day puzzles, but was also a serious form of representation in medieval heraldry

received pronunciation (RP) (p58): an accent traditionally associated with high social status. 'Received' refers to the idea of social acceptance in official circles

reference/referent (p49): reference is the act of referring to something (often called a *referent*). Many words also allow reference to each other and establish cohesive links and patterns across a text (see also → cohesion). Different types of reference include *anaphoric* and *cataphoric* reference. Anaphoric reference points backwards; for example, the grammatical word 'he' in the following sentence: 'I saw the man. *He* was wearing a black jacket'. Cataphoric reference points forwards; for example, the word 'here' in the following sentence: '*Here* is the nine o'clock news'. Reference within a text is generally referred to as endophoric reference; reference to the world outside the text is generally referred to as exophoric reference. 'Demonstrative reference' involves *deictics* such as 'these', 'those', 'here' and 'there' which refer back and forth within a text or speech event. 'Comparative reference' involves reference within a text when one thing is compared to another; for example, 'Ann is *stronger* than William' (see → deixis)

reflexive verb (p183): a reflexive verb is a verb whose direct object is the same as its subject – for example, 'They *prepared themselves*'; 'he *injured himself* badly when he was skiing'. The direct object here is a reflexive pronoun (*themselves, himself, myself* etc.)

register (p97): register is used to describe particular varieties or styles of speaking and writing. Registers vary because the language is used for different purposes, in different contexts and for different audiences. Registers are recognised because of their specialised vocabulary and grammar. The term is often used to refer to occupational varieties of English; for example, there is a legal register, a register of advertising, registers of science and so on

representation (p128): something that stands in place of something else. Representation is how something appears to be, not necessarily how it really is

reverse rhyme (p68): this occurs when parallel sounds occur at the beginning rather than at the end of words. For example, *grating gravel* or *choosing cheese* are examples of reverse rhyme. Half-rhyme or pararhyme or partial rhyme occurs when words almost rhyme (for example: *hall* and *howl*) (see → rhyme)

rhyme (p68): a rhyme is a repetition of similar sounds in two or more words, commonly in the final syllables of lines in poems and songs – for example the words *hall* and *ball* rhyme (see → reverse rhyme)

semantics (p46): the study of meaning. This can refer to meaning in a more limited sense – such as the meanings of individual words and phrases – or meaning in a more holistic sense, the overall meaning of a text

semantic field (p95): a group of words which are related in meaning, normally as a result of being connected with a particular context of use. For example, 'chop', 'sprinkle', 'salt', 'dice', 'wash', 'simmer', 'boil', 'herbs' are all part of a 'word family' in being connected with the semantic field of cookery

semantic profile (p107): describes the way in which certain seemingly neutral words can be perceived with positive or negative associations (sometimes referred to as 'semantic prosody' or 'lexical profile'). For example, the verb *set in* has a negative semantic profile, as can be seen from structures such as *the bad weather set in*; *a deep crisis set in*. By contrast, a verb such as *provide* normally has a positive attitudinal meaning: *they provided support to her when she was ill*

semiotics/semiology (p45): the study of how signs work within human communication. A *sign* consists of the relationship between a 'signifier' which refers to something, and a 'signified', which is the thing or person or idea being referred to. Signs are culturally determined and so their meanings are never fixed. An *iconic* sign involves a picture of a referent, while a *symbolic* sign has no logical connection with the referent, beyond that established by cultural convention (see → symbol)

sentence (p25): sentence is a difficult term to define because the structure of sentences differs according to whether spoken or written language is used. Traditionally a sentence has a subject and a main verb, though in poetry or SMS texts, for example, sentences can commonly be a minor sentence. A minor sentence is a sentence without a main verb and can consist of just a single word. Minor sentences are commonly found in written texts where writers have limited space. Another example of this is recipes – '*egg custard slice: a light pastry case with egg custard dusted with nutmeg*'. In spoken English, utterances such as '*over here*', '*if you like*' and '*perhaps*' are not structurally sentences but as minor sentences they can function as a sentence (see also → clause)

shibboleth (p63): a language item used as a marker or test of group membership

singular (p149): (see → plural)

sound symbolism (p67): the way in which sounds are used to represent ideas – for example, in onomatopoeia, where sounds represent noises. There is no logical connection between the sounds and the ideas they represent

subject (p134): the subject of a sentence is the word or phrase that agrees with the main verb. This is also referred to as 'subject verb concord'. *The city is the capital of the country* has correct subject verb concord and the word *city* is the subject. (In the sentence *The city are the capital of the country* there is an incorrect subject verb agreement or concord.)

subject deletion (p38): subjects are deleted when we cannot tell what the subject or agent in a sentence or utterance is. For example: (1) *Malaysian taxi drivers block bridge in Southern Thailand.* (2) *Bridge blocked in Southern Thailand.* In the second sentence (which is in the passive voice) the subject has been deleted (see → voice)

subordinate clause (p153): (see → clause)

suffix (p89): a suffix is a series of letters added to the end of a word which changes its meaning in some way, usually changing the word-class. For example: *statement; talkative*

symbolic (p49): a symbol is something that stands for something else, with no logical connections between the items

tense (p37): tense refers to the verb form that shows the time of an action, event or state. The present simple tense *walks* contrasts with the past simple tense *walked*

transitive (p128): a transitive verb is a verb that needs an object (*I enjoyed the concert*); an intransitive verb does not need an object (*An hour elapsed*)

vague language (p38): vague language refers to words and phrases that are purposefully unspecific in meaning. Using vague language such as *kind of, that sort of stuff, things like that* can be an important part of social communication (see also → hedges), softening the force of utterances in order to be more polite or more indirect

verb (p128): a verb is commonly used with a subject as the basis of a clause: *The old man smiled.* A verb phrase may contain more than a single verb: *I might have forgotten.* A finite verb is a verb marked for tense (see → finite; see → tense) (see also → reflexive verb)

voice (p135): voice refers to verb forms that are said to be either in the 'active' or 'passive' voice. The passive voice is formed by *be* + the past participle form of the verb and often involves a *by*-phrase. Examples: *She broke the 200-metre world record* is active voice; *the 200-metre world record was broken by her* is passive voice. In the second sentence the focus is on what is broken (the world record) and the performer of the action is identified in the phrase 'by her'. This phrase can be left out (see also → subject deletion)

voiced (p60): some consonants can be voiced or unvoiced depending on whether or not the vocal chords vibrate when making the sound. For example, the consonant /s/ in the word *cups* is voiceless but the consonant /s/ in the word *pens* is voiced

voiceless (p60): (see → voiced)

word (p99): (see → lexis)

word family (p99): (see → semantic field)

word formation (p94): (see → morphology)

World Englishes (p1): varieties of English that are used in different countries around the world, mainly in areas that were formerly colonised such as India and Singapore. These countries have their own versions of standard English

List of texts

	Text	Type of text	Page
2.1	Swedish train seat	public artifact	11
2.2	Nobody was here	graffiti	11
2.3	Waterstones	promotional text	12
2.4	Gone tanning	shop door notice	12
2.5	Ci gusta	advert for food outlet	13
2.6	Researcher's archive	research notes	14
3.1	Tsunami	public sign	16
3.2	Lisbon	photographic image	16
3.3	Telescope	public artefact	19
4.1	Cobuild 'chat' and 'discussion'	corpus searches	22–23
4.2	Voicemail message	digital communication	25
4.3	Personal 'chat' data	digital communication	28
4.4	Business 'chat' data	digital communication	29
4.5	Georgia	travel writing	31
11.1	Dove	greetings card	49
11.2	Call button	public sign	50
11.3	Canadian river sign	public sign	51
11.4	CCTV	building site notice	52
11.5	Emoji	news article about emoticons	53
11.6	Ladder of Years	novel	54
11.7	art'otel	letter	56
12.1	arrrggggh!!	hotel card	65
12.2	Strange Meeting	poem	70
13.1	SSSHHH!!	hotel notice	71
13.2	Hedy's speech	child's speech	78
13.3	Omar's writing	child's writing	79
15.1	Frequent words (writing)	corpus search	82
17.1	Matalan	advertisement	90

LIST OF TEXTS

17.2	Andrex eco roll	advertisement	91
17.3	Comfort on Sale	advertisement	94
18.1	conchas borrachas	recipe	96
18.2	Techno and metal	advertisement	98
20.1	Rodney's Oyster House	restaurant napkin	101
21.1	House & Home	logo	104
21.2	Pokhara hotels	public signs	106
21.3	Concordance of 'cause'	corpus search	107
21.4	UN Women	promotional text	108
21.5	Muscat	travel brochure	110
22.1	Encounters Dating	personal dating website	113
23.1	Jumbled sentences	variety of texts	115
23.2	Two friends	informal conversation	116
23.3	Offerings	poem	117
25.1	simplehuman	guarantee card	125
26.1	Romantic fiction	novel	130
26.2	Menu	menu	131
26.3	Estate agent's advert	advertisement	131
26.4	Bleak House	novel	132
26.5	Environmental injuries	information text	138
26.6	University examination regulations	information text	138
27.1	Frequency list (speech)	corpus search	140
27.2	Like	greetings card	144
28.1	Political speech: Obama and 'Yes, we can'	political speech	148
29.1	TV review	newspaper article	152
30.1	SMS conversation	digital communication	153
30.2	Two SMS examples	digital communication	154
31.1	Popcorn-can cover	poem	156
31.2	for Goodness sake	promotional text	157
31.3	Exeter Cruises	information notice	158
31.4	Burger me	advertisement	158
31.5	Orange my day	promotional text	159
31.6	Job ad for a proofreader	job advertisement	159
32.1	Instruction	spoken instructions	190
32.2	Student chat	digital communication	192
32.3	Sales chat	digital communication	192
32.4	Coffee cup	promotional text	194

32.5	Ordinary Thunderstorms	novel	195
32.6	61 Hours	novel	196
32.7	Jump	promotional text	199
33.1	Bathroom notice	instructions	204
34.1	Beer mat	instructions	205
34.2	Afternoon tea	advertisement	206
34.3	Times Higher	magazine cover	207
34.4	clas ohlson	advertisement	208
34.5	Men's Health	magazine cover	210
35.1	GO TO: GREAT CHRISTMASDEALS	promotional text	213
35.2	Scandinavian Metro	newspaper article	215